The Cold War and the Americas 1945–81

Vivienne Sanders

HODDER
EDUCATION
AN HACHETTE UK COMPANY

The material in this title has been developed independently of the International Baccalaureate®, which in no way endorses it.

The Publishers would like to thank the following for permission to reproduce copyright material:

Photo credits: p30 Pictorial Press Ltd/Alamy; **p33** A 1947 Herblock Cartoon, copyright by The Herb Block Foundation; **p60** Getty Images; **p72** Hungerford Cy, artist. 'An Uncomfortable Situation.' December 3, 1953. Prints and Photographs Division, Library of Congress; **p84** Time & Life Pictures/Getty Images; **p98** Bettmann/Corbis; **p109** Nick Ut/AP/Press Association Images; **p114** Eddie Adams/AP/Press Association Images; **p115** Bettmann/Corbis; **p139** Roger Viollet/Getty Images; **p155** Cecil Stoughton. White House Photographs. John F. Kennedy Presidential Library and Museum, Boston; **p173** Copyright by Bill Maudlin (1965). Courtesy of Bill Maudlin Estate LLC; **p176** Bettmann/Corbis; **p194** Roger Viollet/Getty Images; **p210** AFP/Getty Images; **p228** Edmund Valtman, artist. Prints and Photographs Division, Library of Congress.

Acknowledgements: p23 *Foreign Affairs*, Council on Foreign Relations, Inc. for an extract from an article published in 1947; **p49** *Saturday Evening Post* for an extract from an article published in 1950; **p78** Westview Press for an extract from Henry Raymont, *Troubled Neigbors: The Story of US–Latin American Relations from Roosevelt to the Present*, 2005; **p78** Oxford University Press for an extract from Robert Holden and Eric Zolov (editors), *Latin America and the United States*, 2000; **p85** Simon & Schuster for an extract from Stephen Ambrose, Nixon*: Volume 1 – The Education of a Politician 1913–1962*, 1987; **p113** Oxford University Press for an extract from Robert Holden and Eric Zolov (editors), *Latin America and United States*, 2000; **p141** The New York Times Company, *New York Times* for an extract from an article by Herbert Matthews, 1957; **p144** *New Republic* for an extract from an article by Jean Daniel, 1963; **p148** *Suddeutsche Zeitung* for an extract from an article by Hans Ulrich Kempski, 1960; **p158** *Foreign Affairs*, Council on Foreign Relations, Inc. for an extract from an article by Eduardo Frei Montalvo, 1967; **p172** Random House for an extract from William Fulbright, *The Arrogance of Power*, 1966; **p182** Oxford University Press for an extract from Robert Schulzinger, *U.S. Diplomacy Since 1900*, 2002; **p189** Duke University Press for an extract from Tulio Halperín Donghi, *The Contemporary History of Latin America*, 1996; **pp218 and 231** Duke University Press for extracts from Gilbert Joseph and Daniela Spenser (editors), *In From the Cold: Latin America's New Encounter With the Cold War*, 2008; **p233** Cambridge University Press for an extract from Boris Fausto, *A Concise History of Brazil*, 1999.

Every effort has been made to trace all copyright holders, but if any have been inadvertently overlooked the Publishers will be pleased to make the necessary arrangements at the first opportunity.

Although every effort has been made to ensure that website addresses are correct at time of going to press, Hodder Education cannot be held responsible for the content of any website mentioned in this book. It is sometimes possible to find a relocated web page by typing in the address of the home page for a website in the URL window of your browser.

Hachette UK's policy is to use papers that are natural, renewable and recyclable products and made from wood grown in sustainable forests. The logging and manufacturing processes are expected to conform to the environmental regulations of the country of origin.

Orders: please contact Bookpoint Ltd, 130 Milton Park, Abingdon, Oxon OX14 4SB. Telephone: (44) 01235 827827. Fax: (44) 01235 400401. Lines are open 9.00–5.00, Monday to Saturday, with a 24-hour message answering service. Visit our website at www.hoddereducation.co.uk

© Vivienne Sanders 2012

First published in 2012 by
Hodder Education,
An Hachette UK Company
338 Euston Road
London NW1 3BH

Impression number   5 4 3 2 1
Year   2016 2015 2014 2013 2012

Cover photo: © Bettmann/Corbis
Illustrations by Gray Publishing
Typeset in 10/13pt Palatino and produced by Gray Publishing, Tunbridge Wells
Printed in Italy

A catalogue record for this title is available from the British Library

ISBN: 978 1444 156591

Contents

Dedication

Keith Randell (1943–2002)

The original *Access to History* series was conceived and developed by Keith, who created a series to 'cater for students as they are, not as we might wish them to be'. He leaves a living legacy of a series that for over 20 years has provided a trusted, stimulating and well-loved accompaniment to post-16 study. Our aim with these new editions for the IB is to continue to offer students the best possible support for their studies.

Introduction

This book has been written to support your study of HL option 3: Aspects of the history of the Americas: The Cold War and the Americas 1945–81 of the IB History Diploma Route 2.

This introduction gives you an overview of:

✪ the content you will study for The Cold War and the Americas 1945–81

✪ how you will be assessed for Paper 3

✪ the different features of this book and how these will aid your learning.

 ## What you will study

The Cold War between the USA and the Soviet Union (roughly from 1946 to 1989) affected virtually every country in the Americas. Motivated primarily by Cold War anti-Communism, the USA worked to undermine governments that had the support of a large proportion of the population in countries such as Guatemala, Cuba, the Dominican Republic, Chile and Nicaragua. In some of these countries, and in others such as Argentina and Bolivia, dictatorial regimes were supported by the USA, even as they terrorized and oppressed their own people.

The desire to contain Communism led the USA to intervene militarily in nations in the Americas, such as the Dominican Republic and Cuba, and in Asia, where the USA sent hundreds of thousands of American soldiers to fight in Korea and Vietnam.

This book covers the impact of the Cold War on the Americas:

● It begins by providing an overview of US foreign policy in the Americas and Asia before 1945 (Chapter 1).
● It examines how the Cold War began and how Truman's policy of containing Communism developed. It also investigates the rise of McCarthyism and its impact on US domestic and foreign policy (Chapter 2).
● It looks at the causes, course and consequences of the Korean War (Chapter 3).
● It assesses President Eisenhower's 'New Look' in defence and foreign policy, and looks at Eisenhower's reactions to leftist regimes in Guatemala and Cuba (Chapter 4).
● It covers the involvement of the USA in Vietnam from 1950 to 1973 (Chapter 5).
● It studies Cold War Cuba in depth (Chapters 6 and 8).

- It analyses US policy toward the Americas in the Kennedy, Johnson, Nixon and Carter presidencies (Chapter 7).
- The book ends by drawing some conclusions about the impact of the Cold War on Latin America (Chapter 9).

 # How you will be assessed

The IB History Diploma Higher Level has three papers in total: Papers 1 and 2 for Standard Level and a further Paper 3 for Higher Level. It also has an internal assessment that all students must do.

- For Paper 1 you need to answer four source-based questions on a prescribed subject. This counts for 20 per cent of your overall marks.
- For Paper 2 you need to answer two essay questions on two different topics. This counts for 25 per cent of your overall marks.
- For Paper 3 you need to answer three essay questions on two or three sections. This counts for 35 per cent of your overall marks.

For the Internal Assessment you need to carry out a historical investigation. This counts for 20 per cent of your overall marks.

HL option 3: Aspects of the history of the Americas is assessed through Paper 3. You must study three sections out of a choice of 12, one of which could be The Cold War and the Americas 1945–81. These sections are assessed through Paper 3 of the IB History diploma which has 24 essay questions – two for each of the 12 sections. In other words, there will be two specific questions that you can answer based on the Cold War.

Examination questions

For Paper 3 you need to answer three of the 24 questions. You could either answer two on one of the sections you have studied and one on another section, or one from each of the three sections you have studied. So, assuming the Cold War and the Americas is one of the sections you have studied, you may choose to answer one or two questions on it.

The questions are not divided up by section but just run 1–24 and are usually arranged chronologically. In the case of the questions on the Cold War, you should expect numbers 19 and 20 to be on this particular section. When the exam begins, you will have five minutes in which to read the questions. You are not allowed to use a pen or highlighter during the reading period. Scan the list of question but focus on the ones relating to the sections you have studied.

Remember you are to write on the history of the Americas. If a question such as, 'Discuss the impact of the Cold War on the society of one country of the region,' is asked do *not* write about the USSR. You will receive no credit for this answer.

Command terms

When choosing the three questions, keep in mind that you must answer the question asked, not one you might have hoped for. A key to success is understanding the demands of the question. IB History diploma questions use key terms and phrases known as command terms. The more common command terms are listed in the table below, with a brief definition of each. More are listed in the appendix of the IB History Guide.

Examples of questions using some of the more common command terms and specific strategies to answer them are included at the end of Chapters 2–8.

Command term	Description	Where exemplified in this book
Analyse	Investigate the various components of a given issue	Page 90
Assess	Very similar to evaluate. Raise the various sides to an argument but clearly state which are more important and why	Page 39
Compare and contrast	Discuss both similarities and differences of two events, people, etc.	Page 129
Evaluate	Make a judgement while looking at two or more sides of an issue	Page 150
In what ways and with what effects	Be sure to include both ways and effects in your answer – that is how an event took place and what the repercussions were	Page 220
To what extent	Discuss the various merits of a given argument or opinion	Page 67
Why	Explain the reasons for something that took place. Provide several reasons	Page 190

Answering the questions

You have two-and-a-half hours to answer the three questions or 50 minutes each. Try to budget your time wisely. In other words, do not spend 75 minutes on one answer. Before you begin each essay, take five to seven minutes and compose an outline of the major points you will raise in your essay. These you can check off as you write the essay itself. This is not a waste of time and will bring organization and coherency to what you write. Well-organized essays that include an introduction, several well-supported arguments, and a concluding statement are much more likely to score highly than essays which jump from point to point without structure.

The three essays you write for Paper 3 will be read by a trained examiner. The examiner will read your essays and check what you write against the IB mark scheme. This mark scheme offers guidance to the examiner but is not comprehensive. You may well write an essay that includes analysis and evidence not included in the mark scheme and that is fine. It is also worth remembering that the examiner who will mark your essay is looking to reward well-defended and argued positions, not to deduct for misinformation.

Each of your essays will be marked on a 0–20 scale, for a total of 60 points. The total score will be weighted as 35 per cent of your final IB History. Do bear in mind that you are not expected to score 60/60 to earn a 7; 37–39/60 will equal a 7. Another way of putting this is that if you write three essays that each score 13, you will receive a 7.

Writing essays

In order to attain the highest mark band (18–20), your essays should:

- be clearly focused
- address all implications of the question
- demonstrate extensive historical knowledge
- demonstrate knowledge of historical processes such as continuity and change
- integrate your analysis
- be well structured
- have well-developed synthesis.

Your essay should include an introduction in which you set out your main points. Do not waste time copying the question but define the key terms stated in the question. Best essays probe the demands of the question. In other words, there are often different ways of interpreting the question.

Next, you should write an in-depth analysis of your main points in several paragraphs. Here you will provide evidence that supports your argument. Each paragraph should focus on one of your main points and relate directly to the question. More sophisticated responses include counter-arguments.

Finally, you should end with a concluding statement.

In the roughly 45 minutes you spend on one essay, you should be able to write 3–6 pages. While there is no set minimum, you do need to explore the issues and provide sufficient evidence to support what you write.

At the end of Chapters 2–8, you will find IB-style questions with guidance on how best to answer them. Each question focuses on a different command term. It goes without saying that the more practice you have writing essays, the better your results will be.

The appearance of the examination paper

Cover

The cover of the examination paper states the date of the examination and the length of time you have to complete it: 2 hours 30 minutes. Please note that there are two routes in history. Make sure your paper says Route 2 on it. Instructions are limited and simply state that you should not open it until told to do so and that three questions must be answered.

Questions

You will have five minutes in which to read through the questions. It is very important to choose the three questions you can answer most fully. It is quite possible that two of the three questions may be on the Cold War, especially after mastering the material in this book. That is certainly permissible. After the five minutes' reading time is over, you can take out your pen and mark up the exam booklet:

- Circle the three questions you have decided to answer.
- Identify the command terms and important points. For example, if a question asked, 'To what extent did Eisenhower's foreign policy towards Latin America differ from Kennedy's' underline 'to what extent' and 'foreign policy'. This will help you to focus on the demands of the question.

For each essay take 5–7 minutes to write an outline and approximately 43–45 minutes to write the essay.

 # About this book

Coverage of the course content

This book addresses the key areas listed in the IB History Guide for Route 2: HL option 3: Aspects of the history of the Americas: The Cold War and the Americas 1945–81. Chapters start with an introduction outlining key questions they address. They are then divided into a series of sections and topics covering the course content.

Throughout the chapters you will find the following features to aid your study of the course content.

Key and leading questions

Each section heading in the chapter has a related key question which gives a focus to your reading and understanding of the section. These are also listed in the chapter introduction. You should be able answer the questions after completing the relevant section.

Topics within the sections have leading questions which are designed to help you focus on the key points within a topic and give you more practice in answering questions.

Key terms

Key terms are the important terms you need to know to gain an understanding of the period. These are emboldened in the text the first time they appear in the book and are defined in the margin. They also appear in the glossary at the end of the book.

Sources

Throughout the book are several written and visual sources. Historical sources are important components in understanding more fully why specific decisions were taken or on what contemporary writers and politicians based their actions. The sources are accompanied by questions to help you dig deeper into the history of the Cold War.

Key debates

Historians often disagree on historical events and this historical debate is referred to as historiography. Knowledge of historiography is helpful in reaching the upper mark bands when you take your IB History examinations. You should not merely drop the names of historians in your essay. You need to understand the different points of view for a given historiographical debate. These you can bring up in your essay. There are a number of debates throughout the book to develop your understanding of historiography.

Theory of Knowledge (TOK) questions

Understanding that different historians see history differently is an important element in understanding the connection between the IB History Diploma and Theory of Knowledge. Alongside some of the debates is a Theory of Knowledge-style question that makes that link.

Summary diagrams

At the end of each section is a summary diagram that gives a visual summary of the content of the section. It is intended as an aid for revision.

Chapter summary

At the end of each chapter is a short summary of the content of that chapter. This is intended to help you revise and consolidate your knowledge and understanding of the content.

Examination guidance

At the end of Chapters 2–8 is:

- Examination guidance on how to answer questions, accompanied with advice on what supporting evidence you might use, and sometimes sample answers designed to help you focus on specific details.
- Examination practice in the form of Paper 3-style questions.

End of the book

The book concludes with the following sections:

Timeline

This gives a timeline of the major events covered in the book that is helpful for quick reference or as a revision tool.

Glossary

All key terms in the book are defined in the glossary.

Further reading

This contains a list of books and websites that may help you with further independent research and presentations. It may also be helpful when further information is required for internal assessments and extended essays in history. You may wish to share the contents of this area with your school or local librarian.

Internal assessment

All IB History diploma students are required to write a historical investigation that is internally assessed. The investigation is an opportunity for you to dig more deeply into a subject that interests you. This gives you a list of possible areas for research.

CHAPTER 1

US foreign policy pre-1945

This chapter looks at US foreign policy in the Americas and Asia before 1945 and gives important background to the topics covered in this book. You need to consider the following questions throughout this chapter:

✪ Why and with what results was the USA interested in Latin America before 1945?

✪ When and why did US–Canadian relations improve?

✪ What was the US relationship with China prior to 1945?

1 The USA and Latin America pre-1945

▶ **Key question:** Why and with what results was the USA interested in Latin America before 1945?

The USA and Latin America pre-1933

The Monroe Doctrine 1823

The USA first declared its position on Latin America in 1823, when President Monroe (1817–25) stated that any European attempts to interfere in the Western hemisphere (North and South America) would be 'dangerous' to the 'peace and safety' of the USA. This declaration became known as the Monroe Doctrine. Although the USA was a weak and insignificant country in 1823, the Monroe Doctrine signalled a special US interest in Latin America and opened the way to future intervention there if the USA, once it grew more powerful, felt its interests were at stake.

Cuba and the Canal Zone

In the late nineteenth and early twentieth centuries the USA was developing into the most powerful nation in the world. It began to intervene in Latin America, causing growing fear and resentment there toward 'the **Colossus of the North**'. In 1898, the USA made Cuba a US **protectorate** (see page 133) and took over Puerto Rico. In 1903, President Theodore Roosevelt (1901–9) decided to build a canal in Panama that would link the Atlantic and Pacific oceans and facilitate US trade and communications. The USA imposed a treaty on Panama in which the Americans acquired the Panama Canal and the territory on each side of it.

◀ When, why and with what results did the USA intervene in Latin America from 1895 to 1933?

 **KEY TERM**

Colossus of the North Phrase used to signify the greater power of the USA relative to its southern neighbours.

Protectorate Country whose foreign affairs and domestic stability are 'looked after' by another more powerful nation.

The Roosevelt Corollary

In the Roosevelt Corollary (1904), Theodore Roosevelt developed the Monroe Doctrine from a warning to Europeans not to intervene in the Western hemisphere into an American commitment to intervention in Latin America in certain cases (see Source A).

SOURCE A

Extract from the Roosevelt Corollary of 1904.

Flagrant cases … [of] chronic wrongdoing or an impotence which results in a general loosening of the ties of civilized society … may ultimately require intervention by some civilized nation … [and] force the United States, however reluctantly, to the exercise of an international police power.

? Quoting the language used in Source A, how would you describe Theodore Roosevelt's attitude to the people of Latin America?

Under Presidents Taft (1909–13) and Wilson (1913–21), the USA exercised its 'police power' (see Source A) and intervened in the Dominican Republic (1910–24), Haiti (1915–34) and Nicaragua (1912–33) when they defaulted on their debts. Wilson repeatedly intervened in Mexico because he was dissatisfied with Mexican governments. Latin American complaints about the American 'right to intervene' and protectionist tariffs encouraged President Franklin D. Roosevelt (1933–45) to promise to be a **'good neighbor'**.

KEY TERM

'Good neighbor' President Franklin Roosevelt's repudiation of past US use of force in Latin America.

Was the USA a 'good neighbor' to Latin America under Franklin Roosevelt?

'Good neighbor' 1933–45

The 'good neighbor' and political influence

Roosevelt halted direct US intervention in Latin America but indirect intervention continued in the form of the US creation, training and equipping of local forces to keep the peace and thereby facilitate political and economic development. After Roosevelt withdrew American troops, individuals such as Batista in Cuba (1933–44, 1952–9), Somoza in Nicaragua (1936–56), and Trujillo in the Dominican Republic (1930–61) gained control of those local forces. These dictators were further assisted in the consolidation of their power by the economic emergencies generated by the **Great Depression**. So, despite an oft-professed desire to help build democracies south of the border, the USA contributed to the creation of repressive Central American dictatorships. Roosevelt supposedly said, 'They may be sons of bitches, but they are our sons of bitches.'

KEY TERM

Great Depression World-wide economic depression starting in 1929.

? Using your own knowledge and Source C, why do you suppose the Latin American states demanded the inclusion of Article 8 in the Convention, and why did the USA accept the inclusion?

SOURCE C

In Montevideo, Uruguay, 1933, the USA, along with all the Latin American states, signed the Convention on Rights and Duties of States, including Article 8.

ARTICLE 8

No state has the right to intervene in the internal or external affairs of another.

SOURCE B

Map to show dates of US international involvement pre-1945.

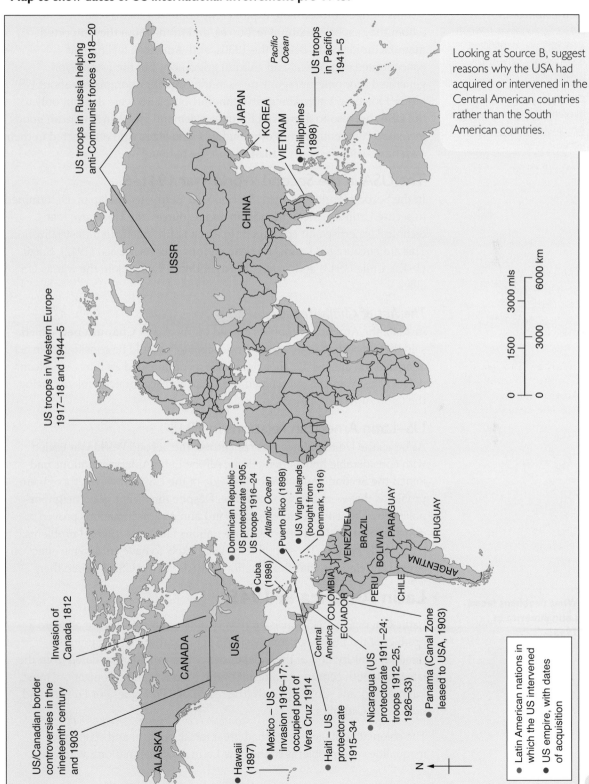

Looking at Source B, suggest reasons why the USA had acquired or intervened in the Central American countries rather than the South American countries. ?

The 'good neighbor' and economic influence

The Great Depression convinced many Latin Americans that they were victims of **neo-colonialism**, exploited by countries such as the USA, to whom they exported natural resources, and from whom they imported manufactured goods. Before the 1930s, anti-American feeling had concentrated on political and cultural grievances, but the Depression generated economic antagonism, as in the Argentine complaints about US tariffs. However, Latin American economic problems were due not only to the USA, but also to decreased European demand for Latin American goods, increased competition from other nations, and élites who often acted in their own narrow interest rather than that of the nation.

The USA in the Second World War 1941–5

In the Second World War the USA opposed Germany and Japan. Determined to secure Latin American friendship and resources, the USA gave loans, technical expertise and equipment to assist Latin American industrialization. This aid encouraged Latin American nations such as Mexico (1942), Brazil (1942), Chile (1943) and, belatedly, Argentina (1945), to join the war as US allies.

The Act of Chapultepec

In 1945, the American republics agreed on the Act of **Chapultepec**, which said that any act of aggression on one signatory would be considered an act of aggression against all. The conference recommended an inter-American defence treaty and also discussed the social and economic problems facing the Latin American nations.

US–Latin American relations in 1945

As far as the United States was concerned, the Second World War ended with considerable hemispheric unity. All the Latin American nations had joined the Second World War on the side of the USA. However, there were problems that were likely to resurface. Despite the recent 'good neighbor' policy, the US history of intervention in Latin American nations proved difficult to forget. Furthermore, those nations had great internal problems, particularly poverty. Those problems were likely to have an adverse effect on American relations with those nations, but as yet the USA ignored them.

> **What problems faced Latin America in 1945?**

Latin America in 1945

Latin America in 1945 consisted of very different countries, but all were a product of the European conquest and colonization that began in the fifteenth century, and of the independence movements that dated from the late eighteenth century. As a result of the conquest and colonization, most Latin Americans spoke Spanish (the rest spoke Portuguese or French) and most were Catholics.

The colonial heritage bequeathed great racial, political and economic inequalities and problems to the new Latin American nations, where the descendants of the European conquerors and colonists remained politically, socially and economically dominant, and where national armies had often replaced the crown as the major centralizing force in politics.

Political problems

Before 1945, only a few Latin American nations, such as Chile, had a tradition of some degree of democratic government. According to historian Edwin Williamson (2009), the armed forces were 'the decisive power-brokers' in twentieth-century Latin American politics. Sometimes the armed forces assisted the accession of others to power, as with Getúlio Vargas in Brazil, and sometimes the officers themselves gained power, as with Juan Perón in Argentina.

Economic problems

The white élite owned most of the land and dominated agriculture, but there were vast numbers of impoverished peasants and ever increasing numbers of urban workers, professionals and businessmen in the cities of Latin America. Latin American politics often reflected the tensions between these groups.

Many Latin American economies were predominantly agricultural and often dangerously dependent on one crop, so most Latin American nations were concerned to industrialize and diversify their economies.

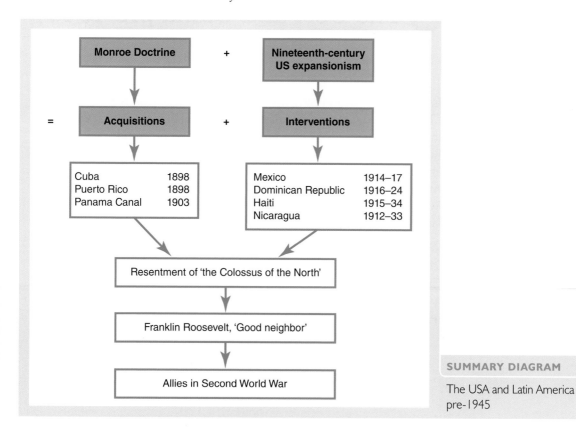

SUMMARY DIAGRAM

The USA and Latin America pre-1945

② The USA and Canada pre-1945

▶ **Key question:** *When and why did US–Canadian relations improve?*

After the Americans declared their independence from Britain in 1776, Canada remained loyal to Britain. US–Canadian relations were tense in the nineteenth century. During the war of 1812 between the USA and Britain, the United States invaded Canada, which made Canada uneasy about possible American aggression and domination, especially as some Americans dreamt of acquiring Canada.

Memories of 1812 and border controversies fuelled the Canadian perception that the USA was threatening, while the USA feared Canada's connection with Britain and British imperialism. So, during the 1920s, Canada and the USA developed secret plans to defend their borders against each other. However, during the Second World War they worked closely together, and while Canada remained suspicious of American imperialism, by 1945 it seemed likely that there would be further co-operation in the event of international uncertainty.

③ The USA and China pre-1945

▶ **Key question:** *What was the US relationship with China prior to 1945?*

In the nineteenth and early twentieth centuries, the USA felt kindly toward China, which was weak, but increasingly fearful of Japan, which was strong. In 1931, Japan invaded China and during the Second World War, President Roosevelt publicly proclaimed Chiang Kai-shek's China as an important ally against Japan but was privately frustrated by China's inept performance. Americans could not understand why Chiang's **Chinese Nationalists** and Mao Zedong's Chinese **Communists** failed to unite to concentrate on the Japanese threat.

When the Second World War ended in 1945, the USA was optimistic about friendship with Chiang Kai-shek's China, although unrealistic about Chiang's prospects in his struggles with Mao Zedong's Communists. While good post-war relations with China seemed likely, good Japanese–American relations seemed unlikely.

 KEY TERM

Chinese Nationalists Chiang Kai-shek's party, the Guomindang.

Communists Supporters of the ideology that emphasized large-scale redistribution of wealth in order to attain economic equality.

Chapter summary

US foreign policy pre-1945

In 1823, President Monroe warned Europeans not to interfere in the Western hemisphere. In the late nineteenth and early twentieth centuries, the USA grew more powerful and took over some Latin American countries and intervened in others at will. Latin Americans resented US imperialism, so President Franklin D. Roosevelt introduced a 'good neighbor' policy, which repudiated previous US use of force in Latin America. This helped to ensure that the Latin American nations supported the USA in the Second World War, although they remained sensitive about 'Yankee imperialism'. They had great internal problems such as poverty and governmental stability.

The Second World War reinforced US perceptions of Japan as an aggressor and China as a friend, but greatly improved the US relationship with Canada.

CHAPTER 2

President Truman and the Cold War

Between about 1946 and 1989, the USA and the USSR engaged in an arms race and in a struggle to win other nations over to their side. They were never in direct military opposition. This chapter investigates the reasons for this Cold War. You need to consider the following questions throughout this chapter:

✪ What was the American response to Communism 1917–45?

✪ Was a post-Second World War breakdown in Soviet–American relations inevitable?

✪ Why did the Cold War begin?

✪ What was the significance of the Truman Doctrine for US foreign policy?

✪ How did the Truman Doctrine impact on Latin America?

✪ How and why did the Cold War affect American society and culture?

① The USA and Communism pre-1945

▶ **Key question:** *What was the American response to Communism 1917–45?*

When Russia became Communist during the First World War, the USA responded with anxiety. For most Americans, Communism was a political system that had to be opposed, because Communists suppressed human rights at home and were expansionist abroad. The USA feared for its safety if the Communist ideology were to spread. In a world full of Communist governments, with their state-controlled economies, with whom would the USA trade? If the world were full of one-party Communist states, with expansionist ideas, what would happen to multi-party democracies such as the USA?

KEY TERM

USSR Communist Russia called itself the Union of Soviet Socialist Republics (USSR).

As historian Martin McCauley emphasized (2003), the USA and the **USSR** were two competing systems, each convinced of their own rectitude and of the expansionist plans of the other. Each saw the other as a threat to its existence and, from the first, both engaged in behaviour that confirmed the other's fears. In 1918, American troops intervened in Russia in an unsuccessful attempt to prevent a Communist regime (some historians offer alternative but less persuasive reasons for that intervention). Convinced that the USSR was promoting world-wide Communist revolutions, the USA refused to recognize its existence until 1933. Then, desperate for trading partners in the Great Depression, and hopeful of using Russia to counter-balance the increasing power of Japan, President Franklin D. Roosevelt finally gave diplomatic recognition to the USSR. Relations remained uneasy, but when Adolf Hitler declared war on the USA in December 1941, Roosevelt and the **Soviet** leader Josef Stalin (1926–53) became allies in the struggle against Nazi Germany.

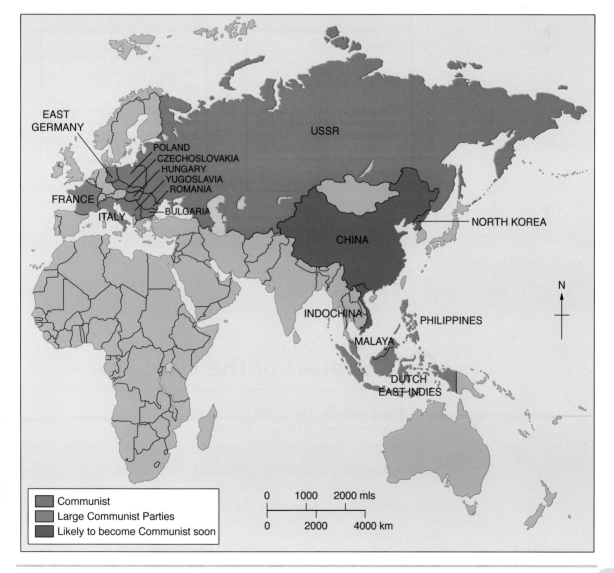

KEY TERM

Soviet Pertaining to the USSR.

Looking at Source A, why do you suppose the USA was so fearful of Communism in 1945?

?

SOURCE A

A map of Europe, Asia and Africa in 1945 showing countries that were Communist or about to become Communist.

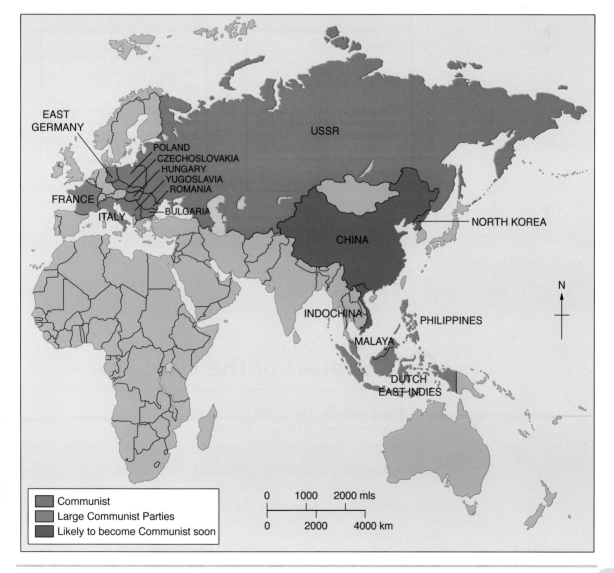

The situation in 1945

According to some contemporaries and some historians, the prospects for continuing co-operation between the USA and the USSR in 1945 were hopeful. These historians highlight the positive aspects of the relationship during the Second World War. Others, however, look at events from 1917 to 1933, see the wartime alliance between the USA and the USSR as a mere 'marriage of convenience', emphasize the tensions during the Second World War, and see the post-war **Cold War** conflict as inevitable. Coupled with the past suspicions based on ideological antipathy and the points of clash in the Second World War was the prospect of a traditional great power struggle.

USA		USSR
• Multi-party state	vs	One-party state (as the Communist Party is the party of the people, they only need the one party)
• Capitalist economy – minimal government intervention, wide variations in wealth	vs	Communism – state-controlled economy, wealth equally distributed
• USA safer if other countries not Communist	vs	USSR safer if other countries are Communist

1918	– US intervention in Russia
1933	– USA finally recognizes USSR
1941–5	– Allies in Second World War

SUMMARY DIAGRAM

The USA and Communism pre-1945

② The start of the Cold War

▶ *Key question: Was a post-Second World War breakdown in Soviet–American relations inevitable?*

In 1945, the USA and the USSR were allies, but within a few years they were enemies. Suggested causes of that enmity include the personalities of the leaders, the relative power of the two nations, and their differing ideologies.

Roosevelt, Truman and Stalin

Hitler attacked the USSR in summer 1941 and, when Japan's attack on **Pearl Harbor** in 1941 prompted its ally, Germany, to declare war on the USA, the USSR joined the USA and Britain together in the 'Grand Alliance' (1941–5).

The Grand Alliance

Given the uneasy Soviet–US relationship before the Second World War, it is not surprising that the Grand Alliance did not always operate smoothly. The greatest sources of tension, and surely the proof that the Cold War was inevitable, lay in the atomic bomb and Eastern Europe. During the war, the USA kept its Communist ally in the dark about the development of the atomic bomb, but shared (albeit reluctantly) the information with its democratic, capitalist British ally. Thanks to his spies, Stalin knew about and bitterly resented this American secrecy. For his part, Stalin ensured that as the Soviet army advanced towards Germany from 1944, Communist regimes were established in Eastern Europe, which he considered to be a Soviet security zone won with the blood of millions of Russians. What the Soviets saw as a question of national defence was perceived as aggression by the USA.

Such co-operation as there was within the Grand Alliance could be interpreted in two ways. For example, after repeated pleas from Roosevelt, Stalin promised to enter the war against Japan three months after Germany was defeated. He kept his promise. However, just before he declared war on Japan, the US use of atomic weaponry had already ensured Japan's defeat. So, Stalin's behaviour could either be seen as that of a helpful ally, or as that of a greedy and aggressive opportunist, moving to get his share of the spoils when Japan was defeated.

The power of the USA in 1945

The death of President Franklin Roosevelt in April 1945 left his relatively inexperienced vice president, Harry Truman, in charge of a nation with unparalleled economic and military might. The USA was by far the most powerful country in a world in which the war had drained the power and resources of all potential rivals: America's enemies Germany and Japan would soon be defeated; America's allies Britain and Russia were exhausted by the struggle. Around 30 million Russians had died in the Second World War. Much of western Russia's industry and agriculture had been severely damaged by the German invasion, in contrast to US territory, which (with the exception of Pearl Harbor) had remained untouched.

The USSR in 1945

The end of the Second World War saw the USSR triumphant, facing a world in which two traditional threats, Germany and Japan, were destroyed, and in which Poland, Czechoslovakia, Romania, Bulgaria, Hungary and the Soviet zone of occupied Germany, were developing at various speeds into

What was the Soviet–US relationship in 1945?

🗝 KEY TERM

Pearl Harbor The US naval base in Hawaii.

Grand Alliance The USA, USSR and Britain were allied to oppose Nazi Germany in the Second World War.

Communist states. Nevertheless, the USSR came in a distant second to the USA in the great power rankings. The phenomenal economic power of the USA was frightening enough, but American possession of the atomic bomb left Stalin terrified. The world balance of power had dramatically changed.

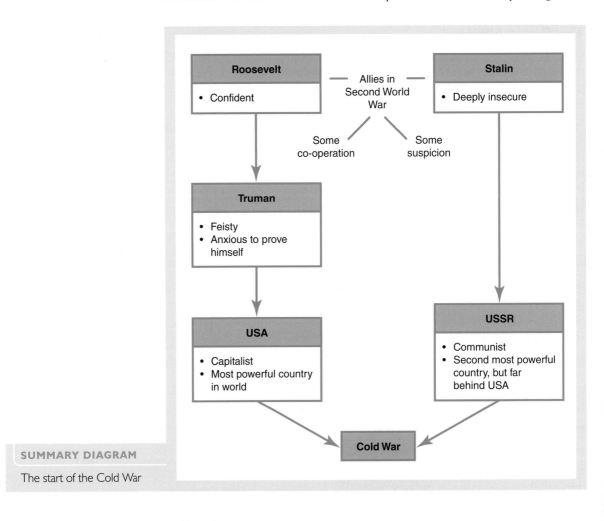

SUMMARY DIAGRAM

The start of the Cold War

3 Key debate

▶ *Key question: Why did the Cold War begin?*

There can be no doubt that when the Second World War came to an end, none of the major participants desired another war, whether 'hot' or 'cold'. Nevertheless, within two years of the end of the Second World War, the Cold War was underway. Historians have differing views on why it began. Some historians see the USA as the aggressor, some see Stalin as the aggressor, and some blame both.

The orthodox interpretation

Not surprisingly, many Westerners writing during the Cold War blamed Stalin. An early example of this **orthodox** approach was Arthur Schlesinger. Orthodox historians emphasize Stalin's aggression, especially his takeover of Eastern Europe.

The revisionist interpretation

Beginning in 1950 with William Appleman Williams, a **revisionist** group of American historians blamed their own country for the Cold War, emphasizing the American desire to export freely both US products and the American capitalist system. So, their argument goes, the Soviet takeover of Eastern Europe was ominous, as it would shut off potential markets for US products.

The post-revisionist interpretation

Post-revisionist historians apportion blame relatively equally to the USA and the USSR, as when Martin McCauley (2003) wrote of the inevitability of a clash between these two 'competing systems'. Post-revisionists also point out that mutual incomprehension and misunderstandings played an important role, as when the USA mistakenly believed that Stalin was assisting the Greek Communist Party after the Second World War.

Historians changing their minds

Some American historians who started out as revisionists became more orthodox and conservative in their viewpoints over the years, for example, Stephen Ambrose and John Lewis Gaddis.

Conclusions

The post-revisionists are surely right when they apportion blame equally. Both countries had expansionist ideologies, and the two greatest powers in the world at any given time are unlikely to get along. The role played by differing personalities was important. Roosevelt was more ingratiating and confident than the feisty Truman who tried to hide his insecurities behind an aggressive stance toward the USSR. Those who emphasize personality also attribute a great deal of responsibility to Stalin's insecurities, which arguably made him unjustifiably suspicious of the USA.

KEY TERM

Orthodox In the Cold War context, a Western historian who sees the West as always right and blames the USSR for the conflict.

Revisionist In the Cold War context, a Western historian who blames the USA for the conflict.

Post-revisionist In the Cold War context, a historian who argues that both the USA and the USSR bore responsibility for the Cold War.

T O K Which school of thought (orthodox, revisionist, or post-revisionist) do you find the most convincing? Why? (History, Reason.)

The Truman Doctrine and containment

> ▶ *Key question: What was the significance of the Truman Doctrine for US foreign policy?*

In 1947, President Truman made a speech to **Congress** in which he enunciated what became known as the **Truman Doctrine**. The speech could be considered to be a declaration of Cold War.

 ## Background to the Truman Doctrine

Why did Truman declare the Cold War in 1947?

Between August 1945 when Japan was defeated and March 1947 when Truman made his Truman Doctrine speech, Soviet–American relations deteriorated. There were tensions over Stalin's creation of a Communist Eastern Europe, Iranian oil, the Allied occupation of Germany, and Greece and Turkey.

The civil war in Greece provides an excellent example of how misunderstandings helped trigger the Cold War. Despite the **Western** conviction to the contrary, Stalin did not help the Greek Communists to foment revolution.

The second great cause of tension in the eastern Mediterranean was Stalin's behaviour over Turkey, which could be interpreted either as justifiable or as aggressive. During the Second World War, Roosevelt and Churchill had indicated that they would always recognize Stalin's interests in Turkey, where Istanbul stood astride the narrow Soviet exit from the Black Sea to the Mediterranean. Stalin therefore felt justified in putting pressure on Turkey for naval access after the war, but as post-war tensions increased, the Western position changed and in March 1947, Truman went before Congress to obtain $300 million for Greece and $100 million for Turkey, so that those countries could combat the Communist threat. **Republican** Senator Arthur Vandenberg told him he would have to 'scare the hell out of the country' in order to get Americans behind him. The **Democrat** Truman obliged. His speech (Source B) depicted a world divided between free people and unfree people, a world in which the USA would now champion and defend the free when threatened by Soviet Communism. It is hard to pinpoint each protagonist's definitive 'declaration' of Cold War, but Stalin's speech about the superiority of Communism in early 1946 and the Truman Doctrine speech in March 1947 are good candidates.

🔑 KEY TERM

Congress Elected US legislative body consisting of the Senate and the House of Representatives.

Truman Doctrine Truman's March 1947 speech that said the USA would help any country under attack from Communists.

Western Cold War term for the anti-Communist alliance led by the USA.

Republican US political party that tends to favour minimal government and big business.

Democrat US political party that tends to favour big government in matters relating to the health and welfare of the population.

SOURCE B

Truman's speech before Congress, 12 March 1947 (the Truman Doctrine speech).

At the present moment in world history nearly every nation must choose between alternative ways of life. The choice is too often not a free one. One way of life is based upon the will of the majority, and is distinguished by free institutions, representative government, free elections, guarantees of individual liberty, freedom of speech and religion, and freedom from political oppression. The second way of life is based upon the will of a minority forcibly imposed upon the majority. It relies upon terror and oppression, controlled press and radio, fixed elections, and the suppression of personal freedoms. I believe that it must be the policy of the United States to support free peoples who are resisting attempted subjugation by armed minorities or by outside pressures.

Do you think that the words in Source B would have been an effective prelude to Truman's request for aid for Greece and Turkey?

The Truman Doctrine and containment

In February 1946, the **State Department**'s Soviet specialist George Kennan's 'long telegram', sent from Moscow, urged US resistance to Soviet expansionism. In July 1947, Kennan reached a wider audience with an influential article (Source C) written under the pseudonym of 'Mr X' in the prestigious journal *Foreign Affairs*. Kennan claimed Moscow's foreign policy was based on traditional Russian expansionism, revolutionary Communist ideology, and Stalin's paranoid suspicions. He said the USA should 'contain' the USSR. The Truman administration decided Kennan had got it right and implemented this policy of **containment** of Communist expansionism.

🔑 KEY TERM

State Department The US federal government department that deals with foreign affairs.

Containment The Truman administration's policy of preventing the spread of Communism.

SOURCE C

'The Sources of Soviet Conduct', an article published in 1947 in *Foreign Affairs* under the pseudonym 'Mr X'.

It is clear that the main element of any United States policy towards the Soviet Union must be that of a long-term, patient but firm and vigilant containment of Russian expansive tendencies … It is clear that the United States cannot expect in the foreseeable future to enjoy political intimacy with the Soviet regime. It must continue to regard the Soviet Union as a rival, not a partner, in the political arena. It must continue to expect that Soviet policies will reflect no abstract love of peace and stability, no real faith in the possibility of a permanent happy coexistence of the Socialist and capitalist worlds, but rather a cautious, persistent pressure towards the disruption and weakening of all rival influence and rival power.

Using Source C and your own knowledge, explain why 'Mr X' wrote this article, and why it was significant.

The results and significance of the Truman Doctrine and containment

← **What impact did the Truman Doctrine have on US foreign policy?**

The Truman Doctrine was in effect a declaration of Cold War and it had a dramatic impact on US society and culture (see page 31) and on US foreign policy, which it dominated for nearly half a century. It was the major cause of

A map showing crises in the Cold War world.

> Using Source D, what inferences can you make in relation to Latin America and great Cold War crises?

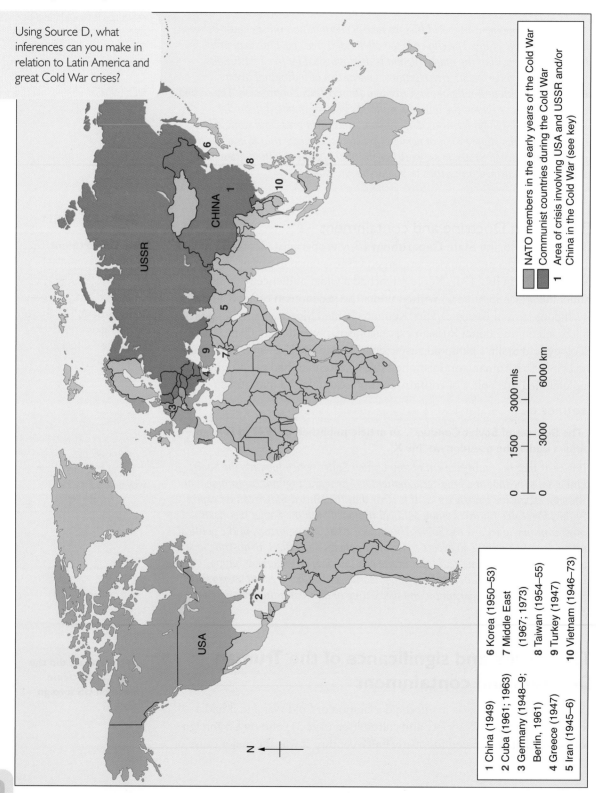

Key

- NATO members in the early years of the Cold War
- Communist countries during the Cold War
- 1 Area of crisis involving USA and USSR and/or China in the Cold War (see key)

1 China (1949)	6 Korea (1950–53)
2 Cuba (1961; 1963)	7 Middle East
3 Germany (1948–9;	(1967; 1973)
Berlin, 1961)	8 Taiwan (1954–55)
4 Greece (1947)	9 Turkey (1947)
5 Iran (1945–6)	10 Vietnam (1946–73)

0   1500   3000 mls
0   3000   6000 km

the US involvement in two wars in Asia, the Korean War (see Chapter 3) and the Vietnam War (see Chapter 5). It helped to generate an extremely expensive and tense arms race with the USSR, and a race to win the hearts and minds of the governments of countries on every continent.

Increased involvement in Europe

The Truman Doctrine led to increased American involvement in Europe. Under the **Marshall Plan**, $13 billion was given to West European nations in order to revitalize them as allies and trading partners of the USA. The political and economic association was militarily cemented from 1949, with the establishment of **NATO**. The creation of NATO was partly a response to Stalin's blockade of the American, British and French zones of Berlin, which lay within the Soviet zone of Germany. The West overcame the blockade by a sustained airlift of supplies to West Berlin during 1948–9. The Berlin blockade hastened the development of a West German state that was politically and militarily integrated into the Western anti-Soviet alliance.

KEY TERM

Marshall Plan US economic aid programme for post-war Western Europe, also known as Marshall Aid.

NATO The North Atlantic Treaty Organization, established in 1949, as a defensive alliance against the USSR.

SOURCE E

A map showing Cold War Germany in 1948.

Infer from Source E why there were Cold War crises over Berlin.

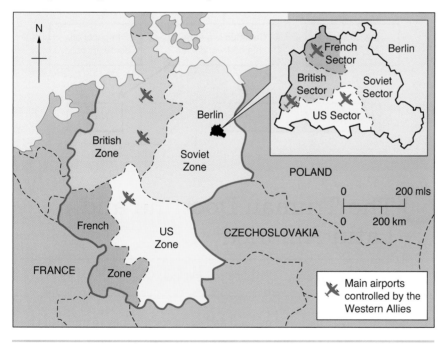

Criticisms of the Truman Doctrine

Contemporaries and historians have disagreed as to whether Truman and Kennan got it right. A case can be made that the USSR was an aggressively expansionist power that had to be contained. However, it can also be argued that Truman and containment led the USA into unimportant, undesirable and unaffordable commitments all over the globe.

Journalist Walter Lippmann criticized the Truman Doctrine as 'a global policy', a call to an 'ideological crusade' that 'has no limits'. He feared containment would engage the USA in 'recruiting, subsidizing, and supporting a heterogeneous array of satellites, clients, dependants and puppets', and would result in perpetual 'Cold War' with the USSR.

Whether right or wrong, the Truman Doctrine and containment revolutionized American foreign relations, with an impact not only on Europe and Asia, but also on Latin America.

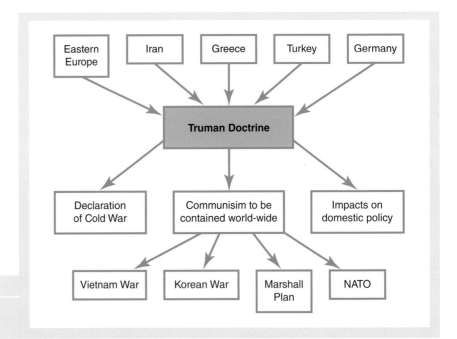

SUMMARY DIAGRAM

The Truman Doctrine and containment

5 The Truman Doctrine and Latin America

> ▶ **Key question:** *How did the Truman Doctrine impact on Latin America?*

President Roosevelt had worked hard and quite successfully to improve US–Latin American relations, but President Truman faced a new and different challenge in the Cold War that had an adverse impact on the relationship.

US and Latin American goals after 1945

How did US and Latin American post-war aims differ?

US foreign policy goals after the Second World War diverged from those of the Latin American nations. Truman sought an anti-Communist alliance but the Latin American nations had very different priorities. Their post-war goal was to obtain economic and technological aid in order to industrialize and diversify their economies. They believed that the great threat to Latin American stability was poverty, not Communist imperialism.

Within months of the Truman Doctrine speech, a conference of the American nations was held in Rio de Janeiro in September 1947. Truman sought a **collective security** system, while the Latin Americans sought American economic aid. The Latin American nations hoped that if they co-operated with Washington's plans for a regional security system, they might gain Marshall Aid for the Americas.

The Rio Conference, 1947

The participants at the Rio Conference signed the Rio Treaty. They agreed that an attack on one American nation would constitute an attack on all and merit resistance if two-thirds of them agreed on action. Having achieved this collective security system, which it thought necessary to combat Communism, the USA considered the Rio Conference to be a great success. US fears of Communism found some echoes in Latin America, as with the Argentine and Brazilian governments. Brazil, Chile and Cuba banned Communist organizations and cut off diplomatic relations with the USSR in 1948. However, many Latin Americans were deeply disappointed by the Rio Treaty: the Mexican journalist Narciso Bassols García disliked the way it made Latin American nations 'compulsory automatic allies of the United States'. Others felt that they had gone along with Truman's containment policy and got nothing in return (US **Secretary of State** George Marshall had explained at Rio that there must be no discussion of economic aid because European recovery took precedence over Latin American economic development).

SOURCE F

On the eve of the Rio Conference in 1947, Truman responded to a press conference question as to whether the USA was taking any notice of Latin American demands for economic aid.

I think there has always been a Marshall Plan in effect for the Western Hemisphere. The foreign policy of the United States in that direction has been set for one hundred years and is known as the Monroe Doctrine.

SOURCE G

A 1947 US State Department Policy Planning Staff memorandum to George Marshall.

To Latin American countries economic development is the foremost objective of national policy. The United States has repeatedly stated its desire to assist in the development program, but in their eyes performance by the United States has been disappointing … Their dissatisfaction has been increased by the United States [pre-] occupation with [European Reconstruction and Marshall Aid] and other foreign aid programs which they feel were crowding out consideration of their needs and will delay still further their plans.

KEY TERM

Collective security System whereby nations promised to intervene to help if one of them was a victim of aggression.

Secretary of State US government official with responsibility for foreign affairs.

How and why do Truman and the State Department Policy Planning Staff memorandum in Sources F and G differ on the relationship between Latin America and the Marshall Plan?

Pan-American Covering
North and South America.

OAS Organization of
American States, established
in 1948 to combat
Communism.

CIA The Central Intelligence
Agency was established in
1947 to conduct counter-
intelligence operations
outside the USA.

? How and why would the
Latin American nations and
the USA have a different
attitude toward this part of
the charter in Source H?

The Organization of American States, 1948

Several **Pan-American** conferences were held in the nineteenth and early
twentieth centuries. The participants became known as the Pan-American
Union. At Bogotá, Colombia, in 1948, the Union of American Republics was
reconstituted as the Organization of American States (**OAS**). The OAS laid
down the administrative machinery for hemispheric consultation and
military strategy, which pleased the Truman administration. To the USA, the
OAS represented hemispheric unity in the struggle against Communism, a
struggle in which the USA would take the lead. However, fearful lest US
leadership be equated with US domination, the Latin American nations
successfully insisted that the charter of the OAS included a statement of the
principles that would govern hemispheric relations (see Source H).

SOURCE H

Extract from the charter of the OAS.

*No State or group of States has the right to intervene, directly or indirectly, for
any reason whatever, in the internal or external affairs of any other State … No
State may use or encourage the use of coercive measures of an economic or
political character in order to force the sovereign will of another State and obtain
from it advantage of any kind.*

During the Cold War, the USA tended to view everything from a Cold War
perspective, which frequently led to misinterpretations of events in other
countries, as with the US perspective on the Colombian riots during the 1948
Bogotá conference. The riots were triggered by the assassination of a liberal
politician, Jorge Eliécer Gaitán. Many Latin American leaders saw these riots
as the products of Latin American economic problems, but the Truman
administration interpreted them as organized by Communist subversives.

How far did the
Truman
administration
sympathize with Latin
American problems?

→ Truman and aid to Latin America

At both Rio and Bogotá, the Latin American nations pressed the USA for
improved trading arrangements and financial aid. The American response
was to urge them to rely on their own private sectors and private US
investment. In 1948, the US ambassador to Brazil, Herschel Johnson,
explained that Western Europe got far more than Latin America because it
was like 'a case of smallpox in Europe competing with a common cold in
Latin America'. The USA did not see Latin America as under immediate
threat from Soviet expansionism, although a **CIA** document of October 1949
said, 'The general state of political instability continues to be adverse to U.S.
interests in Hemisphere solidarity.'

In 1949, Truman asked Congress to authorize his Point IV Technical Assistance
Program, which aimed to promote technological, scientific, managerial and
economic self-help programmes in less developed countries. While Roosevelt
had flattered Latin Americans into thinking that the region was a top priority
in US foreign policy, the Truman administration grouped Latin America with

Asia and Africa in this programme. The downgrading of Latin American importance was statistically confirmed in that between 1949 and 1953, the 20 Latin American republics received $79 million, while the rest of the world received $18 billion. The $79 million was insignificant compared to Marshall Aid. The Latin American nations felt the USA placed far greater value on the nations of Western Europe and Japan, which received billions of dollars for reconstruction. 'You evidently do not perceive the depth of our economic crisis,' wrote Brazilian President Getúlio Vargas to Truman. Vargas's complaint was echoed by State Department official, Louis Joseph Halle, whose anonymous *Foreign Affairs* article (1950) criticized the Truman administration for insufficient economic support to Latin America, as a result of which a rising tide of anti-Americanism was being created in Latin America.

ECLA

Despite US opposition, the **United Nations** (UN) set up the Economic Commission for Latin America (ECLA) in 1948. ECLA criticized US financial and economic policies, arguing that Latin American poverty owed much to its perceived role as a supplier of raw materials to the industrial nations that made more profitable manufactured goods.

SOURCE I

An extract from *The Economic Development of Latin America and its Principal Problems*, a 1950 report for the UN written by Argentine Raúl Prebisch, executive secretary of ECLA 1949–63.

The outdated schema of the international division of labour … achieved great importance in the nineteenth century and … continued to exert considerable influence until very recently. Under that schema, the specific task that fell to Latin America … was that of producing food and raw materials for the great industrial centres. There was no place within it for the industrialization of the new countries … Two world wars in a single generation and a great economic crisis between them have shown the Latin American countries their opportunities, clearly pointing the way to industrial activity … The enormous benefits that derive from increased productivity have not reached the periphery in a measure compatible to that obtained by the peoples of the great industrial countries. Hence, the outstanding differences between the standards of living of the masses of the former and the latter.

SOURCE J

In 1952, National Security Council Planning Paper Number 141 set out the objectives of the Truman administration with regard to Latin America.

In Latin America we seek first and foremost an orderly political and economic development which will make Latin American nations resistant to the internal growth of Communism and to Soviet political warfare … Secondly, we seek hemisphere solidarity and support of our world policy and the cooperation of the Latin American nations in safeguarding the hemisphere through the individual and collective defense measures against external aggression and internal subversion.

KEY TERM

United Nations
International organization established after the Second World War to work for international peace, co-operation and progress.

In Source I, what reason does Raúl Prebisch give for Latin America's poverty relative to countries such as the USA?

Using your own knowledge, how far had Truman's Latin American policies achieved the objectives stated in Source J?

'The lady in the tutti-frutti hat'

Carmen Miranda (1909–55) was a Portuguese-born Brazilian who became a leading radio and movie performer in Brazil in the 1930s. She specialized in the samba music of Brazil's black slums. Her trademark costumes (colourful turbans, bangles and exposed midriff) were characteristic of some of the impoverished women in those slums. She was offered a Hollywood movie contract and arrived in the USA in 1939. She was invited to the White House because the Roosevelt administration saw her visit as facilitating the 'good neighbor' relationship between the USA and Latin America. By 1946 she was the highest-paid Hollywood star. Nicknamed the 'Brazilian Bombshell' or 'the lady in the tutti-frutti hat', she made 14 Hollywood movies between 1940 and 1953 and to many Americans she represented a typical Latin American. On a visit to Brazil in 1940 she was greatly criticized for 'selling out' to American commercialism and making Brazil look foolish with her towering 'tutti-frutti hats'. Her movie roles had become increasingly stereotypical. On film, she always played a 'vulgar, flashy, hyperkinetic, language-mangling Latin', according to *Bright Lights Film Journal* (1996). In order to sustain her career, she did not resist her typecasting, although she found it humiliating. Her Hollywood career illustrates American interest in, but also stereotyping of, Latin America, along with Brazilian resentment at that demeaning image.

SOURCE K

Carmen Miranda posing in her costume in 1948.

? Judging from Source K, how did Hollywood portray Latin American women?

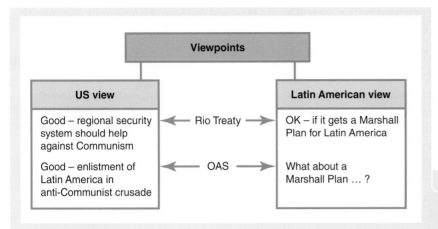

6 The Cold War and American society and culture

▶ **Key question:** *How and why did the Cold War affect American society and culture?*

Background to the Red Scare under Truman

The American people disliked Communism because it was atheistic and seemed to threaten the 'American Dream' that everyone was free to get ahead and to get rich. The historian James Patterson (1996) noted that Americans have 'periodically lashed out at radicals, alleged subversives, aliens, immigrants, blacks, Catholics, Jews, and other vulnerable groups who could be blamed for complex problems'. The first American **Red Scare**, which followed the Bolshevik Revolution of 1917, was one such outburst.

During the poverty-stricken 1930s, right-wing politicians and intellectuals feared **socialism** and Communism might gain popularity so the House of Representatives Committee on Un-American activities (HUAC) investigated **left-wingers**. During the Second World War, there was even less tolerance of different ideas, as in 1940 when the Smith Act targeted advocates of revolution, including Communists. President Roosevelt encouraged **FBI** director J. Edgar Hoover to check on possible Communists and initiated programmes in 1942 that sought out those who were a 'security risk'.

A new Red Scare

At the end of the Second World War, the vast majority of Americans regarded Communism as an alien ideology that was godless, repressive, aggressive and socialistic. This traditional ideological aversion, the surge of patriotism

KEY TERM

Red Scare An outburst of anti-Communist hysteria, in which Communists (real and imagined) were seen everywhere ('Reds under the bed').

> **Is it surprising that a Red Scare gripped the USA under Truman?**

KEY TERM

Socialism Political philosophy that advocated redistribution of wealth. Some contemporaries used the words Communism and socialism interchangeably.

Left-wingers Those sympathetic to the ideals of socialism and Communism, favouring government activism.

FBI The Federal Bureau of Investigation was established in 1935 in order to investigate federal crime and to collect intelligence.

> **Who or what was to blame for the Red Scare?**

generated by the Second World War, and the fear of Soviet military strength combined to generate a second Red Scare, an era of unprecedented anti-Communist hysteria.

HUAC

In 1945 Congressman John Rankin suggested HUAC be made permanent and given broader powers in order to deal with domestic subversion (he was convinced it was a Communist plot when the Red Cross did not label blood according to race). In 1947 the Republicans won control of Congress and of HUAC and began investigating a supposed Hollywood-centred Communist conspiracy to overthrow the government. The 'Hollywood 10', a group of writers and directors who had been or were members of the American Communist Party, were convicted of contempt of Congress and given one-year jail sentences. The hysterical pursuit of suspects then moved to Broadway (New York City's theatre district) and in 1948 the courts moved against Communist Party officials.

Truman's responsibility for the new Red Scare

In 1950, the McCarran or Internal Security Act said members of Communist-affiliated organizations had to register with the federal government or face jail or fines. Those who registered could be denied passports or deported. President Truman was torn between trying to defend his administration from charges that they were lax on security, and the desire to defend civil liberties. On the one hand, he tried (but failed) to veto the Internal Security Act, saying, 'In a free country we punish men for the crimes they commit, but never for the opinions they have.' On the other hand, soon after declaring the Truman Doctrine, he had contributed to the Red Scare by ordering Executive Order Number 9835, which ordered a loyalty investigation into federal employees.

The **Justice Department** and particularly the FBI were greatly involved in hunting Communists. Determined to root out Communism from the USA, J. Edgar Hoover ordered his men to follow up all leads on supposed subversives, however trivial. He was especially interested to hear about the sexual activities of those being investigated. Estimates of the numbers affected vary, but it has been suggested that between 1947 and 1952, there were 3000 investigations, 14,000 enquiries, over 1000 dismissals and several thousand resignations proffered in order to pre-empt investigations. Leading Democrat Clark Clifford recalled that Truman thought the Communist scare 'was a load of baloney. But political pressures were such that he had to recognize it.' Privately, Truman compared Hoover and the FBI to the *Gestapo*.

Communist successes, 1949–50

As advised by Senator Vandenberg, Truman had 'scared the hell' out of the American people with his Truman Doctrine. Americans grew even more anxious in 1949 when the Soviets exploded their first atomic bomb and

SOURCE L

'It's Okay – We're Hunting Communists'. A 1947 cartoon on HUAC, published in the *Washington Post*. (A 1947 Herblock Cartoon, copyright by The Herb Block Foundation.)

Look at Source L. What is the cartoonist's attitude towards HUAC?

China became Communist. In February 1950, Klaus Fuchs, who had worked on the development of the atomic bomb, was arrested in Britain for betraying atomic secrets to the Soviets. Other arrests followed in North America, including Ethel and Julius Rosenberg and State Department official Alger Hiss in January 1950.

Republican Party ambitions

Democrats had occupied the White House since 1933, so the Republicans needed an issue. Patriotism in the face of the Soviet threat required foreign policy consensus, so all the Republicans could do was to attack the

Democrats for not waging the Cold War with sufficient vigour. Beginning with the Republican successes in the 1946 congressional elections, the strategy worked. A spring 1948 poll found 73 per cent of Americans considered Truman too soft on the Soviets. In this already paranoid atmosphere, Republican Senator Joseph McCarthy convinced many Americans that the Truman administration contained Communists, although the Red Scare was obviously not just McCarthy's fault.

The Rosenbergs

Communists Ethel and Julius Rosenberg were the only American citizens executed for espionage in the Cold War. They were 'shopped' by Ethel's brother David. Like Julius, David was a Soviet spy. In 1996, David confessed that he had lied about his sister being a spy in exchange for the freedom of his wife (also a spy). Julius died after the first series of electrocutions, but when the attendants removed Ethel's strapping and other equipment after the normal course of electrocutions, it was found that her heart was still beating. Three more courses of electrocution were applied, after which smoke rose from Ethel's head. Doctors then attested that she was dead. No relatives would adopt the Rosenbergs' two orphaned sons, but a Jewish songwriter did so. It has been suggested that anti-Semitism played a part in the fate of the Rosenbergs.

What was the significance of McCarthy and McCarthyism in Cold War America?

→ McCarthy and McCarthyism

Born to a poor Irish farming family in central Wisconsin, Joseph McCarthy survived serious criticisms of his performance and behaviour as a county judge. In 1946, his successful campaign for the Senate owed much to his lies about his war record. He claimed his limp was due to a war wound but it was the result of falling down stairs at a party.

A 1949 poll of Washington correspondents voted McCarthy the worst US senator. Needing some good publicity, McCarthy presented himself as a diligent patriot, making a series of speeches in early 1950 in which he said there were card-carrying Communists in the State Department (the numbers he said he could name varied from speech to speech). The Senate then established a special committee under Millard Tydings, a conservative Democrat from Maryland, to investigate McCarthy's charges. The Tydings Committee quickly reported that McCarthy's lies were 'a fraud and a hoax', but McCarthy supporters in Maryland retaliated by circulating a fake photograph showing Tydings conversing animatedly with US Communist Party leader Earl Browder. Tydings failed to get re-elected in November 1950.

Investigations during the McCarthy hysteria

In 1952, McCarthy headed congressional committees that investigated Communist subversives in the USA. By 1953, these congressional investigations covered the media, the entertainment industry, colleges and

SOURCE M

A faked photograph of Senator Millard Tydings supposedly talking to Communist Party leader Earl Browder.

Can you tell that the photograph in Source M has been doctored? What does this photograph tell you about photographic evidence? **?**

universities. State legislatures joined in the witch hunt, and around 500 state and local government employees and 600 school teachers and 150 college professors lost their jobs. McCarthyites attacked **US Information Agency** libraries because they had exhibited the work of 'radicals' such as Mark Twain (1835–1910), the creator of two fictional characters much loved by American children, Huckleberry Finn and Tom Sawyer. The nation that considered itself to be the world's leading democracy was stifling freedom of speech and censoring books.

McCarthy and the presidential election of 1952

In 1952, McCarthy helped ensure the defeat of many Democrats ('Commie-crats'), including presidential candidate, Adlai Stevenson ('I'd like to teach patriotism to little Ad-lie'). Future president Richard Nixon had made his name in the second Red Scare-era investigations. He defeated Helen Gahagan Douglas in the California Senate race, mostly by accusing her of being a Communist, '**pink** down to her underwear' (she retaliated by christening him 'Tricky Dick', a nickname that stuck). In 1952, Nixon mocked 'Adlai the appeaser', graduate of the Truman administration's 'cowardly College of Communist Containment'. This anti-Stevenson feeling owed much to class hatred (McCarthy and Nixon came from poor backgrounds). Newspapers with working-class and/or right-wing editorship and readership were particularly hard on Stevenson. The New York *Daily News* called Adlai 'Adelaide', and said he 'trilled' his speeches in a 'fruity' voice. In a homophobic age, it was quite usual to smear establishment figures with supposed Communist sympathies with suggestions of homosexuality.

> 🔑 **KEY TERM**
>
> **US Information Agency** Established by President Eisenhower in 1953 to educate foreigners about the USA.
>
> **Pink** Cold War Americans referred to Communists as 'Reds' or as 'pink'.

How did McCarthy get away with it?

McCarthy terrorized many Americans with his untrue accusations. He got away with his lies because of the tradition of hysterical anti-Communism, the spy scares, Communist successes and expansionism (as demonstrated in Korea), and because of the Republican desire to regain control of the presidency and Congress ('20 years of treason'). Democrats felt they dare not defend the accused lest they be called Communist sympathizers and draw down McCarthy's fire on their own heads. Senators who did stand up to McCarthy suffered defeat in the 1952 congressional elections. McCarthy maintained good relations with many reporters, and the press was rarely hostile to him. Truman's Republican successor, Eisenhower (1953–61) said that he did not want to 'get into a pissing contest with that skunk'. In 1950, Harvard sociologist David Reisman summed it up, describing Cold War Americans as mindless, timid conformists.

The fall of McCarthy

McCarthy always had critics and he eventually fell from grace. When in one speech in Congress, he accused Secretary of State Dean Acheson (whom he described as 'this pompous diplomat with his striped pants and phoney British accent') and Second World War hero and Secretary of Defense George Marshall of Communism, all but three senators left the Senate chamber in disgust. The final straw was the 'Army–McCarthy' hearings, in which McCarthy frequently appeared unshaven and drunk. When McCarthy investigated a supposed spy ring on the army base at Fort Monmouth, New Jersey, the army filed charges against him, and his poll ratings slumped. In March 1955, the Senate finally censured him. He died in 1957, supposedly of cirrhosis of the liver.

Conclusions about the importance of McCarthy

Much of the paranoia and persecution that afflicted Cold War America was due to McCarthy, who also influenced American foreign policy and defence policy. Along with the Truman Doctrine and containment, McCarthy played an important part in getting the USA involved in the Korean War (see Chapter 3). Historian James Patterson (1996) credits him with making any attempt at negotiation with the USSR or China 'politically perilous': when Stalin died, the new Soviet regime sought **détente**, but no one in the Eisenhower State Department wanted to annoy McCarthy.

How did the Cold War change the USA?

→ The impact of the Cold War on American life

The Cold War had a massive impact on American society and culture. In a country that considered itself to be the world's leading democracy, states and towns banned Communists from government jobs. The struggle with the USSR led to an anti-Communist hysteria in which the American ideals of freedom of thought and freedom of expression were damaged. Thousands of innocent people suffered: several thousand lost their jobs, several hundred were jailed and over 150 were deported.

Children

The Cold War affected everyday life. In preparation for a nuclear attack, schoolchildren practised hiding under their desks like the government-sponsored cartoon character 'Bert the Turtle'. Bert knew to lower his head when threatened, so American schoolchildren would lower their heads when the teacher shouted 'Drop!' in the nuclear fallout drill. Many parents bought backyard bomb shelters. Even children's favourite comic-strip characters were drafted into the anti-Communist ranks. In *Annie*, Daddy Warbucks blew up a plane carrying an H-bomb toward America.

Entertainment

The impact on American culture was sometimes stultifying. On the one hand, many important books had little to do with Communism, as with J.D. Salinger's *The Catcher in the Rye* (1951). Similarly New York City was a world-beating centre of artistic and architectural creativity in the Truman years. On the other hand, popular culture was greatly affected, as demonstrated in Hollywood. Depression-era films explored social and economic problems, but Cold War Hollywood avoided such issues. Anti-Communist films abounded, including *The Iron Curtain* (1948), *The Red Menace* (1949) and *My Son John* (1952), who was betrayed to the authorities by his own anti-Communist mother. Hollywood played on fears of a nuclear holocaust: science-fiction movies were popular in an age that anticipated facing the horrors of the unknown. 'Subversives' from the world of entertainment who found themselves increasingly unemployed included outstanding musicians such as Leonard Bernstein and Aaron Copland, actor Edward G. Robinson and actor and singer Paul Robeson. British-born silent movie superstar Charlie Chaplin was no longer welcome in the USA after 1952. All had demonstrated leftist sympathies.

Religion and education

Religion underwent a renaissance in the Cold War era. Evangelical preacher Billy Graham warned great crowds against Communism. In 1954, Bishop Sheen denounced Communism to an audience that reached 25 million per week and the Catholic Knights of Columbus lobbied for a change to the Pledge of Allegiance, uttered daily by schoolchildren, hand on heart, facing the flag of the USA. Congress added to the pledge that the USA was one nation 'under God'.

Education was affected in other ways. The 1958 National Defence Education Act funded more opportunities for would-be scientists, mathematicians and linguists who could invent the weapons to defeat the Communists and speak the languages necessary to spy on them and to convince other nations to oppose them.

The Korean War

The Cold War led to the USA fighting in Korea (see Chapter 3). An estimated 36,000 Americans died there and the war cost the American taxpayer

$67 billion. The increased defence expenditure boosted the gross national product, but also generated inflation and a rise in the cost of living. On the other hand, the Korean War benefited African Americans because it sped up the desegregation of the army. At this time, African Americans in the southern United States were not allowed to vote or to sit in the same schools or restaurants as white Americans, but under the pressure of war, the American forces in Korea were integrated. Short of manpower and slowed up by having to run a black and the white army, both the army top brass and ordinary soldiers realized that segregation hurt them. However, the beneficial impact of the Cold War for African Americans in the armed forces was the exception rather than the rule. In a Cold War in which the USA considered itself to be the champion of freedom against repressive Communist regimes, American society ironically became more conformist and oppressive.

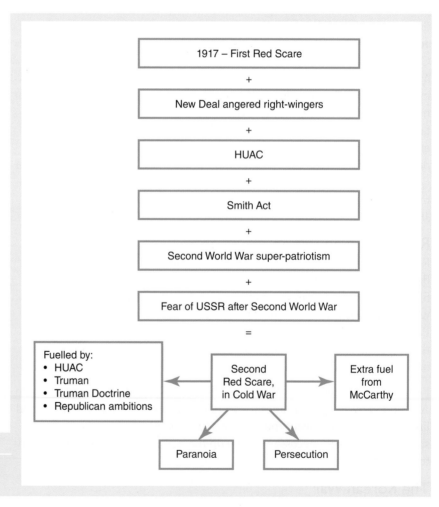

SUMMARY DIAGRAM

The Cold War and American society and culture

Chapter summary

President Truman and the Cold War

The Cold War developed soon after the end of the Second World War. Historians disagree over its origins. Although allied, there were Soviet–American tensions in the Second World War. Suggested causal factors of the Cold War include Truman's aggression, the US atomic bomb, Stalin's aggression and insecurities, the Soviet takeover of Eastern Europe, ideology, and a traditional great power struggle. The Soviet threat to Greece and Turkey prompted the Truman Doctrine, in which Truman depicted the USA as good and the USSR as evil, and sought aid to help Greece and Turkey against the USSR. Truman implemented the policy of containment in order to halt Soviet expansionism, although critics said he was setting unrealistic goals for the USA. The Truman Doctrine led to massive American aid to Europe and the establishment of NATO. In the search for Cold War allies, the USA wooed Latin America and masterminded the Organization of American States, but Truman did not want to give Latin Americans the large-scale economic aid that they sought.

The Cold War had a great impact on American society and culture. The first American 'Red Scare' occurred soon after the Bolshevik Revolution of 1917, the second after the Second World War. This second Red Scare owed much to traditional American anti-Communism, the exaggerated patriotism generated by war, Soviet military strength, HUAC, the Truman administration, spy scares, the loss of China, the Soviet bomb, Republican political ambitions, the Korean War and Senator McCarthy. McCarthy lost credibility by 1954, but along with the Cold War, he had greatly affected American lives. Some people lost their jobs, and popular culture was often propagandist and not particularly thoughtful.

 # Examination advice

How to answer 'assess' questions

Questions that ask you to assess want you to make judgements that you can support with evidence, reasons and explanations. It is important for you to demonstrate why your own assessment is better than alternative ones.

Example

> Assess the impact of the Cold War on US politics during Truman's presidency.

1. For this question you need to consider how the Cold War affected US politics from 1945 to 1953. One way to consider 'politics' is to think of it as the balance of power between the Democrats and the Republicans. You should also consider the role McCarthyism played in Washington. Finally, events taking place outside the USA, for example in Korea, are worth examining. How did they have an impact on political decisions in Washington, DC?
2. First, take at least five minutes to write a short outline. In this outline, you could list the various ways in which the Cold War had an impact on US national politics. For example, you might include the following:

- *Truman asked Congress for hundreds of millions of dollars for Greece and Turkey. Gave speech before Congress. Known as Truman Doctrine speech*
- *Not all agreed. Some felt Truman was about to embark on a global ideological crusade. But most agreed that Communism must be contained – here, there was Republican/Democratic consensus.*
- *Marshall Plan. $23 billion for Europe, little for Latin America*
- *1949: Truman asked Congress for millions for less developed nations, including Latin America.*
- *Red Scares: late 1940s, early 1950s. Impact on Congressional elections. Republicans won control of House and Senate in 1946 elections. Republicans also controlled House Un-American Activities Committee. Republicans claimed to be able to wage the Cold War more efficiently – here, the Cold War polarized US politics.*
- *1950: McCarran Act. Hunt for subversives.*
- *Senator McCarthy claimed Truman administration had Communist sympathizers in it. Witch hunts began.*
- *Tydings Committee. Tydings was smeared with false accusations of Communist ties and lost seat.*
- *McCarthy helped defeat many Democratic candidates in 1952 elections including Adlai Stevenson.*
- *FBI role in searching for subversives.*
- *Even though McCarthy ended his career in disgrace, much damage had been done.*
- *Voter anxiety about the Cold War helped propel the USA into the Korean War and across the 38th parallel. This war greatly damaged Truman's presidency.*

3. Your introduction should state your thesis which might be something like: 'The Cold War had a significant impact on Truman's presidency. This was partly due to the fear of Communism which, in some quarters, reached hysterical proportions.' Be sure to raise the main themes you will discuss in detail in the body of your essay. These could include Truman's policy of containment, how the Cold War influenced the 1946 and 1952 elections, and the role played by Senator McCarthy. An example of a good introductory paragraph for this question is given on the next page.

Soon after he became president in 1945, Truman was entangled in the Cold War. The Cold War had a great impact on US politics, sometimes creating political consensus, such as when Democrats and Republicans agreed that Communism must be opposed, but sometimes polarizing politics, such as when the Republicans (especially McCarthy) accused the Democrat Truman of weakness in the face of the Communist threat. The Cold War affected the result of congressional elections (1948, 1950 and 1952) and the presidential election of 1952 (Cold War fears propelled the USA into the Korean War, which greatly damaged Truman's presidency).

4. In the body of your essay, try to explain the relationship between the Cold War and US politics from 1945 to 1953. You might devote one paragraph for each theme. These themes could be both domestic (for example, McCarthyism, US elections) and international (crises in Greece and Korea, see Chapter 3). Be sure to discuss the relative impact of each theme you raise. One strategy would be to begin with the ones you think had the greatest impact and end with those that had the smallest.
5. In the conclusion, you should tie together the ideas you have explored and come to a judgement about how much impact the Cold War had on US politics during the Truman's presidency.
6. Now try writing a complete answer to the question following the advice above.

Examination practice

Below are two exam-style questions for you to practise on this topic.

1 To what extent was the USA to blame for the Cold War?
   (For guidance on how to answer 'to what extent' questions, see page 67.)

2 Analyse Truman's foreign policy towards Latin America.
   (For guidance on how to answer 'analyse' questions, see page 90.)

CHAPTER 3

The Korean War 1950–3

This chapter looks at what began as a Korean civil war but became the international 'Korean War' when the USA and the United Nations (UN) entered on the side of South Korea. You need to consider the following questions throughout this chapter:

✪ Why did the USA and the UN intervene in a Korean civil war in 1950?

✪ What military developments occurred in Korea in 1950?

✪ How far did other nations contribute to the Korean War?

✪ How and why did the Korean War come to an end?

✪ How did the Korean War affect US politics and diplomacy?

 Causes of the outbreak of the Korean War

> ▶ **Key question:** Why did the USA and the UN intervene in a Korean civil war in 1950?

Japan controlled Korea from 1895 to 1945. During the Second World War, the USA and the USSR agreed that at the end of the war, the Japanese surrender in Korea would be taken by the Soviets in the north and the Americans in the south. The origins of the Korean War owed much to these pragmatic military decisions, which became highly significant because of the development of the Cold War.

How and why did two Koreas develop?

→ Korea 1945–9

As Soviet–American relations deteriorated during 1945–6, they failed to agree on Korean reunification. As both powers had troops stationed in Korea, it is not surprising that the USA tried to create a southern Korean state in its own image, and the USSR did likewise in the north.

The establishment of South Korea

In search of international approval for its policies and ambitions for Korea, the USA encouraged UN-supervised elections in the south in 1948. These elections made the pro-American anti-Communist Syngman Rhee (1875–1965) leader of the newly established Republic of Korea (the ROK or South Korea). American troops put down a major rising against him in October 1948, then left in 1949.

The establishment of North Korea

In September 1948, the Democratic People's Republic of Korea (the DPRK or North Korea) was established under the leadership of the Communist Kim Il Sung. Many believe that if free national elections had been held in Korea, Kim would have won.

The Korean desire for unification

The creation of two Korean nations moulded in the image of the two Cold War protagonists made a Korean war likely, especially as both Rhee and Kim desired reunification (naturally each wanted it on his own terms). By the time Soviet troops left in 1948, North Korea was armed to the hilt. Fearful that Rhee might attack North Korea, the USA gave him far less military equipment.

In June 1950, North Korea attacked South Korea. Most historians now agree that the two Koreas were already waging civil war before this attack. There had been frequent border clashes, mostly initiated by South Korea. They began in the summer of 1948, and peaked in the summer of 1949. Given the anti-Rhee rising in 1948, Kim Il Sung probably thought that his June 1950 invasion of South Korea would inspire popular rebellion there. However, at the time the US perception was that the USSR and China were behind North Korean aggression..

The US entry into the Korean War

<table>
<tr><td>

What were the reasons for the US participation in the Korean War?

</td></tr>
</table>

Reason 1: American anti-Communism

The underlying reason for US entry into the Korean War was fear of an ideology that rejected capitalism and multi-party states. The USA believed its security would be threatened in a world where more and more countries became Communist. Communist countries might try to export their ideology (either by persuasion or by force) to other countries, including the USA, and/or refuse to trade with the USA and thereby damage the American economy.

Reason 2: the world balance of power

By the summer of 1950, it seemed to the USA that the world balance of power was beginning to tilt in favour of Communism. US anxiety about the loss of Eastern Europe (see page 19) was exacerbated by several events between 1948 and 1949, including Stalin's unsuccessful blockade of the Western zones of Berlin, the Soviet atomic bomb test, and the Communist victory in China.

By June 1950, Communism seemed to be entering a dynamic expansionist phase in Asia. China was now Communist, North Korea had attacked South Korea, and there were Communist insurgencies in French Indochina, British Malaya and the Philippines. Some historians emphasize the Cold War credibility of the USA as a major cause of American entry into the Korean War: the USA had to be seen to be able to contain Communism.

? Looking at the map in Source A, suggest reasons why the USA considered a friendly South Korea to be important.

A map showing Korea and East Asia in the 1950s.

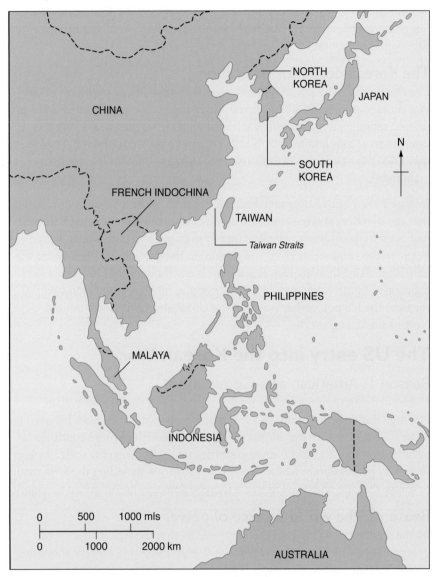

Loss of China

After the defeat of Japan in the Second World War, China was ravaged by civil war in which Chiang Kai-shek's Nationalists fought Mao's Communists. Initially the USA continued to give financial and military aid to Chiang, but this was cancelled in December 1948. In 1949 Mao's Communist forces were triumphant and Mao declared the establishment of the People's Republic of China (PRC). Chiang and the remnants of his Nationalist forces fled to the island of Formosa, now more commonly called Taiwan.

Reason 3: McCarthyism and domestic political concerns

Having depicted Communism as a terrifying evil in his 'Truman Doctrine' speech of March 1947 (see pages 22–3), Truman was vulnerable to Republican accusations that by ceasing aid to Mao's rival Chiang Kai-shek, he was responsible for the **'loss of China'** (see box on page 44) in 1949. After McCarthy's February 1950 accusations that there were Communists in the State Department (see pages 34–5), Truman needed to be seen to be tough on Communism, especially as his party faced the congressional elections in November 1950. As wars tended to make the American people rally around their president, Truman's political motivation in entering the Korean War has long been stressed by some historians, although denied by others.

Reason 4: NSC-68

Early in 1950, Truman commissioned the National Security Council to produce a planning paper to suggest how the USA should handle the Communist threat. **NSC-68** depicted a polarized world, in which the enslaved (in Communist countries) faced the free (in countries such as the USA). NSC-68 claimed that the USSR had a 'fanatic faith' and that its leaders wanted total domination of the Eurasian landmass. It recommended that the USA develop a more powerful bomb, build up its **conventional forces** to defend its shores and enable it to fight limited wars abroad, raise taxes to finance the struggle, seek allies, and mobilize the American public in a united Cold War consensus. These recommendations make it easy to see why the USA was ready to intervene in Korea.

Reason 5: fears for Japan

After the Second World War, the US occupation under General Douglas MacArthur had revitalized Japan, which began to develop from American foe into American friend. Only about 100 miles from South Korea, Japan's safety would be jeopardized if it were faced by a totally Communist Korean peninsula with Communism on the march. The Defense Department told Truman that Japan was vital for the defence of the West against Communism.

Reason 6: the UN and lessons from history

Truman and his contemporaries believed that the failure of the **League of Nations** had played a role in the outbreak of the Second World War and showed that collective security must be supported and **appeasement** avoided. When North Korea attacked South Korea, Truman believed that the UN was being tested and that if he failed to support it and appeased aggressors, the result might be another world war.

 **KEY TERM**

'Loss of China' Belief that Truman could have prevented Communist victory in China in 1949 with more aid to Chiang Kai-shek.

NSC-68 Sixty-eighth National Security Council planning paper.

Conventional forces Soldiers, tanks, ships, etc.

League of Nations A global organization, set up in 1920, to resolve international disputes.

Appeasement Policy of conciliating a potential aggressor by making concessions, as Britain and France did to Nazi Germany in the 1930s, before the outbreak of the Second World War.

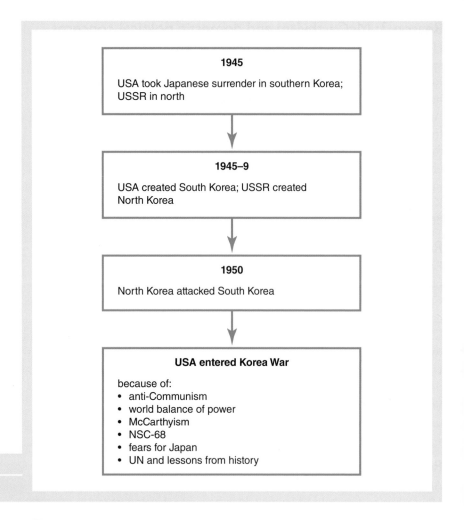

Causes of the Korean War

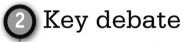 **Key debate**

> ▶ **Key question:** *Why did the Korean War begin?*

The changing Western viewpoint

For many years, the traditional orthodox viewpoint among Western historians was that this was a war of Communist aggression. However, the revisionist historian Bruce Cumings (1981, 1990) emphasized that this was initially a Korean civil war. The current consensus is that the North Korean attack was motivated more by Korean nationalism and the desire for the reunification of the peninsula than by Communist aggression. Cumings also emphasized that the USA bore a great deal of responsibility for that Korean civil war, and therefore for the Korean War, because the USA stopped a left-wing revolution in South Korea in 1945 and imposed a reactionary regime there that Kim Il Sung expected to overthrow with relative ease.

US intervention

The traditional interpretation

According to the still popular traditional interpretation (for example, the historians Michael Dockrill and Michael Hopkins, 2006), the USA was motivated by anti-Communism and containment.

The revisionist interpretation

Revisionist historians such as Robert Wood (2005) claim US policy was motivated by **economic imperialism**.

The emphasis on one factor

Some historians emphasize specific factors. According to Melvyn Leffler (2001), the USA believed it had to intervene in Korea for two reasons. First, because Japan's economic revival required access to markets and raw materials in other countries such as Korea and Malaya. Second, to demonstrate to Japan that the USA was a credible power and ally. John Lewis Gaddis (2005) stressed that the American intervention was a response to a Communist 'challenge to the entire structure of post-war collective security', and quotes Truman 'repeatedly' telling his advisers, 'We can't let the UN down.'

3 The course of events in the Korean War in 1950

▶ *Key question: What happened in Korea in 1950?*

The internationalization of the war in summer 1950

On 25 June 1950, North Korea attacked South Korea. In the absence of the USSR (which was boycotting the UN because Communist China did not have a seat) and encouraged by the USA, the UN **Security Council** passed a resolution that declared that the UN should oppose North Korean aggression.

Truman sent US air and naval forces to help South Korea, telling Americans that Communism had to be resisted. Although he did not ask Congress to declare war, as he was supposed to do under the US constitution, Congress was very supportive in what Truman said was not a war but 'a police action under the United Nations'.

When the US commander in the Pacific, General Douglas MacArthur, warned that without American troops the Communists would take over the whole of Korea, Truman sent US ground troops to Korea and ordered the US

KEY TERM

Economic imperialism
Dominating other countries through trade rather than by territorial conquest.

T O K Investigate Chinese and Korean historians' perspectives on the causes of the Korean War. How do these differ from the views of the historians mentioned here? How are they similar? What might explain these similarities and differences? (History, Social Science, Ethics, Emotion, Perception, Language, Reason.)

← **How did Truman react to the North Korean attack on South Korea?**

KEY TERM

Security Council UN body that has responsibility for the maintenance of international peace and security. It has five permanent members and 10 non-permanent members. Each member can veto an action.

7th Fleet to the Taiwan Straits (see the map on page 44). When the UN asked Truman to appoint a commander for the United Nations Command (UNC), Truman appointed MacArthur. The UN sought direct access to MacArthur, but Truman insisted that he communicate only with Washington.

The significance of the US entry into the Korean War

The US entry into the Korean War was highly significant:

- **Joint Chiefs of Staff** (JCS) chairman General Omar Bradley doubted that the USSR and China would get involved in the war, but warned that if they did, there could be a third world war.
- When Truman ordered tens of thousands of American forces to Korea he was 'significantly expanding and militarizing' American foreign policy in Asia, according to historian James Patterson (1996).
- The historian Gordon Chang (1990) argued that when Truman sent the 7th Fleet to the Taiwan Straits, he re-injected the USA into a Chinese Civil War from which it had previously extricated itself when it stopped aiding Chiang Kai-shek (see page 44). While the dispatch of the 7th Fleet was motivated by the American fear that a Chinese Communist takeover of Taiwan would threaten US security, Communist China interpreted it as an aggressive move. Chinese fears were confirmed when, to the dismay of the State Department, MacArthur visited Chiang Kai-shek on 30 July and publicly praised him. Although Secretary of State Dean Acheson said that the American war aim in Korea was simply to get North Korea out of South Korea, American allies such as Britain pointed out that the combination of the fleet deployment and MacArthur's public support for Chiang suggested that the USA also aimed to defend Taiwan and perhaps even to promote Chiang's aggression against Communist China.
- MacArthur was likely to prove problematic. Already commander of US forces in the Pacific, with a reputation as a great soldier and an expert on East Asia, he seemed to be the logical choice as UNC commander. However, Republican foreign policy expert John Foster Dulles warned Truman that MacArthur was tactless. JCS Chairman Omar Bradley considered MacArthur to be arrogant, and in a 1945 diary entry, Truman described MacArthur as 'Mr Prima Donna, Brass Hat', a 'play actor and bunco [swindler, trickster] man'. There were major tensions between MacArthur and Truman. Truman wanted a limited, defensive war in South Korea; MacArthur wanted to go all out against North Korea and, later, against China. Truman rejected MacArthur's strategy as risking a dangerous war with the USSR and China that would distract the USA and leave Europe more vulnerable to Soviet pressure.
- The war was likely to cause problems within the USA. Although early polls showed three-quarters of Americans approved of Truman's assistance to South Korea and members of Congress stood up and cheered when they heard he was sending troops and when he asked them for $10 billion in July 1950, Truman never obtained a congressional

declaration of war. Senator Tom Connally, head of the influential Senate Foreign Relations Committee, assured him that he did not need this, 'as Commander in Chief and under the UN Charter'. However, should the war go badly, it would give Truman's opponents the opportunity to call the Korean War, 'Truman's war'.

The summer and autumn of 1950

How well did the US/UN/ROK forces do in the summer and autumn of 1950?

American troop preparation

Unprepared for the North Korean attack, the US/ROK forces were on the defensive and struggled throughout the summer, despite the experienced and aggressive US commander, Major General Walton 'Bulldog' Walker. The US Army had been rapidly run down after the Second World War, and the 8th Army had gone soft on occupation duty in Japan (see Source B).

SOURCE B

In October 1950, when the US forces were doing better, Lieutenant-Colonel John 'Iron Mike' Michaelis told the *Saturday Evening Post* about some of his troops' initial problems in Korea.

When they started out, they couldn't shoot. They didn't know their weapons. They have not had enough training in plain old-fashioned musketry. They'd spent a lot of time listening to lectures on the difference between Communism and Americanism and not enough time crawling on their bellies on maneuvers with live ammunition singing over them … The U.S. army is so damn road bound that the soldiers have almost lost the use of their legs. Send out a patrol on a scouting mission and they load up in a three-quarter ton truck and start riding down the highway.

How far would you trust Source B's evaluation of the quality of American troops at the start of the Korean War?

American morale and motivation

Initially, American morale was high. US General George Barth said the American troops had 'overconfidence that bordered on arrogance'. However, as the war dragged on, fighting a limited war for ideology made it difficult to maintain morale. There was no attack on American soil to motivate US forces or any traditional attachment to Korea. Korean conditions were particularly difficult. In August, the temperature was over 38°C (100°F), accentuating the smell of the *kimchi* (fermenting cabbage) buried along the roadsides and of the 'honey wagons', ox-drawn carts of human excrement used to fertilize Korean rice paddies. Thirsty American soldiers, ignorant of Korean agricultural methods, drank water from those rice fields, and then suffered from dysentery. There were also communication problems. Americans could not tell who was North Korean or South Korean or, later, Chinese. Also, US air and ground co-ordination was very poor early in the war. An American soldier wounded by an attack by his own air force, asked, 'What kind of screwy war is this?' All that inspired many American soldiers was the desire to stay alive and the determination not to let their fellow American soldiers down.

Retreat to the Pusan Perimeter, July–August 1950

American military planners believed Korea's mountains and rice paddies made it unsuitable for tanks, so none had been given to Syngman Rhee. As a result, US/ROK forces were unable to halt the North Korean tanks and were forced into a chaotic retreat. Inexperienced troops frequently fled the battlefield, a phenomenon that became known as 'bugout fever'.

The North Koreans were a tough enemy and the fighting was brutal. Of the 4000 Americans who fought at Taejon, one in three ended up dead, wounded or missing. There was great American bitterness about North Korean tactics and atrocities, such as when they used South Korean refugees as human screens from behind which they could throw hand grenades.

By September, there had been 8000 American casualties, and although 50 countries had pledged some kind of support, only the British had arrived. The retreating US/UN/ROK troops were pinned behind the **Pusan Perimeter**, within which were the only port and airfield left where the USA could land more troops and supplies. It was vital to make a stand and Walker managed it ('There will be no more retreating'). By now the North Koreans also had problems. They had lost 58,000 men in their charge to the south and were outnumbered and down to around 40 tanks, with overstretched supply lines. The Americans still controlled the skies and seas, and within the Pusan Perimeter had less territory to defend, and more troops with which to defend it. The arrival of six US tank battalions soon made a great difference, but most importantly, the military situation was miraculously transformed by MacArthur's brilliant and successful assault on Inchon in September 1950.

Inchon, September 1950

MacArthur's plan was to bypass enemy strongholds with an **amphibious assault** that would leave enemy forces cut off and surrounded. The JCS insisted it would fail because of problems with the tides, the sea wall and the weather. However, MacArthur won Truman's support. The assault went ahead and Inchon and the South Korean capital Seoul were speedily taken. MacArthur had triumphed, which would have dramatic political and military implications in the months to come.

How and why did US war aims change in September 1950?

Changing US war aims

The USA had entered the war to restore the *status quo* by evicting the North Koreans from South Korea, but following Inchon US/UN/ROK forces crossed the **38th parallel** (see the map on page 51) into North Korea. The new war aim was 'the destruction of the North Korean armed forces', which would result in the reunification of the Korean peninsula. There were several reasons for the change. First, military momentum and a surge of optimism made stopping at the 38th parallel seem ridiculous to most Americans and South Koreans who desired revenge for all their dead and wounded. Second, MacArthur recommended the change and his advice was taken very

---

KEY TERM

Pusan Perimeter An area 100 by 50 miles in the south-eastern corner of the Korean peninsula, where retreating US/UN/ROK troops were pinned around the port of Pusan in summer 1950.

Amphibious assault Attack in which land and sea forces combine.

38th parallel Line of latitude dividing northern Korea from southern Korea.

SOURCE C

A map showing the course of events in Korea.

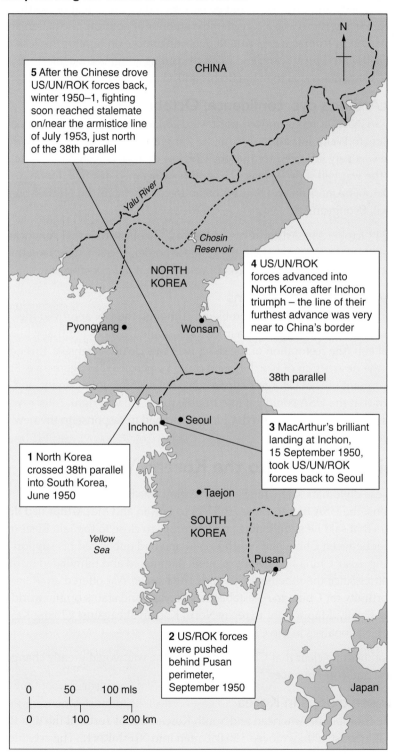

5 After the Chinese drove US/UN/ROK forces back, winter 1950–1, fighting soon reached stalemate on/near the armistice line of July 1953, just north of the 38th parallel

CHINA

N

Yalu River

Chosin Reservoir

NORTH KOREA

4 US/UN/ROK forces advanced into North Korea after Inchon triumph – the line of their furthest advance was very near to China's border

Pyongyang ●

● Wonsan

38th parallel

Inchon ●   ● Seoul

3 MacArthur's brilliant landing at Inchon, 15 September 1950, took US/UN/ROK forces back to Seoul

1 North Korea crossed 38th parallel into South Korea, June 1950

● Taejon

SOUTH KOREA

Yellow Sea

Pusan ●

2 US/ROK forces were pushed behind Pusan perimeter, September 1950

Japan

| 0 | 50 | 100 mls |
| 0 | 100 | 200 km |

Looking at Source C, can you infer why MacArthur's landing at Inchon was 'brilliant'?

?

seriously, especially after his success at Inchon. Third, Korea had come to represent US determination to stand up to Communism and it was felt that US credibility and prestige would be best served by the defeat of North Korea. Finally, there was a considerable amount of political calculation and motivation in Truman's decision. Republican attacks on him for the 'loss' of China, the McCarthy scare, and the forthcoming congressional elections, made Truman anxious to maintain his anti-Communist credentials.

MacArthur's overconfidence, October 1950

As US/UN/ROK forces moved northwards, MacArthur remained confident. He flew to **Wake Island** to discuss the war with Truman, assuring him that there was 'very little' chance that the Chinese or Soviets would intervene and that 'the war will soon be over'. His optimism seemed justified, for on 19 October American and South Korean forces 'liberated' the North Korean capital, Pyongyang.

On 24 October MacArthur reversed his mid-October order that American forces should not operate near the Chinese border. The JCS described this great change in policy as 'a matter of concern', but did not stop him.

New aims, new problems

The new war aims presented problems. Although the UN approved the decision to invade North Korea in October, some US allies felt that while the initial aim (the restoration of the *status quo*) was clearly defensive, this new aim (the destruction of North Korea) could be perceived as aggressive. State Department official George Kennan considered Korea unimportant, and feared that the USA could get into trouble there. He was right. After several warnings that Truman ignored, China intervened in response to the new American war aims.

→ China's entry into the Korean War

Chinese diplomats said Chinese intervention was motivated by security reasons: the USA had sent the 7th Fleet to Taiwan and MacArthur had defied orders that said he should not send US troops to close to the Yalu River (the border between China and North Korea) and had publicized his support for Chiang. Also, China had been exploited, dominated and humiliated by other countries since the nineteenth century. The Korean War offered an opportunity for China to re-establish its prestige and status on the world stage. Finally, Mao sought to repay North Korean aid against Chiang Kai-shek's Nationalists in the Chinese Civil War.

It soon became clear that China's entry into the war would greatly change its course and consequences.

Chinese troops in Korea

While triumphant American and South Korean troops reached the Yalu River, the Chinese stealthily moved 150,000 men into North Korea. These battle-

KEY TERM

Wake Island A US base in the middle of the Pacific Ocean.

Why and with what results did China intervene in the Korean War?

hardened troops had fought a bitter civil war for many years and they proved to be formidable opponents.

The US/UN/ROK forces were soon in trouble, surprised by the North Korean winter (they had not yet received the proper winter clothing) and the arrival of the Chinese. Deluding himself that the Chinese were in retreat, MacArthur decided that a big offensive would end the Korean War.

November offensives, 1950

MacArthur's November offensive was disastrous. Walton Walker knew he had insufficient supplies and MacArthur foolishly broadcast the battle plan on Armed Forces Radio, letting the Chinese know what to expect. Acheson subsequently explained why the president's advisers did nothing: 'It would have meant a fight with MacArthur, charges by him that they had denied his victory.' The Chinese responded with their own offensive, in which 300,000 Chinese and 100,000 North Koreans outnumbered 270,000 US/UN/ROK forces. Colonel Paul Freeman said the Chinese were 'making us look a little silly in this God-awful country'.

SOURCE D

A Chinese commentator in 1950 declaring a low opinion of the US ground troops.

[The American] infantry is weak. Their men are afraid to die … They depend on their planes, tanks and artillery … Their habit is to be active during the daylight hours. They are very weak at night … When transportation comes to a standstill, the infantry loses the will to fight.

Using Source D and your own knowledge, how far would you trust Source D? **?**

The retreating American troops were astounded by the cold, which was sometimes as low as –30°C, and frequently froze motor oil and weapons. Warming tents had to be used to defrost the men before they were sent out into the cold again. Hair oil and urine kept frozen rifles going some of the time. Plasma froze in the tubes of the medics, who had to dip their fingers into patients' blood in order to keep their hands warm. 'The only way you could tell the dead from the living was whether their eyes moved. They were all frozen stiff as boards,' said one American surgeon. The Chinese suffered even more. Many froze to death in their foxholes. One Chinese officer was surprised to see thousands of snowmen on the horizon: on closer inspection, they turned out to be entire platoons of Chinese soldiers who had frozen to death on the spot.

'Frozen Chosin'

One of the hardest fought battles was that waged by 25,000 Americans surrounded by 120,000 Chinese in the mountains of North Korea, near the Chosin reservoir. Their chief of staff criticized the 'insane plan' that had sent them there. One captain felt as if they had run 'smack into what seemed like most of the Chinese from China. I always wonder why they sent us up into all that.' US air supremacy saved many American lives at 'frozen Chosin', but

12 soldiers were burned by **napalm** dropped from their own planes. 'Men all around me were burned. They lay rolling in the snow. Men I knew, marched and fought with begged me to shoot 'em. I couldn't,' said one private. In one division, 'Many were crying and hysterical. Some were sick and vomiting. Some had so many wounds you could hardly touch them.' Six thousand Americans were killed, wounded or captured, while 6000 others suffered from severe frostbite, a casualty rate far higher than in the Second World War. Survivors of 'frozen Chosin' told the American press that the Chinese burned wounded **POWs** alive and danced around the flames, then bayoneted others who tried to surrender.

US/UN/ROK retreat

The US/UN/ROK forces retreated so rapidly in 'the big bugout' that the Chinese, who were on foot, could not keep up. However, General Smith scolded the press when they used the word 'retreat': 'We are not retreating. We are merely attacking in another direction.'

MacArthur and Truman in trouble

Truman wanted no further escalation of the war so he rejected MacArthur's requests to bomb Manchuria, to use atomic weapons, to 'unleash' Chiang Kai-shek's forces, or to send more troops (none were available in the USA or in any other UN nation). MacArthur complained that he was having to fight with 'an enormous handicap … without precedent in military history'.

Truman too was struggling. His poll ratings were falling, the Democrats did badly in the November 1950 elections and there was panic in Washington. The JCS feared a Soviet attack in Europe, so Truman declared a state of national emergency in December. Then Truman said he had 'always' considered using atomic weapons in Korea, and that 'the military commander in the field will have charge of the use of weapons, as he always has'. British Prime Minister Clement Attlee rushed to Washington, fearful that MacArthur had his finger on the nuclear button. Truman hastily reassured everyone that he did not.

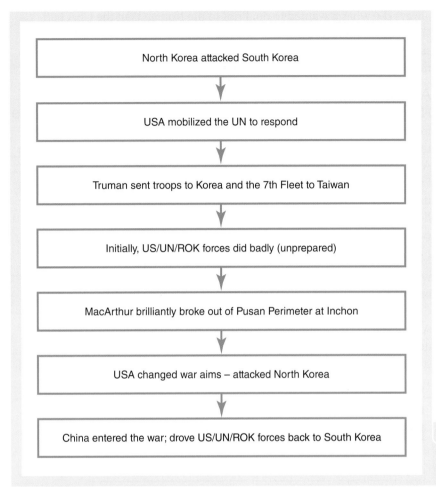

North Korea attacked South Korea

↓

USA mobilized the UN to respond

↓

Truman sent troops to Korea and the 7th Fleet to Taiwan

↓

Initially, US/UN/ROK forces did badly (unprepared)

↓

MacArthur brilliantly broke out of Pusan Perimeter at Inchon

↓

USA changed war aims – attacked North Korea

↓

China entered the war; drove US/UN/ROK forces back to South Korea

SUMMARY DIAGRAM

The course of events in Korea in 1950

 # A UN war

▶ *Key question: How far did other nations contribute to the Korean War?*

There has long been disagreement as to whether the Korean War was a UN war or a US war. There is a good case to be made for each contention.

A US war or a UN war?

A US war

The USA and South Korea provided 90 per cent of the fighting men, and although MacArthur headed UNC, Truman never let him communicate with the UN. Furthermore, although allies disagreed with the USA over issues such as the dispatch of the US 7th Fleet to the Taiwan Straits, the USA

> Was the Korean War a US war or a UN war?

always did what it wanted to do. Prior to the Korean War, the USA had shown little interest in the UN, and the American desire for organizations such as NATO and the OAS suggested little faith in the ability of the UN to maintain world peace and a preference for regional security agreements.

A UN war

Harry Truman often described the Korean War as a UN 'police action' and US troops painted 'Harry's police' on the sides of their tanks and Jeeps. Forty thousand troops from other nations (Britain, Australia, New Zealand, South Africa, Canada, France, Netherlands, Belgium, Colombia, Greece, Turkey, Ethiopia, the Philippines, Thailand and Luxembourg) fought in Korea. India, Italy, Norway, Denmark and Sweden sent medics, while Chile, Cuba, Ecuador, Iceland, Lebanon, Nicaragua, Pakistan and Venezuela sent food and economic aid, and Panama provided transportation.

MacArthur never communicated directly with the United Nations but there were difficulties enough in co-ordinating the war effort. Communications between forces of different nationalities proved difficult. When the British Commonwealth Brigade tried to free some ambushed Americans, the Americans did not know the British radio frequency. The Turks could not understand what the US commanders were telling them, and they sometimes captured South Koreans instead of Chinese.

SOURCE E

US/UN/ROK deaths in the Korean War.

Country	Deaths
South Korea	227,800
USA	54,246
Turkey	717
UK	710
Canada	516
Australia	291
France	288
Greece	169
Colombia	140
Ethiopia	120
Thailand	114
Netherlands	114
Belgium/Luxembourg	97
Philippines	92
New Zealand	24
South Africa	20

?

In relation to the debate as to whether this was a US war or UN war, what can you infer from Source E?

The contribution from the Americas

← **How did Canada and the Latin American nations respond to the Korean War?**

Canada and the Korean War

Although Canada had co-ordinated its defence planning with the USA for the first time in the Second World War in the Permanent Joint Board on Defence, traditional Canadian fears of US domination led Canada to favour entry into multilateral organizations such as the UN where American influence could be diluted. Soviet spying operations in Canada in 1945 helped convince Canada that Communism ought to be opposed. Canada therefore joined NATO (1949), and although not all Canadians were keen, played an important part in the UN effort in the Korean War. After the USA and the UK, Canada's 27,000 soldiers, sailors and airmen constituted the third largest UN contingent in Korea, and 516 Canadians died there. The historian William Stueck (1997) said the Canadians and British 'provided counterweights to tendencies in Washington to start along a road of escalation in Korea that could have ended in World War III'. When there were temporary tensions between Britain and the USA in 1951, Canada was the closest confidant of the USA.

Latin America and the Korean War

From the first, the Latin American nations dutifully voted with the USA on resolutions relating to Korea in both the UN and the OAS. Several contributed war equipment, but in general they felt that Korea was totally irrelevant to their problems of poverty and political instability.

When the US/UN/ROK forces were struggling in the winter of 1950–1, Truman appealed to Bolivia, Brazil, Chile, Mexico, Peru and Uruguay in particular to 'establish the principle of sharing our burdens fairly'. The Bolivian government promised to send troops then reversed its position after a public outcry. Uruguay seemed to be on the verge of sending troops, but pressure from the opposition party and from Argentina, Chile and Mexico halted the process. Peru and Brazil expressed interest in sending troops but only in return for substantial US military and economic aid. Colombia was the only Latin American nation to send troops.

Colombia

Anti-Communism, economic ties, hopes for US aid, and a tradition of US–Colombian co-operation help explain Colombia's contribution of 6200 men to the Korean War. American coffee drinkers had long constituted Colombia's main export market and back in the 1920s, Colombia's President Marco Fidel Suárez's *Respice Polum* (*Follow the North Star*) policy had linked Colombia to the USA. Relations between Bogotá and Washington had been good during the Second World War as Washington particularly valued Colombia's strategically important position near the Caribbean and the Panama Canal.

Reasons for non-involvement of other Latin American nations
Latin American nations refused to send troops to the Korean War because:

- They had no tradition of involvement in regions thousands of miles away (only Brazil and Mexico had sent troops abroad in the Second World War).
- Most were poor and resentful of US neglect. During the Korean War, the US Congress became increasingly reluctant to grant foreign economic aid. What they did grant made it quite clear where US priorities lay. In the mutual security programme for 1953, the US Congress voted $4.4 billion for Western European defence, $811 million for Asia and the Pacific, $680 million for the Near East and Africa, and only $72 million to Latin America.
- The Korean War increased US demand for Latin American products, but it was often US corporations that made the great profits, as they dominated mineral exploitation in Latin America.
- The conditions that the USA attached to its military aid agreements caused great controversies in Brazil, Chile, Mexico and Uruguay, as when the USA demanded greater access to Latin America's strategically important resources.

There was occasional Latin American resistance to US aims in the Korean War, as when the president of the **General Assembly**, Luis Padillo Nervo called confidently for a different approach to the POW issue (see page 62) but overall, Latin Americans had little interest in and influence on the Korean War.

(see page 62)

KEY TERM

General Assembly UN body where every single UN member has representation.

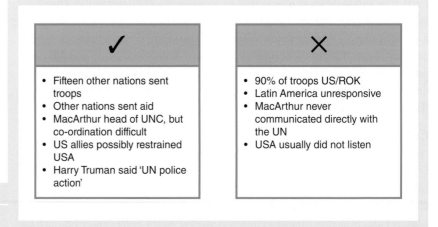

✓	✗
• Fifteen other nations sent troops • Other nations sent aid • MacArthur head of UNC, but co-ordination difficult • US allies possibly restrained USA • Harry Truman said 'UN police action'	• 90% of troops US/ROK • Latin America unresponsive • MacArthur never communicated directly with the UN • USA usually did not listen

SUMMARY DIAGRAM

A UN war

Ending the Korean War, 1951–3

▶ *Key question: How and why did the Korean War come to an end?*

The US recovery in 1951

> **How did Ridgway change the course of the war?**

Although a January 1951 poll revealed that 49 per cent of Americans felt sending troops to Korea had been a mistake, and 66 per cent believed the USA should abandon South Korea, Truman had no intention of getting out and told MacArthur the bottom line: 'It is important to United States prestige worldwide, to the future of UN and NATO organizations, and to efforts to organize anti-Communist resistance in Asia that Korea not be evacuated unless actually forced by military considerations.'

Saving South Korea was not easy. US **ground commander** Walton Walker died in December when his jeep collided with a truck (Truman graciously declined Syngman Rhee's offer to put the South Korean truck driver to death) and by the time the Chinese re-took Seoul in January 1951, morale was very low amongst American troops. However, Walker's replacement was Matt 'Old Iron Tits' Ridgway (he had a hand grenade taped on the right side of his chest, and a first-aid kit on the left), a superb and inspirational leader.

According to one US officer, 'Ridgway took that defeated army and turned it around.' Also, the Chinese supply lines had reached their outer limits and the flatter lands of South Korea favoured the tanks and artillery that Ridgway possessed in abundance. By February, US/UN/ROK forces were moving forward again. By March they had re-taken Seoul and were back at the 38th parallel.

KEY TERM

Ground commander MacArthur was in overall charge of the UNC, but Walker then Ridgway were in charge on the ground in Korea itself.

Tickertape parade When national heroes returned to the USA, New Yorkers would shower them with bits of paper (tickertape) as they drove through the streets of the city in an open-top car.

MacArthur's dismissal

> **Why was MacArthur's dismissal important?**

MacArthur opposed Truman's doctrine of containment (which he likened to appeasement) and his policy of limited war in Korea ('There is no substitute for victory'). He repeatedly publicized his disagreement with the president, which violated the December 1950 JCS directive that all government officials had to obtain clearance before they published any comments on the war.

MacArthur's supporters

When Truman dismissed MacArthur in April 1951, the president's approval rating sank to 26 per cent as the old general returned to a hero's welcome in the USA. MacArthur was met by over half a million supporters in San Francisco and given a record-breaking **tickertape parade** in New York City (see Source F). His farewell speech to Congress was brilliantly dramatic and drew repeated applause (see Source G). Some congressmen wept openly. A conservative Republican said, 'We heard God speak here today, God in the flesh, the voice of God.'

SOURCE F

Many contemporaries thought the parade in Source F demonstrated MacArthur's popularity. How far would you agree?

MacArthur, standing, being driven along Broadway, New York, for his tickertape parade in April 1951.

A poll revealed that 69 per cent of Americans believed he was wrong to sack MacArthur and over 100,000 letters reached Congress, many demanding Truman's impeachment. Senator McCarthy called Truman a 'son of a bitch' and blamed the firing on Truman and his Missouri friends, all 'stoned on bourbon and Benedictine'.

Truman's supporters

Some contemporaries recognized that MacArthur had fatally underestimated the Chinese. One Democratic senator said: 'I do not know how many thousand American GIs are sleeping in unmarked graves in North Korea. But most of them are silent but immutable evidence of the tragic mistake of "The Magnificent MacArthur" who told them that the Chinese Communists just across the Yalu would not intervene.'

Others felt that as MacArthur had committed acts of insubordination, the president had preserved the constitutional principle of civilian control over the military. The JCS, fearing that MacArthur might deliberately provoke a full-scale **Sino-American** war, supported Truman in the congressional hearings on the war (see Source H). After their testimonies, the MacArthur controversy died down.

 **KEY TERM**

Sino-American Chinese–American.

SOURCE G

MacArthur's address to Congress on his return from Korea, April 1951.

The Communist threat is a global one ... You cannot appease or otherwise surrender to Communism in Asia without simultaneously undermining our efforts to halt its advance in Europe ...

The tragedy of Korea is further heightened by the fact that its military action is confined to its territorial limits [instead of extending the war into China]. It condemns that nation, which it is our purpose to save, to suffer the devastating impact of full naval and air bombardments while the enemy's sanctuaries are fully protected from such attack and devastation ...

I am closing my 52 years of military service. When I joined the Army, even before the turn-of-the-century, it was the fulfillment of all my boyish hopes and dreams.

*The world has turned over many times since I took the oath on the plain at **West Point**, and the hopes and dreams have long since vanished, but I still remember the refrain of one of the most popular barracks ballads of that day which proclaimed most proudly that old soldiers never die; they just fade away.*

And like the old soldier of that ballad, I now close my military career and just fade away, an old soldier who tried to do his duty as God gave him the light to see that duty. Goodbye.

> Using Source G and your own knowledge, suggest reasons why MacArthur's speech was so well received by so many of his congressional audience.

> **KEY TERM**
>
> **West Point** US military academy for officer training.
>
> **Kremlin** Location of the Soviet government in Moscow.

SOURCE H

JCS Chairman General Omar Bradley's testimony before the Senate Armed Forces and Foreign Relations Committee in May 1951.

In view of their global responsibilities and their perspective with respect to the worldwide strategic situation [the JCS] are in a better position than is any single theater commander to assess the risk of general war. Moreover, the Joint Chiefs of Staff are best able to judge our own military resources with which to meet that risk.

Korea, in spite of the importance of the engagement, must be looked upon with proper perspective. It is just one engagement, just one phase of this battle that we are having with the other power center in the world which opposes us and all we stand for ...

*[The] enlargement of the war in Korea to include Red China, would probably delight the **Kremlin** more than anything else we could do. It would necessarily tie down additional forces, especially our sea power and our air power, while the Soviet Union would not be obliged to put a single man into the conflict.*

Red China is not the powerful nation seeking to dominate the world. Frankly, in the opinion of the Joint Chiefs of Staff, this strategy would involve us in the wrong war, at the wrong place, at the wrong time and with the wrong enemy.

> Compare and contrast the ideas of in Sources G and H concerning extending the war in Korea.

Why was the armistice finally signed?

The armistice, 1953

Why the combatants wanted peace

In June 1951, suffering terrible losses, needing to concentrate on its domestic problems, and fearing that the conflict might escalate, China requested an armistice. Soviet loans and materials underlay the Chinese and North Korean efforts, and the Soviets along with the North Koreans were tiring of a war that was clearly not going to obtain the reunification of Korea.

The USA had many reasons to seek peace. An autumn 1951 poll demonstrated that the majority of Americans had turned against 'Truman's war', an 'utterly useless war' that had cost 30,000 American lives and damaged US government finances. Some feared that the conflict might escalate into a third world war and, fearing trouble in Europe, the JCS did not want to be pinned down in Korea. Bradley told Congress that the USSR, not China, was the greatest threat faced by the USA (see Source H). There was pressure from America's allies and from the world community to end the military stalemate, and finally the war was damaging America's international reputation through Communist accusations that the USA was using bacteriological warfare in Korea.

Why peace finally came in 1953

Although China proposed the armistice in 1951, it was not signed until 1953, during which time bitter fighting continued. The delay occurred because both sides feared giving the other any advantage, were preoccupied with saving face, and hated each other. Ridgway could hardly bear to talk to the Chinese, whom he called 'treacherous savages'. The historian Peter Lowe described the Communists as inflexible, Syngman Rhee as obstructive ('Our goal is unification'), and the Americans as simplistic. Truman played a major part in delaying the peace. He refused to allow Communist POWs to be returned to China, insisting that they were Communists who wanted to defect to the '**Free World**'. Some historians attribute Truman's inflexibility to principle and humanitarian motives. Others say he sought a Cold War propaganda victory. It seems unlikely that he sought domestic political advantage, as few Americans cared about the POWs (their impatience to end the war was such that more than half were willing to use the atomic bomb).

New leaders in the USA and in the USSR (Eisenhower became president in January 1953 and Stalin died in March) had neither started nor sustained the war. As their prestige was not at stake in the way that their predecessors had been, the armistice was finally signed.

KEY TERM

Free World The West (countries such as the USA and its allies).

SUMMARY DIAGRAM

Ending the Korean War, 1951–3

 # The diplomatic and political outcomes of the Korean War

▶ *Key question: How did the Korean War affect US politics and diplomacy?*

The Korean War and US politics

The Korean War had a massive impact on US politics. It intensified the McCarthyite hysteria that had begun in February 1950 (see page 34). McCarthy and his followers claimed that the war proved Communist conspiracy, and in this paranoid atmosphere, they led 85 separate probes into Communist influence in the USA between 1951 and 1954.

The war greatly damaged Truman's presidency. It cost the country $67 billion, and this massive expenditure generated inflation which caused over half a million steelworkers to strike for better wages in April 1952. Truman seized the steel mills, which led to a constitutional crisis when the Supreme Court ruled that his actions were unconstitutional. Truman's failure to obtain a congressional declaration of war helped saddle him with all the blame for

> **What was the relationship between the war and US politics?**

'Truman's war', and, according to the historian James Patterson (1996), rendered him 'virtually powerless' either to control Congress or to effectively lead the country. It made him decide against standing for re-election in 1952 and helped ensure the victory of the Republican Dwight D. Eisenhower, a Second World War military hero, whom the American people trusted to bring an acceptable peace in Korea.

US politics affected the war, demonstrating the difficulties of waging war in a democracy. Truman had entered the war partly because of domestic political pressures: he felt threatened by Republican accusations of having 'lost' China and by McCarthy's attacks on the patriotism of his administration. After Inchon, Truman's decision to cross the 38th parallel was affected by the electorate's thirst for revenge on the aggressor, and his anxiety about congressional elections. Then, when the Chinese entered the war and the USA did badly, public pressure made Truman's successor get the USA out of Korea. Thus, public opinion shaped the outbreak and the course of the war. This was particularly evident in the case of MacArthur, whose popularity with the American people probably prevented his earlier dismissal.

How did the Korean War affect and reflect US diplomacy?

The Korean War and US foreign policy

Containment and credibility
In his dismissal of MacArthur for publicly seeking all-out war with China, Truman demonstrated his commitment to containment, and containment could be said to have worked. The USA had proved willing and able to halt Communist expansion, and had 'saved' South Korea. The war also ensured Japan's security and development into a reliable and invaluable US ally. However, although the restoration of the *status quo* in South Korea helped American prestige and credibility, the USA had failed in its attempt to reunify the Korean peninsula, having been effectively held to a draw by an impressive Chinese military performance.

The USA and Asia
The Korean War seemed to signal that Western Europe was more important to US security than Asia. Testifying before Congress in 1951, Bradley made clear his belief that the USSR was the greatest enemy and Europe the greatest prize. Nevertheless, it can be argued that the Korean War had shifted the storm centre of the Cold War from Europe to Asia, as events in Korea convinced Truman that Communism was on the march. He then increased financial aid to the French in Vietnam because they too were fighting Communism (see Chapter 5).

The Korean War inevitably had a big impact on Sino-American relations. Two years of bloody and bitter fighting, coupled with Truman's re-injection of the USA into the Chinese Civil War (see page 48), greatly damaged the relationship. It would be more than two decades before the two nations finally exchanged ambassadors.

The arms race and American alliances

The Korean War prompted a US and Soviet military build-up and was important in escalating their arms race. Truman accelerated the US hydrogen-bomb programme, strengthened NATO, and began the re-militarization of Germany.

The Korean War also had a great impact on US alliances. It dramatically changed the relationship with Germany and Japan, who now became close allies, as did Taiwan and South Korea.

Cold War turning point

Historian James Matray (2001) saw the Korean War as the critical turning point in the whole Cold War, with increased US defence expenditure and commitment to NATO, the poisoning of Sino-American relations and, despite US claims that it fought for democracy in the Cold War, a cementing of the relationship with the 'odious' undemocratic regimes of Syngman Rhee in South Korea and Chiang Kai-shek in Taiwan. Matray sees the 'main legacy' as that the 'United States thereafter pursued a foreign policy of global intervention and paid an enormous price in death, destruction, and damaged reputation', especially in Vietnam.

The USA, the Korean War and Latin America

Any hopes that the Latin American nations had for greater US aid for their social and economic problems were dealt a massive blow by the Korean War, which turned US attention to Asia, confirmed the US marginalization of Latin America and contributed greatly to a US preoccupation with a military response to Communism. For example, the 1951 Mutual Security Act provided $38 million of military assistance to Latin American regimes to combat Communism. This military emphasis helped ensure that the USA would see stability rather than (and often at the expense of) democracy as the key to Latin American resistance to Communism. This was evident in Truman's Bolivian policy. In 1951, Bolivia's ruling rightist government rejected the results of a democratic election. In a 1952 revolution that rightist government was overthrown, but Truman then refused to recognize the leftist government of Victor Paz Estenssoro that had won the 1951 election.

Politics	Foreign policy	
Intensified the McCarthyite hysteria	Containment worked	Shifted US Cold War emphasis to Asia
Damaged the US economy and Truman's presidency	Some prestige	Tied USA to Chiang and Rhee – odious
	Failure to reunify Korea	USA greatly increased defence expenditure and global interventions
Showed the difficulties in waging war in a democracy	Damaged Sino-American relations	
	Showed Europe more important than Asia?	Got Truman into Vietnam

SUMMARY DIAGRAM

The diplomatic and political outcomes of the Korean War

Chapter summary

The Korean War 1950–3

At the end of the Second World War, Soviet troops entered northern Korea, which developed into a Communist state, and American troops entered southern Korea, which developed into a pro-American state. In June 1950, North Korea attacked South Korea and the USA led the UN into the war.

The USA fought in Korea because of anti-Communism, fears about the world balance of power and Japan, McCarthyism, NSC-68, Truman's political problems, and a commitment to the UN. Many UN nations helped the USA in Korea, but US forces and policies were dominant. The US/ROK forces were initially unprepared and the North Koreans drove them behind the Pusan Perimeter. However, MacArthur turned the war around in a brilliant landing at Inchon that led to a change in US war aims. Initially the USA fought to save South Korea, but after Inchon it fought to destroy North Korea.

US forces in close proximity to the Chinese border brought China into the war, which caused a humiliating American retreat in late 1950. A new US ground commander, Ridgway, stabilized the front lines near the 38th parallel. In spring 1951, Truman sacked MacArthur for insubordination because MacArthur publicly favoured all-out war against China, while Truman favoured containment.

When 'Truman's War' dragged on, it became very unpopular. By summer 1951, the USA and China were exhausted, but it took two years of bitter fighting and negotiations before they signed the armistice.

The Korean War exacerbated the McCarthyite hysteria, damaged Truman's presidency and showed the difficulties of waging war in a democracy. It showed Truman's commitment to containment and that containment worked, which helped US credibility, but suggested that the USA should not try to roll back Communism, which did not.

When Truman sent the US 7th Fleet to Taiwan and let American troops go near to the Chinese border, he infuriated the Chinese. Coupled with the bitter fighting between Chinese and American troops, this damaged Sino-American relations for two decades. The war sped up the arms race with the USSR and the US search for more allies, including dictators such as Chiang Kai-shek and Syngman Rhee. It could be argued that the war demonstrated American commitment to the UN, or equally persuasively that it did not. Korea got the USA involved in Vietnam, increasing the focus on Asia that contributed to the further marginalization of Latin America in US foreign policy. The war confirmed or even created a US tendency to militarize the Cold War struggle, reflected in increased military rather than economic aid to Latin American regimes.

Examination advice

How to answer 'to what extent' questions

The command term <u>to what extent</u> is a popular one in IB exams. You are asked to evaluate one argument or idea over another. Stronger essays will also address more than one interpretation. This is often a good question in which to discuss how different historians have viewed the issue.

Example

<u>To what extent</u> was the US involvement in the Korean War a success?

1. Beyond stating the degree to which you agree with the premise, you must focus on the words <u>involvement</u> and <u>success</u> in the question. You should define these terms in your introduction. 'Involvement' is fairly straightforward. You might write that the USA sent hundreds of thousands of soldiers to the Korean peninsula and led a UN-sponsored mission. 'Success' is a bit trickier. Think of how one might measure a successful outcome.

2. First take at least five minutes to write a short outline. In order to gauge success you need to list what the goals of the USA were in Korea. These could include:

  * *The containment of Communism.*
  * *The maintenance of the world balance of power.*
  * *McCarthyism and domestic political concerns.*
  * *NSC-68 recommendations.*
  * *Fears for Japan.*
  * *Support for the goals of the UN.*

Next, consider whether or not these goals were met and what the results of the Korean War were. You might mention some of the following:

  * *The war ended with boundaries that were essentially the same as when the war began.*
  * *Advance of Communism had been checked on the Korean peninsula.*
  * *The threat to Japan ended.*
  * *War was very costly for the USA (higher taxes, casualties), China, and the Koreas.*
  * *More than 15 countries sent troops to help in the UN intervention.*

- Arguably, the US Cold War focus turned to Asia, and military resistance to Communism.
- Truman's presidency was damaged by the war.
- Arms race between the USA and USSR escalated.
- Sino-American relations deteriorated (greatly).

3. In your introduction, briefly state what the US goals were in Korea and to what extent these were met by 1953. Your thesis might be: the US involvement in Korea was a qualified success. Alternatively, you could argue that the USA did not meet its objectives in Korea. While there is no one correct answer to this question, a successful answer will provide ample supporting evidence. An example of a good introductory paragraph for this question is given below.

When the USA led the UN into war in Korea in summer 1950, Truman's aims were to restore the **status quo** in Korea, to contain the spread of Communism, to protect Japan, to empower an anti-Communist UN, and to fend off Republican accusations that he was 'soft' on Communism. In the course of the war, the additional aim of reunifying the Korean peninsula was introduced. While that newer aim was a total failure, it could be argued that the initial foreign policy aims were achieved, although at great cost in lives, money, escalating international tensions and the international reputation of the USA, which became enmeshed with undesirable allies in South Korea, Taiwan and Vietnam. Furthermore, 'Truman's War' greatly damaged his domestic popularity.

4. In the body of the essay, you need to discuss each of the points you raised in the introduction. Devote at least a paragraph to each one. It would be a good idea to order these in terms of which ones you think are most important. Be sure to make the connection between the points you raise and the major thrust of your argument. An example of how one of the points could be addressed is given below.

President Truman was able to contain the spread of Communism in Asia by 'saving' South Korea. This he had promised to do. However, the war had damaged his presidency. The war cost $67 billion; American taxpayers faced higher taxes and increased inflation as a consequence. Truman's failure to obtain congressional approval for going to war angered many. Anti-Communist extremists attacked

Truman for not carrying the war into China and for supposedly not taking a strong enough line against Communism. The frequent attacks led to significant defeats during congressional elections. The Democrats lost control over both houses of Congress in 1946 and they lost the presidency in 1952. These events could be tied to the war in Korea. This demonstrates that the increasingly unpopular war in Korea, at least domestically, was not very successful.

5. In the conclusion, be sure to offer final remarks on the extent to which the Korean War was a successful venture for the USA. Avoid adding any new information or themes in your concluding thoughts. An example of a good concluding paragraph is given below.

*In conclusion, it is clear that the Korean War was only a partial success for the USA. While containment had worked and the Korean **status quo** had been restored, the USA had failed in its revised war aim of the total destruction of North Korean forces. Japan was secured, but the USA had wedded itself to what historian James Matray described as 'odious regimes' in Taiwan and South Korea. Sino-American relations were dangerously antagonistic, the aims race had escalated and Korea had contributed to what would ultimately prove to be a disastrous US involvement in Vietnam. The UN had operated as the USA had desired, but other nations, for example, in Latin America, were uncomfortable with that. The war initially increased Truman's popularity but ultimately destroyed his presidency.*

6. Now try writing a complete answer to the question following the advice above.

 # Examination practice

Below are three exam-style questions for you to practise on this topic.

1 Why did anti-Communists in the USA push for a more aggressive foreign policy?
   (For guidance on how to answer 'why' questions, see page 190.)

2 Why did the USA intervene in Korea in 1950?
   (For guidance on how to answer 'why' questions, see page 190.)

3 Analyse the stages of the Korean conflict.
   (For guidance on how to answer 'analyse' questions, see page 90.)

CHAPTER 4

President Eisenhower and the 'New Look'

This chapter investigates the extent to which US foreign and defence policies changed under President Eisenhower (1953–61). This requires consideration of Eisenhower's 'New Look' defence policy, and of his relationship with the USSR, China, Canada and Latin America. You need to consider the following questions throughout this chapter:

✪ What was 'new' in the Eisenhower era?

✪ To what extent could Eisenhower's relations with Latin America be considered 'new' and successful?

✪ What was the significance of the US intervention in Guatemala?

1 Eisenhower and change in foreign and defence policy

▶ **Key question:** *What was 'new' in the Eisenhower era?*

One of the reasons the Republican Eisenhower won the 1952 presidential election was because he repudiated the Democrat Truman's foreign policy. Eisenhower declared that he had a '**mandate** for change', although as the Cold War continued unabated, the extent of change in US diplomacy and defence policy in his two terms as president is debatable.

Eisenhower's 'New Look' defence policy

> **What were the aims and achievements of Eisenhower's 'New Look' in defence?**

The aim of Eisenhower's '**New Look**' in defence was to reconcile the conflicting demands of the military, which wanted to spend more money, with those of the Treasury, which wanted to spend less. Ironically, Eisenhower was the Cold War president most devoted to slashing the military budget, perhaps because only a trusted ex-general would have dared to attempt this without generating massive opposition. Eisenhower firmly believed that US power depended on economic success rather than weaponry and that continued military expenditure at the Truman administration's level ($50 billion per annum) would lead to inflation and economic ruin. 'We must not go broke,' he said. He did not want a deficit in the federal budget, or an economy dependent on what he called 'the

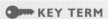

KEY TERM

Mandate Legitimate authority given for action.

New Look Eisenhower's defence policy emphasized the use of nuclear weaponry rather than conventional forces.

military–industrial complex'. He wanted '**more bang for a buck**'. His answer to this conundrum was the 'New Look'.

Under Eisenhower's 'New Look', the USA would have fewer conventional forces, and would rely instead on nuclear weapons. In January 1954, Eisenhower's Secretary of State John Foster Dulles, said the USA would no longer be bound to use only conventional weapons but would use 'massive retaliatory power' to halt aggression. This speech generated great protest: the *New York Times* wrote of **brinkmanship**, of an apparent willingness to go to the verge of nuclear war. In a published article ('dull, duller, Dulles', yawned Washington wits), Dulles explained that 'massive retaliation' meant being 'willing and able to respond vigorously at places and with the means of [our] own choosing'. In March 1954, Eisenhower told the press that the beauty of the policy of mass retaliation was its deliberate vagueness: no one would 'undertake to say exactly what we would do under all that variety of circumstances'.

The 'New Look' and 'massive retaliation' tested

Vietnam
The first test of the policy of massive retaliation came in Vietnam, where Eisenhower discussed using nuclear weaponry to help the French but decided against it (see page 95).

Quemoy and Matsu
A second test of the policy of massive retaliation came in a crisis over of Quemoy and Matsu, islands situated in the Taiwan Straits between Mao Zedong's Communist China and Chiang Kai-shek's island of Taiwan (see page 44).

In August 1954, Communist China pledged to 'liberate' Taiwan and shelled the Nationalist troops on Quemoy. Eisenhower made it clear that while he would not allow a Chinese invasion of Taiwan to go unopposed, Quemoy and Matsu had always been part of mainland China, so he would not bomb the mainland as the JCS requested. Renewed Communist offshore activity in January 1955 raised the Quemoy and Matsu question again. Dulles terrified many people when he said, 'If we defend Quemoy and Matsu, we will have to use atomic weapons.' Two days later he said that the USA possessed 'clean' tactical nuclear weapons that could destroy military targets yet leave civilians unharmed (the Defense Department told him that this was not so). Eisenhower then described the use of tactical nuclear weapons as acceptable; there was 'no reason why' they should not 'be used exactly as you would use a bullet'. The Democrat Adlai Stevenson accused Eisenhower of 'risking a third world war for the defence of these little islands'. Eisenhower backed down, and said nothing more about using nuclear weapons.

KEY TERM

Military–industrial complex Belief that the vested interests of the military and industry encouraged them to escalate tensions and the production of weaponry.

More bang for a buck Eisenhower's belief that greater dependence on nuclear weaponry would save the USA money and protect it as effectively as conventional forces.

Brinkmanship Creating the impression that one is willing to push events to the point of war rather than concede.

Assessment of massive retaliation

Critics of massive retaliation said it was inflexible and left the USA with only one option in a crisis. Supporters said the threat of massive retaliation would mean that there would be no crises. Both sides had a point. American nuclear power certainly helped keep US territory protected. However, if the USA perceived its interests to be threatened in countries such as Vietnam and Taiwan, then massive retaliation was inflexible, dangerous and impractical. In such crises, who would be 'nuked'? The Vietnamese? The Chinese? Supporters of massive retaliation argued that the nuclear threat stopped Communist aggression and expansionism, but events in countries such as Vietnam seemed to prove otherwise (see Chapter 5).

SOURCE A

? What message is the cartoonist in Source A trying to convey?

'An Uncomfortable Situation', a cartoon depicting President Eisenhower (left) and Senator McCarthy (right), originally published 3 December 1953. The artist, Cy Hungerford, was an American cartoonist who produced daily cartoons for the *Pittsburgh Post-Gazette*.

Eisenhower's foreign policy

The USA, the USSR and China

Eisenhower brought about change in that he finally ended the Korean War but that had also been Truman's aim. Although the war had ended, it brought about no change in the extremely hostile relations between the USA and Communist China and the USSR. In the early days of the Eisenhower presidency there was also little change as far as McCarthyism was concerned; when Stalin died and the new Soviet leadership sought *détente*, the Eisenhower administration was unresponsive, partly because of State Department fears of McCarthy.

In the 1952 elections, the Republicans talked of a new policy of '**rollback**' of Communism, but the Eisenhower administration did nothing about Soviet domination of Eastern Europe, despite opportunities afforded in Hungary, where there was an anti-Communist and anti-Soviet rising in 1956. Basically, Eisenhower continued Truman's policy of containment in Europe, although it could be argued that his artificial creation of the state of South Vietnam (see Chapter 5) constituted rollback in Asia.

A new look for US–Canadian relations?

During the Eisenhower years, the USSR developed long-range bombers. A likely route for a Soviet long-range bomber aiming to 'nuke' the USA was across Canadian territory. In order to facilitate US interception of Soviet bombers or missiles over Canada, **NORAD** was established in 1957. From the first, NORAD had an American commander and a Canadian deputy commander. According to historian Joseph Jockel (2007), NORAD was a dramatic new departure for Canada: 'The establishment of NORAD was a decision for which there was no precedent in Canadian history in that it granted in peacetime to a foreign representative operation control of an element of Canadian forces in Canada.'

So, as noted before (see page 57), the Cold War drew the USA and Canada closer together in diplomatic and military terms, although Canadian fears of American domination continued. It took the USA and Canada four years to negotiate this mutual defence agreement, which reflected Canadian unease.

A new world

What was really new in the Eisenhower years were the nationalist independence movements that aimed to sweep the European colonial powers out of Africa and Asia, and a nationalist revolution in Cuba that raised the spectre of America's backyard going Communist (see pages 146–9). Eisenhower's reaction was conservative and unsympathetic. His administration worked to resist reformist left-wing movements in Asia (Vietnam), the Middle East (Iran) and Latin America (Guatemala in 1954 and Cuba in 1959). Some of the methods of resistance, such as the use of **covert operations**, were relatively new.

← **Was there any great change in US Cold War diplomacy under Eisenhower?**

 **KEY TERM**

Rollback Pushing back Communism in places where it was already established.

NORAD North American Aerospace Defense Command.

Covert operations Secret warfare, for example sabotage.

New	Not new
• New look in defence • Covert operations • Some rollback in Vietnam	• Poor relations with China • Poor relations with USSR • Fear of McCarthy • Conservative response to new nationalist independence movements in developing world • Still containment • Talked much of rollback, did little

SUMMARY DIAGRAM

Eisenhower and change in foreign and defence policy

Eisenhower and Latin America

▶ **Key question:** To what extent could Eisenhower's relations with Latin America be considered 'new' and successful?

In his 1952 election campaign, Eisenhower recalled how during the Second World War the USA had 'frantically wooed Latin America'. However, he claimed that the Truman administration had then 'proceeded to forget these countries just as fast', thereby creating 'terrible disillusionment' and making the area vulnerable to Communist subversion. Such words suggested that, if elected, Eisenhower would pursue a more constructive policy. However, the US response to revolutions and Vice President Richard Nixon's visits to Latin America demonstrated the US approach to Latin America was conservative rather than new and constructive.

→ The USA and revolutions

Was Latin America likely to turn Communist?

From sympathy to hostility

After their own American Revolution against the British, Americans were generally sympathetic to similar revolutionaries elsewhere. Subsequently however, the USA's concern for stability in trading partners and fears of Communism combined to make the USA deeply suspicious of most twentieth-century revolutions. The Eisenhower administration inherited that suspicion at a time of nationalist and popular uprisings in the Middle East, Africa, Asia and Latin America. Whereas in Africa and Asia it was European colonial rulers that were removed, in Latin American nations such as El Salvador, Nicaragua and Bolivia, radical nationalists had to fight against native **oligarchies** that were usually supported by the military élite and by the USA.

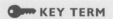 **KEY TERM**

Oligarchies
Unrepresentative élites.

Dealing with revolutionaries

Having just got American troops out of Korea, Eisenhower did not want to get involved in another war, so he used other means to deal with revolutionaries whom he disliked:

- Eisenhower hoped the USSR would refrain from helping revolutionaries for fear of massive retaliation (see page 71).
- Eisenhower sent US military advisers to assist friendly regimes in training native troops to oppose revolutionaries, as in Vietnam (see page 96).
- Dulles organized military alliances such as SEATO (see page 96) to help friendly regimes deal with the Communist threat.
- The CIA used covert operations against revolutionary regimes in Iran and Guatemala. Covert operations were planned against the Cuban revolution in the final months of Eisenhower's presidency.
- Eisenhower 'bought off' Bolivian revolutionaries.

Revolutionary potential in Latin America

Despite the strength of Catholicism in Latin America, it was always likely that Communism might appeal to some of the poor or to **middle-class** idealists such as Fidel Castro and Che Guevara (see pages 137–9). Communist parties were founded in many Latin American republics in the late 1920s. When the Cold War broke out, the party was banned by several countries, including Brazil (1947), Chile (1948) and Costa Rica. Historians disagree over the importance of the Communists. According to historian Edwin Williamson (2009), Communists 'played only a minimal role in Latin American politics' until events in Cuba transformed the situation in the 1960s. However, that was probably a misleading assertion, as the Communists played a part in the governments of several countries, such as pre-1954 Guatemala, and Cuba under Batista. The historian Tulio Halperín Donghi (1996) said the Communist parties played 'a truly important political role' in Brazil, Chile and Cuba in the 1930s, and became 'at least a force to be reckoned with' in countries such as Argentina, Colombia, Venezuela and Uruguay, although they never made as much of a political impact as the 'more radical home-grown movements' in countries such as Mexico and Peru.

The Eisenhower administration watched the growth of Latin American Communist parties with trepidation and in 1953 Dulles admitted that the Truman administration had become 'so preoccupied with Europe and Asia that it had taken South America too much for granted'. He feared that the poverty and inequality in wealth in Latin America could lead to a Communist revolution, as in China. Outside of Costa Rica and Mexico, both of which were democracies, two per cent of the population owned 70 per cent of the agricultural land. As a result, many poor peasants were leaving the countryside and congregating in **shanty towns** at the edge of big cities.

 **KEY TERM**

Middle class Businessmen, professionals, landowners.

Shanty towns Collections of poorly built dwellings containing poverty-stricken populations.

How successful were covert operations under Eisenhower?

Latin American economic development required internal stability and large amounts of outside capital investment and technical and financial aid, but the Eisenhower administration felt that **strongmen** were the best guarantee of internal stability, and while recognizing that a booming economy 'relieves pressures in the world that are favourable to Communism', did not even consider giving the Latin Americans aid such as that received by the Europeans under Truman and the Marshall Plan. The administration felt that investment in Latin America could be left to private capital, but private capital naturally preferred investment in stable areas. So, while private American investment in Latin America was $1.4 billion from 1953 to 1956, it was $3.4 billion in Western Europe.

Eisenhower, covert operations and Guatemala

Most Guatemalans were poor, illiterate Indians who farmed the lands of the whites and *mestizos* who constituted only two per cent of Guatemala's population but owned 70 per cent of its productive land. The inequality was exacerbated by the US United Fruit Company, which since its inception in 1899 had such a stranglehold over the Guatemalan economy that the natives called it *el pulpo* (the octopus). United Fruit gained great concessions from successive conservative Guatemalan governments, including minimal taxes, protection from competition, and the domination of Guatemalan port facilities (see map on page 147), shipping, railroads and communications. United Fruit sent all its profits back to the USA, while paying exceptionally low wages to its 40,000 Guatemalan workers who were forced to purchase the company's medical care, to buy necessities from the company's store, and to rent the company's cramped (if clean) accommodation, incongruously constructed alongside the luxurious homes of the American bosses.

Arévalo, Árbenz and reform in Guatemala

A series of Guatemalan strongmen had prevented any social and economic reforms, but in 1944, student riots and a disgruntled professional middle class prompted a nationalist–liberal revolution led by a philosophy professor, Juan José Arévalo, who became Guatemala's first democratically elected president. His government aimed for greater democracy and the division of the large plantations that dominated Guatemalan agriculture. He initiated a programme of political, labour and land reform and allowed trade unions and strikes. In the 1950 presidential election he supported the candidacy of his defence minister, Jacobo Árbenz Guzmán.

Árbenz enacted further agrarian reform, in which he was supported by the Guatemalan Communist Party. He **expropriated** unused land and gave it to the poorest peasants. He took around 15 per cent of the unused acres belonging to United Fruit and offered to pay the company the $600,000 it had said the land was worth in its 1950 tax return. United Fruit had undervalued the land in order to pay less tax to the Guatemalan government, but faced with expropriation, declared it worth $16 million.

Although John Foster Dulles and his brother, CIA chief Allen Dulles, had shares in United Fruit, the company was not convinced that the American government would help them simply because their land had been taken. So, United Fruit claimed that Árbenz was a Communist. The Eisenhower administration found this persuasive. The US ambassador to Guatemala told a congressional committee, 'I spent six hours with him one evening, and he talked like a Communist, and if he's not one, he'll do until one comes along.' Árbenz responded to the US accusations that he was a Communist by joining in the Communist bloc claims that the USA had used bacteriological warfare during the Korean War.

Nationalism and Guatemalan poverty led Árbenz to reject US demands for proper payment for United Fruit. When Árbenz refused to agree to arbitration, the Eisenhower administration moved to isolate Guatemala diplomatically and then to overthrow him.

Guatemala and the OAS

At an OAS meeting in Caracas, Venezuela, in March 1954, Dulles pushed through a declaration that Communism was 'incompatible with the concept of American freedom'. The signatories vowed 'to eradicate and prevent subversive activities'. The vote on Dulles' resolution was 17 in favour, one against (Guatemala), two abstentions (Mexico and Argentina), and one absence (Costa Rica). Many of the 17 had voted in the hope of gaining US aid and trade. However, the OAS did not give the go-ahead for US intervention in Guatemala. Indeed, most of the delegates gave the Guatemalan representative a standing ovation for his passionately anti-American speech.

The overthrow of Árbenz

From summer 1953, the CIA worked to overthrow Árbenz. At a cost of between $5 million and $7 million, around 100 Guatemalans were given military training. The CIA chose Colonel Carlos Enrique Castillo Armas, an American-trained soldier, to lead the invasion. He was given money, an army, a radio station in neighbouring Nicaragua, and the promise of a US blockade to halt arms imports from the **Soviet bloc**.

Árbenz believed that the USA and the Nicaraguan dictator Somoza were conspiring to overthrow him, so he sought military aid from the USSR. In May 1954, the Soviets let Czechoslovakia's Škoda company export weapons to Árbenz. Allen Dulles said this demonstrated Soviet contempt for the Monroe Doctrine and Soviet plans to establish a military base in the Western hemisphere.

In June 1954, Castillo Armas and his force of around 200 men entered Guatemala. Several small planes piloted by CIA operatives bombed Guatemala City and other key towns. Fearing an invasion by American troops, Árbenz considered arming the peasantry but that upset his middle-class army officers, who demanded his resignation. He also lost the support of the supposedly Communist-controlled **labour unions**. Árbenz therefore

 **KEY TERM**

Soviet bloc The countries in the USSR's Eastern European empire (East Germany, Czechoslovakia, Poland, Romania, Bulgaria and Hungary).

Labour unions Trade unions that negotiated for better pay and working conditions for their members.

fled the country, leaving the way open for Castillo Armas to establish a dictatorship, in which United Fruit got its land back.

? Using your own knowledge and Source B, how far would you trust Castillo Armas' assertions about the US role in Guatemala?

SOURCE B

Journalist Henry Raymont recorded that in a private interview during Vice President Nixon's 1955 visit, Castillo Armas confided in him that 'continued meddling' by the US Embassy was damaging his regime. From *Troubled Neigbors: The Story of US–Latin American Relations from Roosevelt to the Present*, Westview, 2005.

I don't see how I can govern. Most of the government functionaries who knew their job were purged along with Árbenz's followers. I was left with ——. But the authorities in Washington don't seem to care. Your [US] government is always more interested in the earnings of the United Fruit Company than in the welfare of the Guatemalan people.

The results and significance of the overthrow of Árbenz

From the contemporary American viewpoint, the new government in Guatemala was far more acceptable than the previous one, and the covert operations were considered successful. On the other hand, the US involvement alienated Guatemalans who opposed the new regime and also many other Latin Americans. A basic US aim was national security, and the interventions in Guatemala (and subsequently in Cuba) raised the issue as to whether US security was best served by supporting unpopular strongmen or promoting democracy in other countries. The problem was that strongmen were usually reliably anti-Communist, while democratic elections were likely to give Communists a say in government.

? Using Source C and your own knowledge, how far would you trust this assessment of the role of the USA in the overthrow of Árbenz?

SOURCE C

From an interview given in 1974 by Luis Cardoza y Aragón, who served as an ambassador under Arévalo and Árbenz. From Robert Holden and Eric Zolov (editors), *Latin America and the United States*, Oxford University Press, 2000.

With respect to my Guatemala, the key factor, decisively and definitively, is summed up totally in North American Imperialism ... There were no Communists ... And even if there had been a real Communist Party, or if Árbenz' government had been Communist ... they would never have posed the least threat to the United States. Apart from the right of the people to have the government it wishes, etc., the fact is that Árbenz' government was a soft nationalist model (none of the laws, including the agrarian reform, were more than moderate). But to people like Nixon and McCarthy, it was still a bad example on the continent. The U.S. (North American imperialism) squashed a little butterfly that wished to fly a little more freely within the capitalist system, and to emerge from a barbaric, inhumane situation to better living conditions for its people, of all classes ... Keep in mind what sort of beasts Dulles and Eisenhower had to be to destroy a stammer of freedom in a very small, very backward country, which in no way could endanger anyone. That bestiality has to be seen in the clearest perspective, above all else.

The Bolivian Revolution

How did Eisenhower respond to the Bolivian Revolution?

After the Bolivian Revolution in 1952, the revolutionaries nationalized tin mining and instituted radical land reform. However, the USA did not stop this revolution. Eisenhower's response to the Bolivian Revolution was very different from his response to the Guatemalan Revolution because the Bolivians persuaded the Eisenhower administration that they were not Communists. Indeed, some were more like fascists. Furthermore, in comparison to Guatemala, Bolivia was a distant, isolated nation in which the USA had few investments.

Eisenhower's response to the Bolivian Revolution was basically to try to buy it out. Bolivia became the biggest recipient of US foreign aid, which naturally encouraged moderation in the revolutionaries. Here, Eisenhower's policy was far more flexible and far less aggressive than in Guatemala.

Interestingly, despite the conservatism of the Bolivian government, the USA supported a military coup in 1964. The USA had given a great deal of military aid to the Bolivian army, making it steadfastly pro-American and therefore particularly acceptable to the USA in the very tense period after Castro's accession to power in Cuba.

Vice President Nixon's Latin American visits

In what ways were Nixon's Latin American visits important?

American presidents frequently use vice presidents to make the ceremonial and relatively insignificant visits to foreign countries for which the president himself has insufficient time or inclination. Significantly, it was left to Eisenhower's vice president, Richard Nixon, to visit Latin American nations. Nixon's visits, for which he was well briefed by the State Department and the US embassies, demonstrated a lack of US understanding of its southern neighbours.

Nixon's first visit to Latin America

In his first visit, in 1955, Nixon was impressed by two unpleasant and unpopular dictators, the Cuban Fulgencio Batista ('a very remarkable man' who would 'give stability to Cuba') and the Nicaraguan Anastasio Somoza, both of whom would 'deal effectively with the Commies'. Here, Nixon illustrated how the preoccupation with Communism often blinded the USA to the unpleasant nature and unpopularity of dictatorial regimes in Latin America.

On his return, Nixon gave a full report to the Cabinet and the NSC: 'We must keep our eyes on this part of the world. They are close to us, they are our best customers, they buy more from us than all Europe … [However, a major problem is] so much one-man rule … The question facing us is how far is dictatorship necessary? We must deal with these governments as they are and work over a period of time towards more democracy … In these countries, a very few organized people can take over – so we should concentrate on winning them.'

Nixon had a typical Republican viewpoint on Latin America. Republicans wanted stability, anti-Communism, and a favourable climate for US business interests in the region. What was new was the way he pushed hard in the cabinet, in public speeches, in the State Department, and with the Export–Import Bank, for more help for Latin America. Unfortunately, neither Eisenhower nor the press showed much interest in Nixon's visit or ideas. The *New York Times* confined itself to pictures of Nixon's departure from his tearful daughters, and of his return, when one daughter insisted on running up the plane steps to greet her father. Nixon's biographer, Stephen Ambrose (1987), noted that, 'The trouble was that the region was a backwater in the Cold War, hardly of any interest at all to the Eisenhower administration.' Here again, there was little that was new about Eisenhower's foreign policy.

Nixon's second visit to Latin America

It was Nixon's 1958 visit to Latin America that made headlines. The omens were not good on the eve of the visit. Many Latin American economies were highly dependent on US producers and consumers, and a US economic recession in 1957–8 hit Latin American nations hard. Just before Nixon's visit, the Senate Foreign Relations Committee, troubled by United Press reports that Latin American diplomats were deeply dismayed by the US attitude to their continent, had requested testimony from the State Department. The State Department representative reported that 'relations were never better'. On the other hand, at the same time, a **Council on Foreign Relations** report said otherwise (see Source E).

 **KEY TERM**

Council on Foreign Relations American non-profit, non-partisan think-tank specializing in US foreign policy information and publications.

?

Using the content of Sources D and E and your own knowledge, how and why do Dulles and the writer(s) of the report differ on the relationship between Latin America and the USA, and which do you consider more accurate?

SOURCE D

A 1958 Council on Foreign Relations report quoting Secretary of State John Foster Dulles.

I suppose we devote as much time and thought to the problems of the Americas as we do to the problems of any other region in the world.

SOURCE E

After quoting Dulles, the 1958 Council on Foreign Relations report continued.

Despite this unique concern, and despite the long-established tradition of friendship among the 21 republics of the Western hemisphere, few observers have contended that United States–Latin American relations were in satisfactory condition at any time during the post-war period. For the United States there seemed to be no logical way of fitting Latin America into a foreign policy that had come to be so completely dominated by the Soviet–Communist threat in the opposite hemisphere.

Aims of Nixon's 1958 visit

The main stated aim of Nixon's second visit to Latin America was to demonstrate US support for an elected leader, through Nixon's attendance at the inauguration of Arturo Frondizi as president of Argentina. Perhaps the most important unstated aim of the visit was to reassure Latin Americans that they were respected and that the USA did not take them for granted, especially as the Soviets had been wooing Latin America. In 1953, they had made a trade agreement with Argentina, and the USA was concerned about the warm welcome given to Soviet deputy premier Vasily Kuznetsov and his trade-and-aid overtures. Even worse, the pro-US government of General Carlos Ibáñez del Campo in Chile threatened to sell the huge Chilean copper surplus to the USSR unless the USA bought it, prompting Dulles to lament, 'We can't prevent them from selling to the Russians if we refuse to buy. No matter how stupid they act, we must remember that we have to deal with them.' Historian Stephen Ambrose (1987) suggested that the visit was simply 'all about theater', as the vice president was not authorized to make either trade agreements or important pronouncements on US policy.

In some countries, such as Uruguay, Ecuador and Colombia, Nixon's visit went well, although the Colombian policemen concentrated so hard on ensuring a trouble-free visit that Bogotá pickpockets found an exceptional number of victims, including two US Secret Service agents. However, there were problems over Paraguay, and in Argentina, Peru and Venezuela.

Paraguay

The militantly anti-Communist Paraguayan dictator General Alfredo Stroessner brought stability and economic prosperity to Paraguay, but was considered to be one of the toughest and most objectionable strongmen in Latin America. Nixon's trip was supposed to show US support for elected governments, but his visit to Paraguay is an excellent illustration of US ambivalence about dictators who provided stability and were anti-Communist.

Argentina

Argentina was an excellent example of how US economic power frequently impacted on domestic politics in Latin American nations and made relations with the USA uneasy.

In the early twentieth century, Argentina was one of the most prosperous and stable of Latin American nations, but when the US economy crashed in 1929, triggering the Great Depression, army officers became a political force, their nationalism fuelled by **protectionist** practices by countries such as the USA. After an economic boom that owed much to US purchases in the Second World War, Argentina's post-war export earnings plummeted, partly because US competition hit Argentine wheat exports (after 1947 the Marshall Plan stimulated North American grain exports to Europe). Plummeting exports and rising imports (mostly from the USA) led to a

KEY TERM

Protectionist Economic policies designed to protect the domestic economy, for example, through the imposition of tariffs on imports from other countries.

balance of payments crisis so in 1949 the USA gave Argentina $125 million 'credit'. As economic independence was one of President Juan Perón's great aims, he refused to admit that this was a loan. When the economy continued to deteriorate, Perón wanted to open up the oilfields of Patagonia to the American company Standard Oil (Esso) in 1954, but this idea infuriated nationalists. Economic problems and increased violence made civil war seem likely, so Perón went into exile in 1955.

It was in this context, with Argentina only recently rid of an authoritarian and often anti-American leader in Perón, that the inauguration of the democratically elected Frondizi was important. However, Nixon arrived 10 minutes after the oath-taking ceremony and missed the most important part of the inauguration, because the US ambassador misjudged the traffic. Given that the inauguration was the main reason for Nixon's visit to Latin America, this was unfortunate, even unforgivable.

Peru

Economic ties between Peru and the USA were close. American companies dominated Peruvian copper mining and oil fields. The importance of the USA to the Peruvian economy was demonstrated when three days before Nixon's visit, the US Tariff Commission increased export duties and put import quotas on zinc and lead, which further depressed the already plummeting exports of Peru (and also of Mexico and Canada).

Some Peruvian students greeted Nixon with 'Go Home Nixon' or 'Death to Yankee Imperialism'. The State Department recommended that Nixon cancel his visit to the prestigious San Marcos University, but the US ambassador told him it was important not to lose face in front of the Latins. At San Marcos, around 2000 students prevented Nixon from entering the university, crying 'Death to Nixon' and throwing oranges, bottles and small stones. Accompanied by just two American diplomats, Nixon strode in among them. One student said, '*El gringo tiene cojones*' ('The Yankee has balls'). One rock grazed Nixon's shoulder, another broke his companion's tooth, so Nixon retreated to the more conservative Catholic University where there was some hostility, but also lots of cries of '*Viva Nixon*'. On returning to his hotel, spit, fruit and pebbles rained down on him. When one student spat tobacco juice in his face, Nixon retaliated with a kick.

Nixon's Peruvian visit received mostly favourable publicity in the USA. Most Americans felt that the vice president had stood up to what he subsequently described as 'a bunch of Communist thugs', but some at the State Department felt the newly elected Peruvian government had been embarrassed by the scenes and that the whole purpose of the visit (to generate goodwill) had been compromised. Nixon himself had recognized the problem in a press conference in Bolivia, when he said: 'The United States must realize it is not enough to convince government officials. We also must reach peoples. This can't be done in a two-and-a half-week goodwill visit.'

Venezuela

With huge oil resources, Venezuela was one of the more prosperous of Latin American states. It had long been dominated by dictators such as the deeply unpopular General Pérez Jiménez (1948–58), whom the Eisenhower administration decorated (along with his hated police chief Pedro Estrada) for services to anti-Communism. Eisenhower described his government as a model for Latin America and granted him political asylum when he was deposed by a **military junta**.

Nixon arrived in troubled times. After Jiménez's overthrow, people had turned on the police, burning them alive in some working-class districts. The new police force was inexperienced, fearful and demoralized. Eisenhower's support for the unpopular dictator and widespread rumours that the USA was going to cut its imports of Venezuelan oil generated much discontent. The USA was not only unpopular among Communists. In an example of resentment of the US tendency to represent 'the **American way of life**' as the best way, one newspaper had drawn attention to racial inequality in the USA with a photograph of an African American being lynched, captioned 'the American way of life'.

When Nixon, his wife Pat and their small entourage arrived at Caracas airport, a large crowd consisting mostly of teenagers shouted obscenities and 'Go Home Nixon' and threw fruit and other objects. Pat Nixon's red suit was covered with brown spit from tobacco chewers. The motorcade then got stuck for 12 minutes at a roadblock in one of the toughest working-class areas of Caracas, where police had been brutalized in the previous January. Surrounded by a yelling mob of over 4000, who were shouting 'Kill Nixon' and shattering his limousine windows with rocks and fists then rocking it in order to overturn it, Nixon restrained those around him who wanted to start shooting at the students. When the Venezuelan soldiers cleared a path, the limousine sped off, its windscreen wipers going full pelt to clear off the brown spit so that the driver could see where he was going.

'Operation Poor Richard'

When Eisenhower heard that his vice president was in danger of his life, he launched 'Operation Poor Richard' (a title Nixon loathed). US troops and a fleet were put on standby near Venezuela. Meanwhile the Venezuelan army had restored order, so Nixon warned Eisenhower that the Latin Americans would not take kindly to this American show of force, and that they would complain about US '**gunboat diplomacy**'. He was right. Venezuelan radio even talked of a US invasion.

Nixon arrived back at Washington airport to a hero's welcome. The president, cabinet and half of Congress were there to greet him. When Senator Lyndon B. Johnson embraced Nixon at the airport, a reporter reminded him that he had recently called Nixon 'chicken ——'. 'Son,' responded Johnson, 'in politics you have got to learn that overnight chicken —— can turn to chicken salad.' As the vice president left the airport, federal workers, who had been given the afternoon off, lined the streets cheering him.

 **KEY TERM**

Military junta Government by a group of army officers.

American way of life Americans greatly valued their political democracy, economic opportunities and general prosperity.

Gunboat diplomacy Foreign policy aims pursued through military force rather than negotiation.

A photograph of Vice President Nixon's car under attack in Caracas, Venezuela, in 1958.

How far is it fair to conclude from Source F that the USA was unpopular in Venezuela?

The results and significance of Nixon's Latin American visit

Nixon considered his Latin American visit to be a triumph. He felt he had demonstrated US courage. However, as so often, the USA viewed events through a Cold War prism, and in blaming Communists for the anti-American demonstrations, failed to recognize that there were non-Communists who disliked and/or feared the USA. If the visit was 'all about theater', events in Peru and Venezuela played quite well in the USA itself, but did nothing to improve relations with Latin Americans, and perhaps even damaged them.

If the aim of the trip was to demonstrate support for democratically elected leaders, it was unforgivable to have missed Frondizi's inauguration and unwise to visit Stroessner's Paraguay. Significantly, the most violent anti-American demonstrations had taken place in Peru and Venezuela, where unpopular US-supported dictatorships had recently been overthrown. Such demonstrations were in stark contrast to the reception afforded the 'good neighbor' Roosevelt in his 1936 visits to Argentina, Brazil and Uruguay. Nixon's visit had perhaps made the USA a little more aware of Latin American discontent, although events in Cuba (see below) would soon suggest that it was too late.

SOURCE G

Extract from *Nixon: Volume I – The Education of a Politician 1913–1962*, by Stephen Ambrose, Simon & Schuster, 1987.

Nixon proudly quoted FBI chief Hoover as saying that the trip 'made anti-Communism respectable again in the United States' … [but] there were criticisms. Walter Lippmann called the tour 'a diplomatic Pearl Harbor'. The Boston Globe *said it was 'one of the most ineptly handled episodes in this country's foreign relations.' The* New York Post *said that Nixon 'had established his valor in Peru. His insistence on a repeat performance in Venezuela indicates that he was utterly seduced by his press notices, and was incapable of recognizing his own limitations.' James Reston wrote that Nixon had been 'sent south as a substitute for policy,' and added: 'As an exercise in national self-bamboozlement, the reaction here to the Vice President's trip is a classic. A national defeat has been parlayed into a personal political triumph, and even when the Nixons are decorated for good conduct under fire, the larger significance of this event cannot be overlooked.' … Certainly the trip failed to generate anything more than excitement – no good will, no change in policy.*

> **?** To what extent should the assessments in Source G be considered fair? (Use your own knowledge and take care to discuss each extract and its provenance.)

If the aim of Nixon's visit was to improve the economic relationship between the USA and Latin America, then Nixon had some success, as demonstrated by the history of **OPA**.

Juscelino Kubitschek and OPA

According to journalist Henry Raymont (2005), 'There are few better examples of misunderstandings and lost opportunities than the Eisenhower administration's dealings with the Brazilian leader.' Juscelino Kubitschek became president of Brazil in 1956. His support from Brazilian Communists and his vow to champion the poor made Washington distrust him from the first. His Operation Pan America (OPA) plan centred on low-interest US loans and aroused US suspicions that he wanted to blackmail the USA into giving massive financial aid in the style of a Marshall Plan to Latin America. The OPA plan had great support in Latin America, especially from Argentina, Colombia, Peru and Honduras, and Kubitschek took care to place it clearly within the Western camp in the Cold War: 'We hope that the people of the United States realize that continued economic development of the Western hemisphere is vital to the winning of the Cold War, that no matter how strong our bastions are at the "**Iron Curtain**", they will not provide sufficient protection from the dangers we are guarding against if the great masses in Latin America continue to live in poverty and disease.'

Eisenhower's response to the OPA

When Kubitschek first suggested OPA in 1955, Eisenhower's response was cool. In 1956, Eisenhower met Latin American heads of state in Panama. His diary entry was revealing. He was 'unsure' about the democratically elected Kubitschek, but, 'As individuals I thought the presidents of Paraguay [the dictator Stroessner] and Nicaragua [the dictator Somoza] stood out.'

> ← **How did Eisenhower respond to Latin American requests for aid?**

> **🔑 KEY TERM**
>
> **OPA** Brazilian President Juscelino Kubitschek's proposed Operation Pan America was a Marshall Plan for Latin America that never really came to anything.
>
> **Iron Curtain** Former British Prime Minister Winston Churchill used this term in 1946 when he said that Soviets had separated Eastern Europe from the rest of Europe.

The Eisenhower administration warmly endorsed the OPA plan in public, but privately resented the financial demands – Brazil alone sought $3 billion worth of aid. It would have been exceptionally difficult for the Eisenhower administration, rightly concerned about balancing the national budget, to persuade US taxpayers that they had to finance another Marshall Plan for their southern neighbours. The original Marshall Plan had got through Congress because the Communist threat to Western Europe had seemed massive, and because the 'aid' had been deemed vital to US security. In 1958 Latin America looked unlikely to fall to Communism. The USA therefore worked quietly against OPA. In September 1958, the Pan-American Union foreign ministers met in Washington to discuss OPA. Brazil's delegate demanded a 'new deal for the Americas', but the USA reiterated that private initiatives and private capital must play the major role, not US hand-outs. The Brazilian delegate spent five weeks attacking US 'indifference' and 'incomprehension', making headlines throughout Latin America but not in the USA. He also said that the region might be forced to look to the Communist bloc for markets, at which point the US representative called him a Communist.

The Act of Bogotá

As a result of the Washington meeting, the Council of the Organization of American States established a special committee to study measures for economic co-operation. In 1959, Fidel Castro addressed the committee in Buenos Aires, proposing that the USA give $30 billion to fund an economic development programme for Latin America. Vice President Nixon's visit to Latin America, the congressional hearings held to determine why he had received such a hostile reception, and the rise of Fidel Castro in Cuba, combined to prompt Eisenhower to change his stance on this issue, and the Inter-American Development Bank was established in 1959 with $1 billion capital. The OAS committee had its last meeting in September 1960 in Bogotá, Colombia, where it adopted the Act of Bogotá, a series of recommendations for 'measures for social improvements' and 'measures for economic development'. The act gave a 'welcome' to the US government's decision to establish the bank, but the Latin American nations had to wait for Kennedy's Alliance for Progress (see page 154) before there was a little more enthusiasm in the USA for aid to Latin America. Overall, Eisenhower's policy toward Latin America had offered nothing new (unless one counts covert actions) and his response to Árbenz in Guatemala, to OPA and to Cuba (see page 146) was unimaginative and, arguably, endangered US security.

USA	Latin America
• Disliked revolutions • Rich • Liked Latin American strongmen • Intervened in Guatemala • Strongly anti-Communist and other leftists	• Prone to revolutions • Poor • Strongmen usually unpopular • Disliked US intervention • Poverty led to considerable numbers of leftists

SUMMARY DIAGRAM

Eisenhower and Latin America

 # Key debate

▶ *Key question: What was the significance of the US intervention in Guatemala?*

US actions in Guatemala, 1954

← How significant was US intervention in Guatemala?

Historian Walter LaFaber (2008) argued that the US overthrow of Árbenz marked a turning point in American foreign policy. First, the USA misunderstood the Guatemalan situation. Árbenz had been democratically elected and, although reformist, was not a Communist. There were a few Communists in the national legislature and in the labour movement, but they really had little influence on the country's important institutions, which were the presidency, the army, and the Roman Catholic Church. 'Americans,' said LaFaber, 'too easily confused nationalism with Communism.' This error would recur in Vietnam (see Chapter 5). Second, LaFaber argued that as the covert US operation was a great success, the Eisenhower administration wrongly concluded that it could have similar success in Cuba in 1961 (see page 147). Finally, within Guatemala itself, the USA 'won the battle but lost the longer war', according to LaFaber. The USA had replaced Árbenz with a right-wing dictator. Castillo Armas conducted large-scale executions, but still proved so ineffective that he was assassinated by his colleagues within three years. Between 1954 and 1965 the USA gave Guatemala more aid than any other Latin American nation, but a succession of vicious military dictatorships led to the rise in the late 1950s of a **guerrilla movement** far more radical than any group had been in 1954.

 **KEY TERM**

Guerrilla movement
Irregular fighting force that concentrates on activities such as sabotage and raids.

Leslie Bethell and Ian Roxborough (1992) argued that after the Second World War, Latin America experienced a 'continent-wide democratic spring', so that by 1946, only five countries could not call themselves democracies. Roy Rosenzweig (2006) developed that argument further, contending that between 1944 and 1954, Guatemala experienced one of the most ambitious post-war Latin American revolutions, then suffered the first US Cold War direct intervention in Latin American politics, an intervention that toppled Árbenz and definitively ended the hemisphere's post-war democratic opening. Henry Raymont (2005), emphasized that the Guatemalan intervention 'encouraged the tightening of ties with right-wing dictatorships and the Latin American military establishments that supported them'. According to Tulio Halperín Donghi (1996), the intervention represented the end of the 'good neighbor', demonstrated the post-war US impatience with democratically elected Latin American governments that were insufficiently anti-Communist, reaffirmed US domination of Latin America, and appeared to millions of Latin Americans of all political persuasions, to be 'the continuation of a long story of rapacious [US] aggression'.

Significantly, the CIA's own 1983 assessment of the 1954 **coup** in Guatemala concluded that the coup had 'ended a decade of economic and social reforms' and that it had given power to those who believed that 'unpredictable and unmanageable political processes' such as free elections were 'inimical to their interest' and who therefore killed opponents who 'could not be co-opted, silenced or frightened into exile'. That killing was undertaken by 'death squads', to whose training the USA had contributed.

What motivated the United States?

Stephen Schlesinger and Stephen Kinzer (1982) emphasized Eisenhower's desire to support the United Fruit Company. However, Piero Gleijeses (1991) emphasized the activities of the Guatemalan Communist Party as the prime motivation in US intervention. He argued that Guatemala was never more free or democratic than it was between 1944 and 1954. Such disagreements are somewhat exaggerated. The desire to support United Fruit was part of the US desire to support capitalism that underlay US anti-Communism in the Cold War. Washington's motivation, as always, was primarily to defend US national interest.

T
O
K

What would explain these different interpretations? Investigate each historian mentioned in this section (Walter LaFaber, Greg Grandin, Leslie Bethell/Ian Roxborough, Stephen Schlesinger/Stephen Kinzer, Piero Gleijeses, and Nick Cullather). How does your brief research explain the position each historian has taken? You might work in groups or divide up the historians among you. (Language, History, Reason, Emotion, Ethics.)

Tulio Halperín Donghi (1996) noted that 'some observers' pointed out that the USA traditionally justified its domination by reference to outside threats. Donghi said the US intervention had less to do with Communist participation than with Árbenz's refusal to join the anti-Communist crusade of the USA: 'Dulles was correct in believing that if a tiny country like Guatemala was able to ignore with impunity his call for Pan-American unity, US political hegemony over the hemisphere would be severely compromised.'

Was the US role in Guatemala crucial or minimal?

Historian Nick Cullather (1999) showed how the CIA used all available US power to oust Árbenz:

- it used the OAS to isolate Guatemala diplomatically
- it worked with US businesses to create an economic crisis in Guatemala

- it cultivated dissidents within the military, oligarchy, Catholic Church and student organizations
- it funded and equipped an exile invasion force based in Honduras
- it exploited to the full the 'new science of advertising', with rumours, posters and radio shows designed to create panic and acquiescence.

The State Department contributed by threatening to withhold much-needed trade concessions and credits from other Latin American countries unless they acceded to US plans for Guatemala. Cullather concludes that the CIA did not simply want to remove Árbenz, but sought a 'radical, revolutionary change in Guatemalan politics. They sought the reversal of the Revolution of 1944, the termination of land reform, and the replacement of Árbenz with a liberal, authoritarian leader. Afterwards, they foresaw a prolonged period of dictatorial rule during which the regime would depend on United States aid and arms.'

According to Greg Grandin (2006) there is a 'chronic official refusal to reckon seriously with the consequences of U.S. policy in Latin America'. As an example, he cites the respected diplomatic historian John Lewis Gaddis (1998) who claimed that the CIA's intervention in Guatemala 'did little to alter the course of events', as Árbenz's regime was incredibly unpopular. Once again, there is much to be said for both views on the US role in Guatemala. The Cold War in Latin America was not only a product of the conflict between the USA and the USSR. It was also a product of bitterly fought domestic battles over political and economic rights for the people. The vast majority of historians emphasize the importance of the US role in Guatemala, but US actions were superimposed on domestic conditions throughout the Cold War. It was quite easy for the USA to find and to ally with opponents of existing regimes, and this is what happened in Guatemala.

Chapter summary

President Eisenhower and the 'New Look'

Although Eisenhower claimed that his foreign policy was different from Truman's, there was little that was new. Like Truman, Eisenhower was militantly anti-Communist. McCarthyism remained important in the early years of his presidency and Eisenhower did nothing about McCarthy's witch hunts. Relations with the USSR and China remained hostile. The Eisenhower administration talked of the 'rollback' of Communism, although in practice Truman's policy of containment was continued, with the possible exception of Vietnam. Eisenhower's 'New Look' defence policy aimed to save money by depending on the nuclear deterrent. The threat of nuclear weaponry was not used in Vietnam, but it was used over Quemoy and Matsu, and was very controversial.

While Eisenhower's foreign policy was not particularly new, other areas of the world were changing fast. During his presidency, many new nations emerged in Africa and Asia, often through revolutions. The Eisenhower administration was not sympathetic to revolutions, and used covert operations to oppose them in Iran, Vietnam, Guatemala and Cuba (see Chapter 6).

One of the greatest US fears in the Cold War was that Communism might take hold in the Western hemisphere. It could be argued that this was inevitable, given the poverty in Latin America. However, it could also be argued that US policies made Communist success more likely. The Eisenhower administration recognized that the problem of poverty gave Latin America revolutionary potential. Latin Americans argued that they desperately needed US economic aid and investment but support for strongmen was the favoured US solution. The US determination to protect its interests in Latin America lay behind CIA covert operations in Guatemala that helped replace a democratically elected leftist government with a dictatorship. While strongmen sometimes guaranteed the stability that the USA sought, they also served to increase US unpopularity, as demonstrated in Guatemala. US support for unpopular dictatorships and the lack of US aid played a part in the anti-American scenes in Lima and Caracas during Nixon's visit.

Latin America was low on the list of Eisenhower's priorities and it could be argued that his administration's policies there were unimaginative and unsuccessful.

Examination advice

How to answer 'analyse' questions

When answering questions with the command term 'analyse' you should try to identify the key elements and their relative importance.

Example

Analyse why the Eisenhower government overthrew the democratically elected president of Guatemala in 1954.

1. To answer this question successfully, you need to discuss the various reasons why the USA hated Jacobo Árbenz and his government. You should focus on the key reasons and also examine whether or not these were based in reality. Be sure to place the events in historical context; in other words, briefly mention other Cold War events that might have led US decision-makers to make the choices they did.

2. Take several minutes and list the reasons the USA wanted to get rid of Árbenz, what actions it took and the consequences of the overthrow of Árbenz (you can get ideas about the 'reasons' for the US actions by looking at the 'actions' and 'results'). These could include:

Reasons

* Connection between the United Fruit Company and US government officials.
* Election of reformer Árbenz in 1950 and his plans for land reform.
* Seizure of unused United Fruit Company lands.
* Suspicion that Árbenz was a Communist supporter.
* Desire to punish Árbenz's refusal to join the anti-Communist crusade.
* Desire to prevent Communism from spreading in Latin America.
* Guatemala's proximity to the USA.
* Victory of the Viet Minh at Dien Bien Phu (see Chapter 5).
* Preference for military strongmen over reformist presidents.

Actions

* Use of the OAS to condemn Communism and diplomatically isolate Árbenz (1954).
* State Department demands for the return of United Fruit Company land.
* CIA trained and equipped small army under Castillo Armas in Nicaragua beginning in 1953.
* US planes bombed Guatemala City (1954)
* Use of covert action.

Results

* Árbenz left Guatemala.
* United Fruit Company land returned.
* Overreliance on 'illegal' methods.
* Repression in Guatemala.

3. In your introduction, state what you consider to be the main reasons the US wanted to depose Árbenz. These should be ordered from most important to least important. Be sure to provide the historical context, as well. An example of a good introduction is on page 92.

Underlying the US decision to depose Árbenz in 1954 was US anti-Communism. Árbenz's decision to seize land that had belonged to the US-owned United Fruit Company seemed to confirm that he was at the very least a Communist sympathizer. Furthermore, leading figures in the Eisenhower administration had strong connections to United Fruit. Árbenz and his actions constituted a threat to the US vision of an anti-Communist Latin America in which US economic interests were respected. Finally, in 1954, Communism also seemed to be on the march in Asia, so the Eisenhower administration felt that a stand had to be taken. In Guatemala (as in South-east Asia), the USA would feel safer with a 'strongman' in power, rather than a leftist. Historians disagree as to whether the main US motive was fear of Communism or the desire to protect US economic interests, but there should be no such disagreement, as both recognize that the USA was motivated by the promotion of capitalism, which entailed opposition to Communism.

4. For each of the key points you raise in your introduction, you should be able to write one or two long paragraphs. Here, you should provide your supporting evidence. Be sure to also state the connection between what you have written and the reasons why the USA overthrew Árbenz.
5. In the final paragraph, you should tie your essay together stating your conclusions. Do not raise any new points here.
6. Now try writing a complete answer to the question following the advice above.

 # Examination practice

Below are two exam-style questions for you to practise on this topic.

1 The 1950s saw significant political changes in Latin America. Analyse these changes using at least two countries as examples.

2 To what extent was Eisenhower's New Look defence policy different from Truman's?
(For guidance on how to answer 'to what extent' questions, see page 67.)

CHAPTER 5

US involvement in the Vietnam War

This chapter looks at the changing nature of, and reasons for, the US involvement in Vietnam. It traces the domestic effects and explains the end of the war. It also looks at the role played by Vietnam in the Cold War. You need to consider the following questions throughout this chapter:

✪ What was the nature of the US involvement in Vietnam?
✪ How far did the motives of each US president differ?
✪ Why and how far did each US president get involved in Vietnam?
✪ Why was the USA unable to defeat the Communists in Vietnam?
✪ Why, how and with what results did the USA get out of Vietnam?
✪ How did the Vietnam War impact on the US economy, politics and society?
✪ How significant was Vietnam in the development of the Cold War?

① The US involvement in Vietnam, 1950–69

▶ *Key question: What was the nature of the US involvement in Vietnam?*

Late nineteenth-century Vietnam was conquered by the French and became part of the French colony of Indochina. While France was preoccupied with Hitler during the Second World War (1939–45), Japan conquered Vietnam. After Japan's defeat by the USA in 1945, Vietnamese nationalists such as the Communist Ho Chi Minh believed that Vietnam could now become independent, but the French returned. War broke out between the French and the **Vietminh**.

KEY TERM

Vietminh Vietnamese nationalists led by Ho Chi Minh.

President Truman and Vietnam

President Truman (1945–53) helped the French effort to maintain control of Vietnam, because he believed the French were fighting Communism. Truman's aid to the French in their struggle against the Vietnamese Communists was of a primarily financial and military nature. By the end of his presidency, the USA was paying nearly 80 per cent of the French bill for Indochina. Truman gave over $2 billion and a great deal of military equipment and advice to the French and $50 million for economic and technical aid to the Vietnamese people. He invested American money

How did Truman support French colonial rule in Vietnam?

Looking at Source A, and remembering what sustained Americans in the Pusan Perimeter (see page 50), why do you suppose the USA chose to combat Communism in Vietnam rather than in Laos?

A map showing important places in the American era in Vietnam (from about 1956 to 1973).

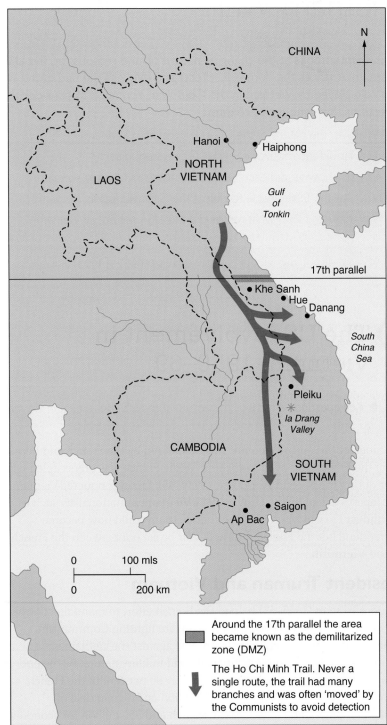

Around the 17th parallel the area became known as the demilitarized zone (DMZ)

The Ho Chi Minh Trail. Never a single route, the trail had many branches and was often 'moved' by the Communists to avoid detection

and prestige in Vietnam, even though one State Department Far East specialist admitted that 'the trouble is that none of us knows enough about Indochina'.

It could be argued that the extent of Truman's commitment was limited, as he was simply supporting the French, but in November 1950 a Defense Department official warned: 'We are gradually increasing our stake in the outcome of the struggle … we are dangerously close to the point of being so deeply committed that we may find ourselves completely committed even to direct intervention.'

President Eisenhower (1953–61) and aid to the French

How did Eisenhower increase the US commitment in Vietnam?

Initially, Eisenhower continued to aid the French. In early 1954 he gave them armaments worth $385 million and US bombers accompanied by 200 American technicians. He told Congress that he disliked putting Americans in danger but that 'we must not lose Asia'. Nevertheless, the French still could not defeat the popular Vietminh, who used effective guerrilla tactics and received weapons from the Chinese.

Struggling in the battle at Dien Bien Phu (1954), France urgently requested a US air strike on the Vietminh. After much consideration Eisenhower decided against helping the French, whom he privately described as 'a hopeless, helpless mass of protoplasm'. Eisenhower subsequently wrote that 'the strongest reason of all' for the USA to stay out was the danger of alienating world opinion by seeming to replace French colonialism with American colonialism. Perhaps more importantly, he tried but failed to get the British support that Congress required before they would approve American military intervention.

The Geneva Accords, 1954

At the Geneva conference in 1954, France and the Vietminh signed the **Geneva Accords**, which said that the French would get out of Indochina, Communists would rule in northern Vietnam and non-Communists in the south. Neither were to make any military alliances with foreign powers and democratic elections for a single government in a re-unified Vietnam would be held in 1956.

The Geneva Accords were rejected by the new premier of southern Vietnam, Ngo Dinh Diem, and by the USA. Neither wanted Vietnam to be under Communist control. Eisenhower chose to misinterpret the temporary ceasefire line of the 17th parallel as a permanent division between a northern state that was Communist and a southern state that was not. Ironically, although the USA saw itself as defending democracy in the Cold War, Eisenhower rejected the idea of national elections in Vietnam in 1956 because he knew that Ho Chi Minh would win around 80 per cent of the votes. Like Korea, Vietnam had been divided because of the Cold War.

 **KEY TERM**

Geneva Accords
Agreements reached at Geneva in 1954 by France, China, Ho Chi Minh and the USSR, that Vietnam should be temporarily divided, with national elections held in 1956.

Nation building in South Vietnam, 1954–61

After the Geneva conference, Ho and the Communists governed North Vietnam (from Hanoi) while Diem governed South Vietnam (from Saigon). Like all Vietnamese nationalists, both would have preferred a united Vietnam.

Eisenhower continued the military nature of the commitment, but introduced two new elements. He incorporated South Vietnam in a defensive military alliance, **SEATO**, and engaged in what the Americans called 'nation building', supporting and encouraging Diem in the creation of the new and 'independent' state of South Vietnam.

Diem's South Vietnam: problems and solutions

In order to contain Communism, Diem and the Americans aimed to create a stable, non-Communist South Vietnamese state. Eisenhower gave Diem a great deal of money, military equipment and nearly 1000 military and civilian advisers. Some Americans advocated **land reform**, but the Eisenhower administration emphasized military solutions rather than social and economic change.

Despite all the US aid, nation building in South Vietnam did not go well. Diem was an upper-class Catholic with little empathy with the Buddhist peasants and his regime was repressive and unpopular. Frequently dissatisfied with Diem, who rejected American advice that his regime needed to reform to survive, Eisenhower nearly withdrew support, but was impressed when Diem sometimes handled opponents well.

Diem faced a great deal of opposition. After 1960, Ho's southern supporters, whom Diem called the **Vietcong**, stepped up their attempts to destabilize his increasingly unpopular regime. Even Diem's army (the Army of the Republic of Vietnam or **ARVN**) contained opponents, some of whom rebelled against him in 1960. Many knowledgeable Americans warned from the first that the struggle against the Communists in Vietnam could not be won with the unpopular Diem.

Eisenhower and Vietnam: conclusions

Eisenhower failed to stop North Vietnam becoming a Communist state during his presidency, but his artificial creation of the 'independent' state of South Vietnam could be considered an example of the rollback of Communism he had promised in 1952 (see page 73). Some historians consider that Eisenhower handled the Vietnam problem quite well, praising him for not aiding the French at Dien Bien Phu (although it was probably only congressional leaders and his British allies that stopped him doing so) and not sending in US ground troops. However, between 1955 and 1961, in defiance of the Geneva Accords, Eisenhower made the USA the guarantor of an independent state of South Vietnam and committed the USA to the defence of a particularly unpopular leader in Diem. He gave Diem $7 billion worth of aid and around 1000 American advisers, nearly half of whom were military. Once such a commitment was undertaken, it was arguable that America had incurred an obligation to see it through. From that point it would prove to be but a short step to putting American soldiers into Vietnam. Eisenhower had massively increased the commitment inherited from Truman.

President Kennedy and Vietnam

← **How far did US policy change under Kennedy?**

Under President Kennedy (1961–3), the nature of the involvement underwent a quantitative change: the USA provided ever more money, weaponry, helicopters and nearly 20,000 'advisers'. Their active involvement in the war, as at Ap Bac, was a new departure.

Ap Bac

In the battle of Ap Bac in January 1963, 2000 ARVN troops (accompanied by 113 American armoured personnel carriers, American-operated helicopters and bombers, and American advisers) refused to attack 350 Vietcong. Five US helicopters and three pilots were lost and the ARVN troops refused to mount a rescue mission. Ap Bac demonstrated the weakness of the ARVN, the extent of US involvement in the fighting in Vietnam, and the uneasy relationship between the ARVN and US forces. Soon after the battle, American officials estimated that Saigon only controlled 49 per cent of the population. The JCS, the National Security Council and Secretary of Defense Robert McNamara recommended putting American ground troops into Vietnam, but Kennedy said no.

SOURCE B

An extract from a 1961 speech by French President de Gaulle warning US President Kennedy.

The more you become involved out there against Communism, the more the Communists will appear as the champions of national independence … You will sink step by step into a bottomless military and political quagmire, however much you spend in men and money.

What value would you put upon the assessment in Source B? **?**

The end of Diem

Some members of the Kennedy administration disliked the emphasis on the military defeat of the Communists and urged Diem to introduce reform. His refusal to reform, coupled with increased American press criticism of his military and political ineptitude, damaged his relationship with Kennedy.

In spring 1963, Diem allowed the flying of Catholic flags in honour of his brother, Archbishop Ngo Dinh Thuc, but banned flags for the celebration of Buddha's birthday. Ten thousand Buddhists protested. Diem sent in soldiers, killing seven Buddhists and prompting several others to burn themselves to death in protest. Kennedy expressed shock: 'How could this have happened? Who are these people? Why didn't we know about them before?' Possibly Kennedy was trying to deflect blame from himself here, but if he really did not know of the Catholic–Buddhist tensions, he had not done his homework on a country to which he had sent several thousand Americans.

As Diem rejected the reform option, and the military option was not working, the USA chose a more ruthless option. When several ARVN generals planned a coup, the USA gave them vital encouragement. Diem was overthrown and killed by his generals. It is possible that the Kennedy administration consented to the assassination.

SOURCE C

A Buddhist priest burns himself to death in protest against Diem's religious policies in 1963 in the central market square of Saigon.

? Why do you suppose the photograph in Source C made headline news and a great impact in the USA?

Kennedy and Vietnam: conclusions

Kennedy's belief that little Vietnam was so important seems ludicrous to us, but many Cold War Americans agreed with him. Securely in the **commitment trap** set by Truman and Eisenhower, Kennedy, despite his frequent uncertainty about the wisdom of US involvement, increased his country's commitment to an unpopular regime that he then helped to overthrow.

Getting rid of Diem did not improve the situation and just confirmed the tendency to believe that in the absence of any other constructive ideas, increased force would somehow do the trick. The US commander in Vietnam, General Westmoreland, said US complicity in the demise of Diem 'morally locked us in Vietnam', greatly increasing America's obligation to subsequent Saigon governments. Kennedy said the same in a cable to his ambassador in Vietnam in November 1963. Kennedy had passed a poisoned chalice to his successor.

KEY TERM

Commitment trap
Historians' theory that successive US presidents were committed to Vietnam by the actions of their predecessors.

President Johnson and Vietnam

President Johnson (1963–9) inherited nearly 20,000 American 'advisers' in Vietnam, but the Saigon regime had still not defeated the Communists. So, Johnson took the first great escalatory step in early 1965, with air strikes of such intensity that they were known as '**Rolling Thunder**'. Bombing the routes taking men and materials to the South would hopefully secure the position of Americans in South Vietnam, decrease infiltration from the North, demoralize Hanoi, and revitalize the unpopular Saigon regime. Sixty-seven per cent of Americans approved of the bombing.

In his second great escalatory step, Johnson sent the first American **ground troops** to Vietnam in spring 1965. General Westmoreland repeatedly requested more troops in order to assist those already there and because he felt more were needed in order to secure victory. There were around 200,000 American soldiers in Vietnam by late 1965, and over 500,000 by early 1968. By sending in ground troops and ordering 'Rolling Thunder', Johnson had dramatically changed the nature of the war.

'Johnson's war'?

The dramatic escalation of the war under Johnson led many contemporaries and historians to blame him for US involvement. However, he inherited a long-standing commitment to Vietnam, in which the USA had invested a great deal of money, prestige and credibility. Furthermore, Congress repeatedly agreed to finance the war, and polls showed that a majority of the public was behind him.

How did Johnson change the nature of the war?

KEY TERM

Rolling Thunder Sustained US bombing of North Vietnam from March 1965 to November 1968.

Ground troops Regular soldiers (rather than just 'advisers') in Vietnam.

President	Involvement	Extent
Truman (1950–3)	• $2 billion military equipment and advice to French	Some money, some US prestige and credibility
Eisenhower (1953–61)	• Defied Geneva Accords • Created South Vietnam • $7 billion to Diem • SEATO	Much money, US prestige and credibility
Kennedy (1961–3)	• Nearly 20,000 'advisers' • Lots of money and military aid	Even more money, prestige, credibility
Johnson (1963–9)	• Rolling Thunder • 500,000 ground troops	Massive money, prestige, credibility

SUMMARY DIAGRAM

The US involvement in Vietnam, 1950–69

The motives behind US involvement in Vietnam

▶ *Key question: How far did the motives of each US president differ?*

Why did Truman and Eisenhower support French colonial rule?

→ Supporting the French, 1950–4

After the Second World War, Soviet domination of Eastern Europe confirmed the American belief that Communism threatened the international free trade and democratic ideals that were important to American well-being and security. The Truman administration considered the French invaluable allies against Communism in both Indochina and Europe and when the French asserted that Ho was part of a world-wide Communist conspiracy that was likely to lead to Soviet domination everywhere, Truman responded positively to their request for aid. Some State Department specialists pointed out that the Vietnamese Communists were *not* subservient to Moscow, but Truman believed that what was at stake in Vietnam was the expansion of Communism, rather than a Vietnamese war for independence. The JCS argued that the world balance of power was at stake in South East Asia, an area full of strategically vital materials such as rubber, where American allies such as Japan and Australia might be vulnerable to Communist attack. The fall of China to Communism in 1949 made Truman fear further Communist expansion in Asia, especially when North Korea attacked South Korea in June 1950 (see page 43).

Truman also had domestic political considerations. Already under attack from the Republicans for having 'lost' China to Communism in 1949 (see page 45), Truman was even more vulnerable after February 1950 when McCarthy (see page 34) convinced many Americans that there were traitors in the Truman State Department.

Eisenhower's first phase: aiding the French

Eisenhower helped the French for the same reasons as Truman, but also had some concerns of his own. The French were threatening to stop fighting the Vietminh without massive US aid and Eisenhower did not want to 'lose' Vietnam as Truman had 'lost' China. Like Truman, he felt it preferable that French rather than American soldiers fight Communists. Also, in his presidential election campaign, Eisenhower had rejected Truman's policy of containment and advocated the rollback of Communism (see page 73). With no rollback as yet, Eisenhower at the very least had to continue containment in Vietnam, where he was in the 'commitment trap'. Most important of all, Eisenhower felt that the loss of Vietnam to Communism would affect the global balance of power. In 1954, he articulated his '**domino theory**'. He said Vietnam was vitally important to America, because if it fell

 **KEY TERM**

Domino theory
Eisenhower believed that if one country fell to Communism, surrounding countries might follow, like falling dominoes.

to Communism, neighbouring countries might follow like dominoes, which would mean the loss of raw materials and millions of people to the Communist world.

Eisenhower, Kennedy and Diem, 1954–63

← **Why did Eisenhower and Kennedy support Diem?**

Eisenhower and nation building

After Geneva, Eisenhower had new reasons to continue and escalate US involvement in Vietnam. As half of Vietnam was now Communist, the USA had to do something to restore its prestige in the area and it was easier to increase the involvement when free of the taint of French colonialism.

Kennedy: containment, commitment and credibility

Like Truman and Eisenhower, Kennedy believed Communism sought world domination and had to be contained for the sake of US security. Kennedy also believed in and quoted the domino theory and considered Vietnam 'a proving ground for democracy … a test of American responsibility and determination in Asia'.

Kennedy was greatly influenced by Secretary of Defense Robert McNamara and Secretary of State Dean Rusk, both great believers in the US commitment to Vietnam. They told Kennedy that as the USA was already committed to help South Vietnam before his presidency, a US departure would result in a loss of face and 'undermine the credibility of American commitments everywhere'. The JCS warned Kennedy that, 'any reversal of US policy could have disastrous effects, not only on our relationship with South Vietnam, but with the rest of our Asian and other allies as well'.

Kennedy had criticized Eisenhower for allowing the rise of Communism in the newly emergent nations of the '**Third World**', which Kennedy (and the Soviet leader Khrushchev) considered to be the new Cold War battleground. The unsuccessful Bay of Pigs invasion of Cuba (see page 162) and the possibility of a Soviet-backed Communist triumph in Laos made Kennedy determined to avoid another Third World failure. 'We just can't have another defeat in Vietnam,' he confided to a reporter. 'Now we have a problem in making our power credible, and Vietnam is the place.'

Domestic political considerations

Kennedy was even more affected by domestic political considerations than Truman and Eisenhower. His militantly anti-Communist presidential campaign rhetoric, designed to win votes, served to limit his foreign policy options once in the White House. Having made much of the need for a more dynamic foreign policy, and highly sensitive about references to his youth and inexperience, Kennedy felt obliged to be assertive in foreign affairs. At a 1961 White House luncheon, a newspaper editor challenged Kennedy: 'We can annihilate Russia and should make that clear to the Soviet government … you and your Administration are weak sisters … [We need] a man on

---

KEY TERM

Third World During the Cold War, the USA and its allies considered themselves the 'first' world, the Communist bloc the 'second', and the less developed nations the 'third'.

horseback … Many people in Texas and the Southwest think that you are riding [your daughter] Caroline's tricycle.' A red-faced Kennedy who retorted 'I'm just as tough as you are' was clearly a president who thought he had much to prove.

Rusk and McNamara knew there would be 'bitter' divisions amongst the American public if Kennedy got out of Vietnam. 'Extreme elements' would make political capital out of the retreat. Kennedy did not want to be accused of 'losing' Vietnam in the way that Truman had 'lost' China. 'There are just so many concessions that one can make to the Communists in one year and survive politically,' he said in 1961. In 1963 he told a journalist friend that: 'We don't have a prayer of staying in Vietnam … These people hate us. They are going to throw our asses out … But I can't give up a piece of territory like that to the Communists and then get the American people to re-elect me.'

Why did Johnson continue and escalate the US involvement in Vietnam?

KEY TERM

Commander-in-chief
Under the US Constitution, the president commands the US armed forces.

Gulf of Tonkin Resolution
Congressional resolution giving the president power to do as he saw fit in Vietnam.

President Johnson: continuation and escalation

For Johnson, there was no question but that he must continue the involvement. A typical American of the Cold War era, Johnson believed in containment and the domino theory and abhorred the idea of appeasing an aggressive enemy. Johnson inherited involvement in a war and as **commander-in-chief** felt duty-bound to listen to the generals, who wanted to continue and intensify the only war they had in order to win. Intensely patriotic, Johnson felt it was a question of national honour for the USA to continue its commitment to its South Vietnamese ally and to stick by SEATO (see page 96). America had always won its wars and defeat by what he called 'that damn little pissant country', 'that raggedy-ass little fourth-rate' North Vietnam was inconceivable.

There were domestic political reasons behind Johnson's continuation of the commitment. Emotionally and constitutionally, he felt bound to continue with the policies and advisers of the assassinated President Kennedy. He retained Kennedy men such as McNamara and Rusk, so no fresh ideas emerged. No one wanted to admit past errors or to have real debate and, although there were doubts about the viability of South Vietnam, many in the administration believed that the USA would somehow triumph. Finally, Johnson did not want to be the first US president to lose a war.

These reasons also explain his decision to escalate.

Escalation

In order to escalate involvement in Vietnam, Johnson needed congressional support. Because of real and imagined attacks on US ships off the coast of North Vietnam in August 1964, Congress passed the **Gulf of Tonkin Resolution**, which gave Johnson the power to do as he saw fit in Vietnam. Armed with this resolution, Johnson took the war to the North. American aircraft bombed North Vietnam for the first time. The escalation made Johnson look tough. His public approval rating rose from 42 to 72 per cent, helping him to win the November 1964 presidential election with a landslide victory. The resolution and the election victory suggested a nation united behind its president in his Vietnam policy, although Congress only passed the resolution after a subsequently much-debated 'attack' on US ships in North Vietnamese waters, and voters thought Johnson's opponent was the candidate more likely to get the USA into war.

Johnson escalated US involvement in Vietnam because Diem's successors (see the table below) were even less effective than Diem in creating a viable South Vietnamese state. In 1964 it was estimated that the Communists controlled half of the country.

Date	President
July 1954 to November 1963	Ngo Dinh Diem
November 1963 to January 1964	General Minh
January 1964 to February 1965	General Khanh
February 1965 to June 1965	Dr Pan Huy Quat
June 1965 to September 1967	Air Vice-Marshal Ky
September 1967 to April 1975	Nguyen Van Thieu

South Vietnamese presidents 1954–75

Working Group recommendations

In autumn 1964, a Working Group was brought together by President Johnson to study Vietnam and make suggestions for future policies. It was made up of experts from the Defense Department, the State Department, the CIA and the JCS and:

- said an independent and anti-Communist South Vietnam was vital to the USA
- reiterated the domino theory
- said American 'national prestige, credibility, and honour' were at stake
- emphasized that escalation was necessary due to the Saigon government ('close to a standstill' and 'plagued by confusion, apathy, and poor morale')
- suggested heavier bombing.

Safety of American personnel

The Vietcong seemed able to strike at will at Americans in South Vietnam. In November 1964, 100 Vietcong attacked and greatly damaged a US airbase near Saigon and the JCS demanded retaliatory air strikes on North Vietnam. In February 1965, the Vietcong attacked a huge American camp near Pleiku. Eight Americans were killed and 100 were wounded. Johnson was furious ('I've had enough of this') and his advisers urged retaliation.

In a speech in April 1965, Johnson summed up the reasons why the USA had to continue and escalate its commitment to Vietnam. He said that:

- The USA needed to fight if it wanted to live securely in a free world.
- North Vietnam was a puppet of expansionists in Moscow and Beijing who wanted to conquer all of Asia, and appeasing them could lead to a third world war.
- Since Eisenhower and Kennedy had helped build and defend South Vietnam, abandonment would dishonour the USA and cause allies to doubt its word and credibility.

President	Motives
Truman (1950–3)	• Containment • Loss of China • McCarthy • Elections • Help NATO ally
Eisenhower (1953–61)	• Containment • Rollback • Loss of China • Rid of taint of French colonialism • Domino theory • Geneva Accords bad for US image
Kennedy (1961–3)	• Containment • Domino theory • Bay of Pigs • Laos • Developing world • Commitment trap • SEATO • Advisers • Elections • Youth and experience
Johnson (1963–9)	• Containment • Domino theory • Kennedy's death and advisers • SEATO • Commitment trap • Elections • Safety of US personnel • First president to lose a war

The motives behind US involvement in Vietnam

③ Key debate

▶ **Key question:** *Why and how far did each US president get involved in Vietnam?*

Why did the USA get involved?

As historian Robert Shulzinger (1997) wrote, 'Had American leaders not thought that all international events were connected to the Cold War there would have been no American war in Vietnam.' There are three main schools of thought amongst historians about why the Cold War presidents got involved there.

The orthodox interpretation

Orthodox historians (see page 21) such as George Herring (1997) saw the USA containing Communist aggression and expansion in Vietnam, and as having little choice but to do so.

The revisionist interpretation

Revisionist historians (see page 21) such as Gabriel Kolko (1985) emphasized aggressive and acquisitive US economic policies. Kolko said the markets and raw materials in South East Asia motivated American interest in Vietnam. Vietnam became important because a Communist, nationalist revolution there posed a threat to the global capitalist system. If this revolution succeeded, others might follow.

The post-revisionist interpretation

Post-revisionist historians (see page 21) such as David Anderson (2005) saw the USA as motivated by a variety of reasons: 'geopolitical strategy, economics, domestic US politics, and cultural arrogance'.

Why did involvement continue and escalate?

The quagmire theory

Journalist David Halberstam (1964) suggested the 'quagmire theory'. Ignorant of Vietnam and overconfident about American power and ideals, US leaders became trapped in an expensive commitment in an unimportant area, unable to exit without losing credibility. J. Schell (1976) pointed out a crucial change from the Eisenhower administration to the Kennedy administration: the 'territorial domino theory' became the 'psychological domino theory' or the 'doctrine of credibility'. It was not so much that other territories would become Communist if Vietnam did, but that the USA would lose credibility.

 **KEY TERM**

Quagmire theory Belief that the USA got slowly and increasingly trapped in Vietnam, due to ignorance, overconfidence and credibility concerns.

Stalemate theory Belief
that the USA continued to
fight an unwinnable war in
Vietnam, simply to avoid
being seen to be defeated.

The stalemate theory

Leslie Gelb and Richard Betts (1979) claimed that the USA continued and
escalated the commitment not to win (hence '**stalemate theory**') but to
avoid being seen to lose by the American voters.

The commitment trap theory

Many historians argue that an inherited commitment to Vietnam made it
harder for the next president to exit without the nation and its leader losing
face. Successive presidents recognized this 'commitment trap': Kennedy told
French President de Gaulle that he had inherited SEATO from Eisenhower
and that it would look bad if the USA dumped it, while Johnson told the
Vietnamese generals, 'Lyndon Johnson intends to stand by our word.'

How far was each president responsible for the involvement?

President Truman

'The Vietnam War was not an American war' during the Truman years,
according to David Anderson, who argued that American dislike of French
colonialism restrained US involvement. However, Mark Byrnes (2000)
argued, 'It was the mindset of the Truman administration which ultimately
led to that tragic and misguided war.'

President Eisenhower

Historians who absolve Eisenhower of any great responsibility for the
American war in Vietnam, such as Stephen Ambrose (1984), tend to judge
presidents by the extent to which they got America committed. As
Eisenhower did not send ground troops to Vietnam, his Vietnam policy is
considered relatively successful.

While sometimes critical of the Eisenhower administration, historian Fredrik
Logevall (2001) said: 'Making a stand in the Southern parts of Vietnam was
not an illogical move in 1954, given the globalization of the Cold War, given
the domestic political realities, and most of all perhaps, given that the costs
seemed reasonable – a few thousand American advisers on the ground, a
few hundred million dollars in aid.'

However, David Anderson (1990) concluded that, 'the Eisenhower
administration trapped itself and its successors into a commitment to the
survival of its own counterfeit creation', a non-viable South Vietnamese state.
Anthony Short (1989) blamed years of conflict in Vietnam on Eisenhower's
refusal to accept the Geneva Accords. Lloyd Gardner (1988) emphasized that
John Foster Dulles welcomed the end of French colonialism after Dien Bien
Phu ('a blessing in disguise') and gladly took the opportunity to replace it,
saying, 'We have a clean base there now, without the taint of [French]
colonialism.'

In an article in 2008, I concluded that Eisenhower played the crucial role in both the US involvement and the US failure in Vietnam: 'Eisenhower's creation of a South Vietnamese state constituted a dramatic break with the past. The U.S. became deeply involved in the war because the Eisenhower administration set up South Vietnam during 1954–5. Problems that were evident then (stemming from an unpopular South Vietnamese regime created, dominated and sustained by the U.S.) were still evident [under Johnson] … In that sense, the main responsibility for U.S. involvement and failure to win the war lay not with Johnson but with Eisenhower. This was not "Johnson's war". It was "Eisenhower's war", and Eisenhower's actions and assumptions had ensured that it would never be a successful one.'

President Kennedy

David Kaiser (2000) emphasized how Kennedy resisted great pressure from his military and civilian advisers to send in ground troops, although that pressure contributed greatly to the increased number of 'advisers'. Kaiser argued that the greatest responsibility for the overthrow of Diem lay with Diem himself, as he had managed to alienate most of his South Vietnamese and American supporters. Kaiser also emphasized how Rusk and McNamara urged continued support of Diem to the very end. On the other hand, historians such as Ellen Hammer (1987) cite US collusion in the coup against Diem as the US government's greatest mistake and probably the single most important cause of the full-scale American involvement in the war.

As Kennedy's assassination cut short his presidency, there is inevitably much **counterfactual** speculation on 'what might have happened if Kennedy had lived'. Kennedy's old friends and associates, such as Arthur Schlesinger Jr, claimed that Kennedy would have got out of Vietnam, which exonerates Kennedy (and them) from blame for what turned out to be a highly unpopular and unsuccessful war. Much depends on which Kennedy pronouncements and/or actions one concentrates on. Persuaded by Kennedy's expressed doubts about involvement, John Newman (1992) contended that, had he lived, Kennedy would have withdrawn American military advisers. Lawrence Freedman (2000) studied Kennedy's Vietnam policies in the context of Kennedy's response to crises in Berlin, Cuba and Laos, and concluded that Kennedy would not have escalated the war, but he made little mention of Kennedy's dramatic increase in the number of advisers sent to Vietnam. Other historians concentrate on the scale of Kennedy's escalation of the involvement and doubt that Kennedy intended to withdraw. 'There had been no official American reassessment of the strategic value of Vietnam. The commitment, in fact, was stronger than ever,' said David Anderson (2005): thousands more advisers were sent and Kennedy had 'embraced the war both in private and in public, making it more difficult for his successor to walk away from it'. Fredrik Logevall (2001) emphasized that American 'public outrage' at Diem's refusal to reform and

KEY TERM

Counterfactual History that asks 'what if' a particular event had or had not happened.

In this chapter, many historians' ideas on US involvement in Vietnam are presented. If they are to be of any use as guides for future actions by policy makers, how would one choose among them? (History, Reason, Ethics.)

mistreatment of Buddhists gave Kennedy 'a plausible excuse for disengaging the USA from Vietnam' – had he wanted to do so.

President Johnson

While some historians put all the blame on Johnson for the escalation, for example, Logevall (1999), it has been seen that others blame Truman, Eisenhower or Kennedy. H.R. McMaster (1997) accused the JCS of dishonestly encouraging escalation. David Schmitz (2005) saw Johnson as a victim of the commitment trap: 'All the logic and rationale of the Cold War and containment called for escalation.'

Why the USA failed in Vietnam

> ▶ **Key question:** Why was the USA unable to defeat the Communists in Vietnam?

The USA failed to defeat the Communists because of the unpopularity of the Saigon regime and of US aims and methods.

→ The Vietnamese

Johnson's methods were to try to advise, support and strengthen the Saigon governments, politically and militarily, but his methods did not bring victory and alienated the South Vietnamese.

The military emphasis

The main reason that the Americans could not defeat the Communists was because Washington and Saigon were unable to win the hearts and minds of the Vietnamese people. Understandably, the military men thought in terms of force. 'Grab 'em by the balls and their hearts and minds will follow' was a favourite military saying. 'Bomb, bomb, bomb – that's all they know,' sighed Johnson.

Losing hearts and minds

Ironically, American firepower was concentrated more on South than North Vietnam. In their search for Vietcong the Americans killed and wounded tens of thousands of civilians who were not necessarily Communist sympathizers. General Westmoreland agreed civilian casualties were a problem, 'but it does deprive the enemy of the population, doesn't it? They are Asians who don't think about death the way we do.'

The war destroyed the social fabric of South Vietnam, uprooting around one-third of the peasant population to the cities (where they could avoid the US bombing) and dividing families. Responding to American demand, poor peasant girls turned to prostitution, dismaying their families despite earning more in a week than the whole family did in a year.

> **Why were the people of South Vietnam so often unsupportive of the Americans and the Saigon regime?**

SOURCE D

One of the most famous photos of the war: 10-year-old Kim Phuc (centre) ran away from her South Vietnamese village, badly burned by napalm dropped by her own side in the war in 1972.

Why do you suppose Source D played an important part in turning some Americans against the Vietnam War?

Unable to tell whether or not villagers were Communist, American soldiers often disliked the people they were supposed to be helping, as shown in the massacre at apparently pro-Communist My Lai on 16 March 1968. Three hundred and forty-seven unarmed civilians were beaten and killed by American soldiers and their officers.

Vietcong strengths

Although ruthless when necessary, the Communists were generally far better at winning the hearts and minds of the peasantry, whom they treated with respect. Furthermore, the Communist military performance was determined and more impressive than that of ARVN. When in 1965 a North Vietnamese regiment clashed with American soldiers at Ia Drang and 305 Americans and 3561 North Vietnamese died, both sides thought they had won, that the other would not be able to sustain such losses. It was the North Vietnamese who would be proved right.

ARVN weaknesses

Many military leaders were appointed for political rather than military reasons and the ARVN performance was affected because Saigon wanted to avoid losses. In February 1971, 30,000 ARVN invaded Laos with orders to retreat if over 3000 died. They retreated, halfway to their objective (see page 119). The Americans described their own tactics as '**Search and Destroy**' but those of the ARVN as 'Search and Avoid'.

 **KEY TERM**

Search and destroy
General Westmoreland's tactics included finding and killing groups of Vietcong guerrillas.

The Saigon regime

After 'American Diem', a succession of military governments, especially those of Ky (1965–7) and Thieu (1967–75), were corrupt, averse to reform, too closely associated with the USA, and generally unpopular. When President Thieu fled Vietnam in April 1975, he carried away millions of dollars in gold, some of which came from American aid that rarely reached the peasants for whom it was primarily intended.

The Americans in Vietnam

American disunity

The American forces were frequently disunited. Ordinary soldiers only served for one year, so units never attained the feeling of unity vital to morale and performance. **Grunts** frequently painted UUUU on their helmets, representing 'the unwilling, led by the unqualified, doing the unnecessary, for the ungrateful'. African Americans were resentful that they constituted a disproportionate number of front-line troops. An American army officer did five months in the front line and would probably be less experienced than some of the soldiers he commanded. Five months was too little to get to know his men properly and disagreement with the war or tactics led to indiscipline. Between 1969 and 1971, there were 730 **'fraggings'**, killing 83 officers who were often simply trying to get their men to fight. Many American soldiers became confused about why they were fighting, especially in the late 1960s, when anti-war feeling grew back home.

The American way of fighting

The US military strategy was often ineffective. By 1967, even McNamara concluded bombing would not bring victory. General Westmoreland emphasized 'search and destroy' missions in which US troops would try to clear an area of Vietcong, but it was difficult to find the guerrillas and the ratio of destruction was usually six South Vietnamese civilians for every Vietcong soldier. The large-scale use of helicopters and the blasting of the zones where they were to land was not conducive to searching out guerrillas, who heard the noise and went elsewhere.

In the Second World War the folk back home cheered soldiers making visible progress towards Berlin. In contrast, some folk back home jeered while the grunts in Vietnam fought for ground, won it, and left knowing the Vietcong would move in again, as when the Americans 'won' the bloody battle for **'Hamburger Hill'** in 1969. Not knowing which Vietnamese were the enemy was also demoralizing.

Wartime comforts

Frustration with the war led many American soldiers to seek comfort elsewhere. Around a quarter of American soldiers caught sexually transmitted diseases. In 1970 an estimated 58 per cent of Americans in

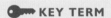

What were the weaknesses of the US military?

KEY TERM

Grunts Ordinary ground troopers or foot soldiers.

Fragging When enlisted men tried to kill officers by throwing fragmentation grenades at them.

Hamburger Hill A 1969 battle where the quantity of blood and guts spilled reminded soldiers of raw hamburgers.

Vietnam smoked marijuana ('pot'), and 22 per cent injected heroin. One colonel was **court-martialled** for organizing pot parties.

Ironically, the American desire to keep their soldiers as comfortable as possible in Vietnam helps explain their defeat. A soldier could be airlifted from the horrors of the jungle to a luxurious base, which led to an air of unreality and disorientation, but Westmoreland said this was the only way you could get Americans to fight.

SOURCE E

An extract from President Nixon's diary in 1972.

If we fail it will be because the American way simply isn't as effective as the Communist way … I have an uneasy feeling that this may be the case. We give them the most modern arms, we emphasize the material to the exclusion of the spiritual and the Spartan life, and it may be that we soften them up rather than harden them up for the battle.

The home front

Johnson and Congress naturally paid great attention to public opinion. Many believe that opposition to the war from the public and in the press was the main reason why Johnson decided on retreat, although the objectors were probably a minority, and supporters of the war also put pressure on Johnson to continue and even escalate the fighting.

1964

Anti-war feeling developed in the universities, but the Gulf of Tonkin Resolution and the presidential election (see pages 102–3) suggested that at this stage Johnson had near unanimous support for his Vietnam policy from the public and most congressmen.

1965

With the introduction of American ground troops to Vietnam, the press and TV networks went there in full force. Vietnam became America's first fully televised war. Johnson was informed that increasing numbers of American reporters in Saigon were 'thoroughly sour and poisonous in their reporting'.

One congressman reported 'widened unrest' in Congress in January, and thousands of citizens participated in protests. In April, 25,000 protesters marched on Washington. The universities were restless: 20,000 students participated in an anti-war rally in **Berkeley**. However, thousands of students signed pro-Johnson petitions, and as yet the opposition had little practical impact on American involvement. Fewer than 25 per cent of Americans believed that the USA had erred in sending troops to Vietnam.

KEY TERM

Court-martialled Tried by an army court for breaking army regulations.

Berkeley University of California at Berkeley, an important state university.

How far would you trust Nixon's explanation in Source E of why the Americans were likely to fail? **?**

← **Did the home front lose the war?**

?

How inspirational would you consider the aims in Source F to be?

SOURCE F

In 1965, an assistant to Defense Secretary McNamara's quantified American aims.

Seventy per cent to avoid a humiliating U.S. defeat (to our reputation as a guarantor). Twenty per cent to keep South Vietnamese (and the adjacent) territory from Chinese hands. Ten per cent to permit the people of South Vietnam to enjoy a better, freer way of life.

1966

Public and congressional support for the war dropped dramatically. Polls showed Johnson's publicly proclaimed war aims, the defeat of Communist aggression and the building of a nation in Vietnam, failed to inspire. Nearly half of those polled were uncertain as to why the USA was fighting. Democrat congressmen blamed Vietnam for losses in the November elections and urged Johnson to end the war, while he limited his public appearances to avoid chants of 'Hey, hey, LBJ, how many boys have you killed today?' On the other hand, there were relatively few protests and Congress continued to fund the war.

1967

This year was something of a turning point. Some influential newspapers and TV stations shifted from support to opposition and tens of thousands protested against tax rises for the war. Some 70,000 protesters marched in Washington, DC and congressmen increasingly pressed Johnson to halt the escalation.

On the other hand, although 46 per cent of Americans polled in October felt that the Vietnam commitment was a mistake, a massive majority wanted to stay there and get tougher. Many middle-class Americans disliked the protesters whose activities, according to Californian **gubernatorial** candidate Ronald Reagan, 'can be summed up in three words: Sex, Drugs and Treason'.

The war was going badly and although publicly optimistic, the Johnson administration was losing confidence, as demonstrated by Secretary of Defense McNamara, who although vital in the formulation of Kennedy and Johnson's Vietnam policies, resigned in autumn. He condemned, 'the goddamned Air Force and its goddamned bombing campaign that had dropped more bombs on Vietnam than on Europe in the whole of World War II and we hadn't gotten a goddamned thing for it'.

In August, McNamara testified before the Senate that the bombing was not worth risking a clash with the Soviets and did not stop Communist troops and supplies moving south on the **Ho Chi Minh Trail.** He said it would take the annihilation of North Vietnam and all its people to stop Hanoi. His replacement as Secretary of Defense, Clark Clifford, began to doubt the domino theory and the wisdom of US involvement. The **Tet** Offensive finally made him conclude that he had to get the USA out.

🔑 **KEY TERM**

Gubernatorial Pertaining to governors.

Ho Chi Minh Trail Route through Cambodia and Laos, by which Hanoi sent troops to South Vietnam.

Tet The most important Vietnamese festival. Americans use the word 'Tet' as shorthand for the 'Tet Offensive'.

SOURCE G

An extract from the 'Final Resolution from the Protest Conference' held at a meeting attended by 50 musicians from around the world at Havana in 1967. From Robert Holden and Eric Zolov (editors), *Latin America and United States*, Oxford University Press, 2000.

[The signatories express gratitude to Cuba for understanding] the important role that we are fulfilling in the struggle for the liberation of the people against North American imperialism and colonialism ... Protest song workers must be aware that song, by its particular nature, is an enormous force for communications with the masses, to the extent that it breaks down barriers like illiteracy ... Everyone today is a witness to the crimes of imperialism against the people of Vietnam, as shown by the just and heroic struggle of the Vietnamese people for their liberation. As authors, performers and scholars of protest songs, we raise our voices to demand an immediate and unconditional end to the bombing of North Vietnam and the total withdrawal of all the forces of the United States from South Vietnam.

> Source G was signed by musicians from Chile, Argentina, Uruguay, Peru, Paraguay, France, Portugal, Mexico, Haiti, Cuba, Britain, Australia, Italy and Spain. How representative would you consider it to be of world opinion?

The Tet Offensive, 1968

In January 1968 Hanoi launched an offensive against South Vietnamese cities and military installations. Saigon, Washington and the American public were shocked that the Communists could move so freely throughout the South. The American ambassador had to flee the embassy in Saigon in his pyjamas. It took 11,000 American and ARVN troops three weeks to clear Saigon of Communist forces: 3895 Americans, 4954 South Vietnamese military, 14,300 South Vietnamese civilians and 58,373 Communist soldiers were killed.

The ordinary South Vietnamese had not rallied to the Saigon regime, so Tet seemed to show that while the USA could stop the overthrow of the Saigon government and inflict massive losses on the Communists, it could not defeat them. The Johnson administration had been claiming that America was winning the war but dramatic TV pictures of Communists in the grounds of the US embassy suggested otherwise. Some consider the media coverage of the Tet Offensive the crucial turning point in the American decision to exit. Walter Cronkite, the most respected TV journalist, had been strongly supportive of the war but was shocked by Tet. 'What the hell is going on?' Cronkite asked. 'I thought we were winning the war.' 'If I've lost Cronkite, I've lost America,' said Johnson.

What Americans saw and read about Tet helped turn many against the war (see Source H). When the journalist Peter Arnett reported a soldier saying, 'We had to destroy the town to save it', many Americans questioned what was being done in Vietnam. Some historians claim that while American reporters presented a uniformly hostile and negative picture of the Tet Offensive that made Americans feel it was a great disaster, Tet was a psychological rather than a military defeat. Tet certainly shook the confidence of the American government and people.

One of the most famous and most misinterpreted photos of the war. South Vietnam's police chief executed a Vietcong in Saigon during the Tet Offensive in 1968. It was later discovered that the captive was a Vietcong death-squad member who had just shot a relation of the general.

?　Why do you suppose that this photograph in Source H helped turn some Americans against the war?

Why was the USA unable to defeat the Communists in Vietnam?

→ # Conclusions about the American failure in Vietnam

The underlying reason for the American defeat in Vietnam was surely that South Vietnam was an artificial state, created and sustained only by the USA. To sustain this artificial creation required the continuation of the US conviction of the importance of Vietnam. When it became clear that the USA could not defeat the Vietnamese Communists without risking a third world war, when the world-wide Communist threat decreased, and when the nature of the warfare and criticism back home led to the apparent collapse of the home front and the American forces in Vietnam, it was inevitable that the USA would decide that Vietnam was not worth it, and would get out and 'lose' the war.

SOURCE I

A massive anti-war protest outside the Pentagon (the US Department of Defense headquarters) in October 1967. The 'war criminal' is President Johnson.

To what extent does Source I suggest there was large-scale opposition to the war?

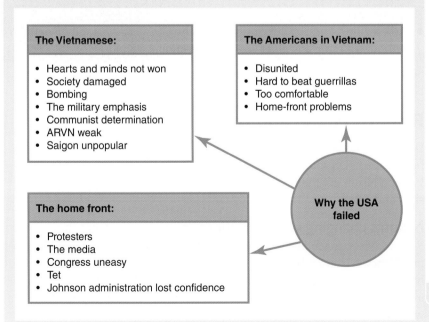

The Vietnamese:

• Hearts and minds not won
• Society damaged
• Bombing
• The military emphasis
• Communist determination
• ARVN weak
• Saigon unpopular

The Americans in Vietnam:

• Disunited
• Hard to beat guerrillas
• Too comfortable
• Home-front problems

The home front:

• Protesters
• The media
• Congress uneasy
• Tet
• Johnson administration lost confidence

Why the USA failed

SUMMARY DIAGRAM

Why the USA failed in Vietnam

⑤ The end of the war

> ▶ *Key question: Why, how and with what results did the USA get out of Vietnam?*

Why did Johnson halt the escalation?

→ **The end of escalation**

After the Tet Offensive, a combination of factors drove Johnson toward a re-evaluation of US policy:

- The Tet Offensive suggested Washington and Saigon were nowhere near defeating the Communists.
- The loss of McNamara had shaken the confidence of the Johnson administration and Congress advocated some kind of retreat in Vietnam after the Tet Offensive.
- The polls were discouraging. Johnson's approval rating fell from 48 to 36 per cent, suggesting he was losing the battle for the hearts and minds of an important percentage of his own people. Seventy-eight per cent of Americans believed that America was not making any progress in the war, 74 per cent that Johnson was not handling it well.
- Taxpayers were increasingly resentful about funding this expensive war. The government deficit rose from $1.6 billion in 1965 to $25.3 billion in 1968, causing inflation and endangering America's economic well-being. The Treasury warned Johnson that this should not go on. The war-induced **balance of payments deficit** dramatically weakened the dollar on the international money market, causing a gold crisis that was the final straw for many Americans.
- Back in 1967, the CIA director had said the USA could get out of Vietnam without suffering any great loss of international standing.

So, after the Tet Offensive, Johnson rejected JCS demands that more troops be sent to Vietnam, halted the escalation and began peace talks.

KEY TERM

Balance of payments deficit When the value of a country's imports exceeds that of its exports.

Why did Nixon decide to get out of Vietnam?

→ **Richard Nixon and the exit from Vietnam**

When Richard Nixon became president in January 1969, there were around half a million US soldiers in Vietnam. Despite having been a notable Cold Warrior, Nixon got the USA out of Vietnam, although the withdrawal was slow and painful.

Nixon's changing views on Vietnam

Richard Nixon made his name as an extreme Cold Warrior. During Johnson's presidency, Nixon said: 'Victory is essential to the survival of freedom. We have an unparalleled opportunity to roll back the Communist tide, not only in South Vietnam but in South East Asia generally and indeed the world as a whole.'

Whatever the Democrat President Johnson did, the Republican Nixon urged him to do more. However, by the time Nixon became president in January 1969, he had changed his mind about Vietnam and was determined to get the USA out. His reasons for reversing his position on Vietnam were the Tet Offensive, the **Sino-Soviet split**, and his desire to be a peacemaker.

The Tet Offensive

The Tet Offensive was a great turning point for Nixon. He realized that there would have to be changes in US policy. He said American forces should be withdrawn and ARVN built up ('**Vietnamization**'). He stopped talking about escalation and a 'victorious peace', and emphasized **'peace with honor'**, to be obtained by heavier US bombing and improved relations with the USSR and China, whom he hoped would persuade Hanoi to accept US peace terms.

The Sino-Soviet split

Nixon recognized that as the Cold War world had changed, an American exit from Vietnam would not jeopardize US security. The Sino-Soviet split made Communism less of a world-wide threat and Nixon hoped he could play Russia and China off against each other and improve relations with both.

Peacemaker

In his inaugural address, Nixon said, 'The greatest honor history can bestow is the title of peacemaker.' Improved relations with China and the USSR and peace in Vietnam would reinvigorate the USA, and ensure Nixon's place in the history books and his re-election in 1972. He knew that the Vietnam War had ruined Johnson's presidency, saying, 'He's been under such pressure because of that damn war … I'm not going to end up like LBJ … I'm going to stop that war. Fast!' The anti-war protests were part of 'such pressure', and although Nixon considered the protesters to be a treasonous minority, they no doubt helped him conclude he must get out of Vietnam and be a peacemaker at home as well as abroad.

The exit from Vietnam

Nixon's aim was a peace settlement that would allow President Thieu to remain in power in an independent South Vietnam. He hoped to achieve this through 'Vietnamization', an improved relationship with the USSR and China, and heavier bombing of North Vietnam. Nixon also sought peace at home. During his presidential inaugural parade, thousands of anti-war demonstrators chanted 'Ho, Ho, Ho Chi Minh, the **NLF** is going to win'. Some burned small American flags and spat at police. Peace in Vietnam would bring peace within the USA.

1969

This was not a successful year for Nixon. He tried a secret bombing offensive against the Ho Chi Minh Trail (see the map on page 94) in Cambodia, hoping in vain to sever enemy supply lines and to encourage Hanoi to agree

 **KEY TERM**

Sino-Soviet split Chinese–Soviet mutual hostility became increasingly obvious to the rest of the world in the 1960s.

Vietnamization Nixon's policy under which South Vietnam's government and forces took the main responsibility for the war.

'Peace with honor' Nixon wanted Thieu's government to stay in power in a viable South Vietnamese state, so that the USA could withdraw from Vietnam with its dignity intact.

NLF Communist National Liberation Front in Vietnam.

to an acceptable peace. Although still insistent that Thieu remain in power, he now agreed that North Vietnamese troops need not get out before American troops, but Hanoi was unimpressed by these improved peace terms. Nixon put pressure on the Soviets, promising *détente* for their help in ending the Vietnam War (he called this exchange '**linkage**') but this too was unsuccessful.

Things were no better on the home front. Although Nixon started to withdraw US troops, adjusted the **draft** so that students were less hard-hit, and tried to keep the bombing of Cambodia secret, he failed to halt the anti-war protests.

Militarily, diplomatically and politically, Nixon made no real progress in 1969, and 1970 was no better.

1970: the Cambodian Offensive

In January, Nixon appeared to be extending the war to Laos and Cambodia when he escalated the air offensive with heavy bombing of the trail in Laos and Cambodia and of North Vietnamese anti-aircraft bases. He believed that demonstrations of US power would counter Saigon's pessimism about American troop withdrawals, help protect the remaining Americans in Vietnam, intimidate Hanoi and gain better peace terms. Nevertheless, the North Vietnamese launched another great offensive in Laos. Desperate for some success, especially as Congress was considering cutting off his money, Nixon sent 30,000 American and ARVN forces into south-western Cambodia (less than 50 miles from Saigon), but they found no Communists and 344 Americans and 818 ARVN died, and 1592 Americans and 3553 ARVN were wounded.

The significance of the Cambodian Offensive

The capture and destruction of vast quantities of Communist war *matériel* in the Cambodian Offensive left Hanoi unable to launch another major offensive in South Vietnam for two years, which Nixon said gave the ARVN time to grow stronger and occupied North Vietnamese troops who would otherwise have been killing Americans. However, Nixon's critics said that the offensive had widened the war. The *New York Times* queried whether the offensive had just boosted Hanoi by revealing American divisions and the restraints on the president. Furthermore, the invasion forced the Communists further inland, where they destabilized the Cambodian government, which became even more unpopular because of bombing by its American ally.

1971

By 1971 the morale of the US Army in Vietnam had plummeted. Eighteen-year-olds were still being asked to fight a war that everyone in the USA agreed was just about finished, in order to allow time for the army of a corrupt dictatorship in Saigon to improve. Nixon had pinned his hopes on 'Vietnamization' and in February, the progress of ARVN was tested in the

Lam Son Offensive. The JCS had long wanted to attack the Ho Chi Minh Trail in southern Laos, arguing that the ARVN could do it if protected by American air power. However, there had been leaks in Saigon so Hanoi was prepared, and Nixon was sending only one ARVN division to do a job that Westmoreland refused to do without four American divisions. Initially the 5000 élite ARVN troops did well, but then the Communists got the upper hand, thanks especially to new armoured units and Soviet equipment. Within two weeks, the ARVN was routed. Half the force died.

While 'Vietnamization' was not working, it seemed as if linkage might be. Nixon's planned *rapprochement* with both the USSR and China was becoming a reality. Both were urging Hanoi not to insist on Thieu's removal as a prerequisite for peace. However, there were problems on the home front. Nixon's approval rating had dropped to 31 per cent and influenced by the spring protests (300,000 marched in Washington, DC), some senators tried to halt all aid to South Vietnam unless there was a presidential election (Thieu held one but he was the only candidate).

1972

In March, the ARVN crumbled in the face of the great Communist offensive, so Nixon decided the 'bastards have never been bombed like they are going to be bombed this time'. Although American bombers hit four Soviet merchant ships in the North Vietnamese port of Haiphong, the Soviet protests were low key. Linkage was working. Moscow was tired of financing Hanoi's war, desperate for *détente*, and impressed by huge American concessions, as when Nixon said North Vietnamese forces could stay in South Vietnam and hinted that he would accept a coalition containing Communists.

Nixon's concessions, Soviet and Chinese pressure, the failure of their offensive to take big cities, the destructiveness of the American bombing, and Nixon's probable re-election all helped drive Hanoi toward a settlement. It was just as well because Nixon was running out of time and money. Troop withdrawals meant that Congress could no longer be shamed into granting funds to help 'our boys in the field'. Nixon begged them not to damage his negotiating capabilities, pointing out that it would be immoral to just walk away from Vietnam. Polls showed that most Americans agreed with him: 74 per cent thought it important that South Vietnam should not fall to the Communists.

Compromise

Both sides had compromised by late 1972. Hanoi said Thieu could remain in power and the USA would let the North Vietnamese Army stay in South Vietnam and not insist on a ceasefire in Cambodia and Laos where the Communists were winning. However, Hanoi insisted on a voice in the Saigon government. Nixon's national security adviser, Henry Kissinger, rejected the coalition idea but offered the Communists representation on a

Committee of National Reconciliation that would oversee a Vietnamese constitution and elections. Kissinger thereby agreed that the Communists were a legitimate political force in South Vietnam, which Thieu had always denied.

Nixon then rejected the terms, fearing accusations that he had given in to protesters, or that peace at this time was an electoral ploy. Some of his advisers feared that if peace came before the election, people might vote Democrat as they were supposedly better at peace-time governing. Furthermore, US Cold Warriors and Thieu opposed a National Council containing Communists.

Re-elected in a landslide victory in November 1972, Nixon bombed North Vietnam again. A thousand civilians died in Hanoi and its port Haiphong. There was no public explanation for this Christmas 1972 bombing, and several Congressmen and newspapers questioned Nixon's sanity, accusing him of waging 'war by tantrum'. Nixon was probably trying to reassure Thieu of American strength and support, to weaken Hanoi so that it could not speedily threaten South Vietnam after peace was concluded, and/or to disguise American retreats and compromises in the negotiations.

The Paris Peace Accords

The settlement agreed in Paris in January 1973 was basically the same as that of October 1972 with a few cosmetic changes (one Kissinger aide said, 'We bombed the North Vietnamese into accepting our concessions'). The Paris Peace Accords declared a ceasefire throughout Vietnam (but not Cambodia or Laos). While American troops would leave South Vietnam, the North Vietnamese Army would not. However, Hanoi had to promise not to 'take advantage' of the ceasefire or increase troop numbers. Thieu remained in power, but the Committee of National Reconciliation contained Communist representation, and would sponsor free elections. Nixon secretly promised billions of dollars worth of reconstruction aid to Hanoi.

How successful were Nixon's policies?

KEY TERM

Watergate scandal In 1973, the Nixon administration tried to cover up the burglary and wiretapping of the Democratic national headquarters at the Watergate building in Washington, DC.

→ Nixon in Vietnam: conclusions

Nixon got US troops out of Vietnam. He did not always get much thanks for it (many criticized his slowness) and he perhaps did not have much choice, but retreating from America's uncompromising and impossibly expensive Cold War militancy was perhaps one of his greatest achievements.

Having decided on retreat in 1968, should he not have done it speedily? Twenty thousand Americans died during a slow four-year retreat that damaged the morale of American forces in Vietnam, antagonized American anti-war activists and, some argue, created the division, discontent and the presidential paranoia that helped to bring about the **Watergate scandal** and cost Nixon the presidency.

However, Nixon felt that American honour and its investment of men and money required that Thieu be left in power with a good chance of survival.

He believed an American defeat would lead to a collapse of confidence in American leadership and to Communist expansion throughout the world. Many understood what he was trying to do and sympathized. Like so many Americans, Nixon believed that the USSR and China presented a threat to the USA and its allies. Given the lack of political freedom within Communist countries, those American fears were comprehensible and vital to understanding why the USA got into Vietnam and insisted on getting out 'with honor'. Although Kissinger and Nixon believed in *détente*, they thought that it was dangerous if the Soviets and Chinese perceived the USA as weak and they were probably right.

Had Nixon achieved 'peace with honor'? He got the American ground forces out without abandoning Saigon and forced Hanoi to let Thieu remain in power with the world's fourth largest air force and an improved ARVN but, knowing that Congress would soon cut off his money, he allowed the North Vietnamese Army to remain in South Vietnam. Overall though, the terms he got in 1973 were better than he could have got in 1969, when Hanoi had been adamant that Thieu should not remain in power. However, he had not really won peace for Indochina. South Vietnam was overrun by the Communists in 1975.

Why Nixon got out

- Tet
- Sino-Soviet split
- Peacemaker

How he got out

- Linkage, *détente*
- Bombing
- Concessions

Impact of the exit

Slow + extra bombing = divided USA
                           = ruined his presidency
                           = loss of life
but … managed retreat from power

Peace with honour?

☺ Still Thieu

☹ North Vietnamese army remained in South Vietnam

SUMMARY DIAGRAM

Why and how did the USA get out of Vietnam?

6 Domestic effects of the war

> ▶ **Key question:** *How did the Vietnam War impact on the US economy, politics and society?*

→ **The US economy**

> **What was the impact of the war on the US economy?**

The war was expensive and caused deficits in the federal government budget and the balance of payments. It could be argued that it was during the Vietnam War that fiscal irresponsibility first set in, as Johnson was the first but not the last president to believe that he could have it all, prosperity at home and interventions abroad, regardless of the impact on the national debt. The war dealt a death blow to Johnson's dream of a **Great Society**: between 1965 and 1973, $15.5 billion was spent on the Great Society, $120 billion on the war.

→ **US society**

> **What was the impact of the war on US society?**

From 1964, the war bitterly divided Americans, as first demonstrated by the protests and the reactions they generated in the Johnson years (see pages 111–12). Families were torn apart, including those of McNamara and Rusk.

KEY TERM

Great Society President Johnson's policy to bring about greater social and economic quality in the USA.

Moratorium In this context, suspension of normal activities, in order to protest.

The Nixon years were the most divisive. Many Americans failed to understand and/or disliked Nixon's apparent escalation of the war in order to disguise a US retreat from power and to gain better peace terms. Ironically, as Nixon fought to get peace with honour, the anti-war protests increased. In October 1969 the campuses were in uproar and in the largest anti-war protest in American history, the '**moratorium**', millions took to the streets in every major city. Some were middle class and middle aged, others were radical and burned American flags.

In November, Nixon delivered one of his best speeches, asking 'the great silent majority of my fellow Americans' to be united for peace, saying only Americans could 'defeat or humiliate the USA'. His approval rating shot up to 68 per cent ('We've got those liberal bastards on the run now') but the protests soon restarted. A quarter of a million peaceful protesters took over Washington.

In April 1970, Nixon tried to defuse the unrest generated by the Cambodian Offensive with a speech in which he said the invasion of Cambodia was not an invasion but a clean-up operation, and that the USA's first defeat in its 190-year existence would be a national disgrace: 'If, when the chips are down, the world's most powerful nation, the United States of America, acts like a pitiful, helpless giant, the forces of totalitarianism and anarchy will threaten free nations and free institutions throughout the world.' The speech proved quite popular, but its success was short-lived. Trouble erupted on campuses across the USA. In May, four students at Kent State University, Ohio, were shot dead by the National Guard. Some had been participating in an anti-war rally, some just changing classes. When student protests escalated, Nixon backed down, declaring that he would get American troops out of Cambodia by June. Students were not the only protesters: 300,000 marched in Washington, DC. Nixon rightly claimed that the protesters were a minority, but they were more vociferous than his silent majority. Despite Nixon's denials, government policy was being made in the streets. It was also being made by a minority, as polls showed 50 per cent approved of his actions, compared to the 39 per cent who disapproved. Indeed, 100,000 people participated in a pro-Nixon demonstration in New York City.

Along with the bitter divisions on the home front, and far more importantly, over 200,000 Americans were killed or wounded in Vietnam and many lives were ruined. Returning veterans had physical and/or mental disabilities that for the most part would remain with them for the rest of their lives. Many came back with drug and alcohol problems.

US politics

The war damaged relations between the president and Congress. Congress resented the way in which the Cold War had increased the power of the commander-in-chief, as demonstrated in the Cambodian Offensive of 1970, which appeared to be a dramatic escalation of the war authorized solely by the president. Throughout 1970 and 1971, the Senate enthusiastically supported bills to stop Nixon waging war in Cambodia, Laos and Vietnam.

It could be argued that the war cost Nixon the presidency. The difficulties of gaining 'peace with honor' in the face of domestic opposition and Vietnamese intransigence accentuated his tendency towards a siege mentality. During 1972, Nixon's Campaign to Re-elect the President (CREEP) indulged in dirty tricks and got caught breaking into the Democrats' offices in the Watergate building. The Watergate scandal simmered relatively quietly in late 1972, but during Nixon's second term it exploded and brought the president down. Had Nixon not felt besieged and battered by the Vietnam War, and had he not believed that Vietnam might cost him re-election, Watergate would probably not have happened.

The war also damaged the presidency. Respect for the office decreased because of Johnson and Nixon's Vietnam policies, and because the war exacerbated the tendency of both men toward dishonesty and dissimulation.

Finally, it could be argued that the Vietnam War made the USA more wary of foreign interventions and adventures, although only for about two decades, as the twenty-first century involvements in Iraq and Afghanistan proved.

How did the Vietnam War impact on US politics?

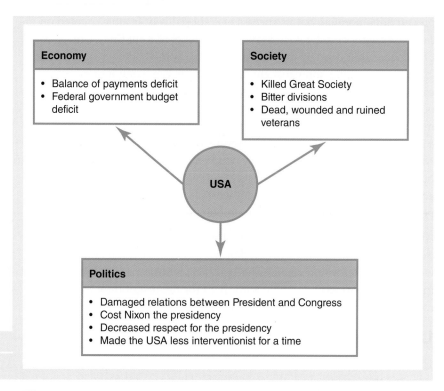

Economy

- Balance of payments deficit
- Federal government budget deficit

Society

- Killed Great Society
- Bitter divisions
- Dead, wounded and ruined veterans

USA

Politics

- Damaged relations between President and Congress
- Cost Nixon the presidency
- Decreased respect for the presidency
- Made the USA less interventionist for a time

SUMMARY DIAGRAM

Domestic effects of the war

---

⑦ The role of Vietnam in the development of the Cold War

▶ *Key question: How significant was Vietnam in the development of the Cold War?*

What was the relationship between Vietnam and the Cold War before 1954?

Vietnam and the Cold War, 1945–54

The US preoccupation with Europe, 1945–9

In the first phase of the deterioration of Soviet–American relations that became known as the Cold War, the USA was preoccupied with Europe. In this first phase, between 1945 and 1949, the developing struggle between the Vietnamese Communists and the French was not of great significance in the Cold War.

Whereas in the 1940s the development of the Cold War depended on events in and rivalry over Europe, in the 1950s, Asia became a second great continental arena for the conflict. Although the USA was keen to maintain France as a bulwark against Communism in Europe, it was not until this second phase of the Cold War, when the US–Communist rivalry focused as much if not more on Asia than on Europe, that the Truman administration first offered to assist the French in their struggle against the Vietnamese Communists.

The US preoccupation with Asia after 1949

It was when China became Communist in late 1949 that the Truman administration turned its attention to the Cold War in Asia, where Communism seemed to be on the march. Not only had China been 'lost', but Communists were active in French Indochina and British Malaya. Communist expansionism in Asia appeared to be confirmed by the North Korean attack on South Korea in the summer of 1950. So, as Vietnam seemed to prove that Communism was a world-wide threat, it played a part in the development of the Cold War into a world-wide struggle that encompassed Asia as well as Europe. However, it was a small part. It was the need to support France (a NATO ally in Europe), the fall of China to Communism in 1949 and the Korean War that made Vietnam significant in the Cold War. When Truman and Eisenhower aided the French in Vietnam, it was a case of developments in the Cold War having an impact on Vietnam more than Vietnam having an impact on the development of the Cold War.

The impact of the Cold War on Sino-Soviet policies

The development of the Cold War affected Soviet and Chinese policy toward Vietnam. At Geneva in 1954, it suited the USSR to put pressure on Ho Chi Minh to retreat from areas his forces already held below the 17th parallel, because the USSR sought peaceful coexistence at this time and was not going to let this hoped-for development in the Cold War be affected by Vietnam and Communist camaraderie. Subsequently, as the US commitment deepened, the USSR and China stepped up their aid to Vietnam because both wanted to be seen to support world Communism and both felt safer with the USA tied down there.

Vietnam and the Cold War, 1955–63

After the French exit from Vietnam, Eisenhower established the 'state' of South Vietnam, and from 1955 to 1963 the war there began to affect the development of the Cold War in Asia and in Latin America. The growing American involvement in Vietnam increased tension in the Pacific in 1954–6 and led to a dangerous crisis. When the Chinese shelled Quemoy and Matsu, the Eisenhower administration seemed to be considering the use of nuclear weapons. The Chinese actions no doubt owed something to Chinese fears of US expansionism in the Pacific, as demonstrated by the establishment of SEATO, an organization set up in part in order to protect South Vietnam. The USA's preoccupation with Vietnam also served to divert funds and enthusiasm away from Kennedy's **Alliance for Progress** with Latin America (see page 169).

Vietnam and *détente*

Hindering *détente*

It was under Johnson, when the USA's commitment to South Vietnam greatly escalated, that the US involvement in Vietnam really affected the development of the Cold War. It is possible to argue that the escalation in

> How did Vietnam affect US relations with China and Latin America, 1955–63?

> **KEY TERM**
>
> **Alliance for Progress** Kennedy's plan to advance economic development, democratic institutions and social justice in Latin America.

> Did the Vietnam War help or hinder *détente*?

Vietnam damaged the chances of an improved relationship with the USSR in the 1960s. It was Vietnam that relegated the only high-level meeting between US and Soviet leaders between 1961 and 1972 to the obscure college town of Glassboro, New Jersey, because Soviet premier Kosygin objected to going to Washington in the middle of the Vietnam War. Politician and foreign policy expert William Hyland noted: 'It was indicative of growing American weakness and Soviet arrogance that Kosygin refused to come to the US capital.'

Vietnam and Soviet expansionism

It was, of course, the enormous US effort expended in Vietnam under Johnson that led to that 'growing American weakness'. Knowing that the involvement was weakening the USA financially, economically, militarily and politically (the country was bitterly divided over the war) no doubt gave the USSR the increased confidence to pursue aggressive policies. In 1968, the Soviets invaded Czechoslovakia to crush the liberalization movement there and in the 1970s they increased their involvement in the 'Third World' in areas such as the Horn of Africa and Afghanistan.

Helping *détente*

The Soviets of course had problems of their own, especially with China. Sino-Soviet relations had been uneasy from the first, and there were border clashes in 1962 and 1969, by which time 658,000 Soviet troops faced 814,000 Chinese troops on their disputed northern borders. Sino-Soviet tensions had a great impact on the course of both the Cold War and the Vietnam War. Sino-Soviet tensions made Nixon less fearful of Communism, which encouraged him to get out of Vietnam and to pursue *détente*, and made the USSR and China far more inclined to respond to Nixon's overtures.

While the Sino-Soviet tensions clearly contributed greatly to *détente*, Vietnam also played a part. Nixon's *détente* policy owed a great deal to his desire for Sino-Soviet assistance in the American exit from Vietnam. US anxiety to get 'peace with honor' in Vietnam helped motivate Nixon's policy of improved relations with China and Russia, and he used their desire for *détente* to get them to exert pressure on Hanoi to allow Thieu to remain in power and to agree to a settlement. So, while Vietnam could be argued to have delayed the development of *détente* in the 1960s, it then played a part in hastening the *détente* process under Nixon, because of the increasing Sino-Soviet tensions and the US desire to extricate itself.

How did the war affect US alliances?

→ Vietnam and US allies

The American preoccupation with Vietnam affected US relations with countries other than the USSR and China, alienating American allies (such as Canada and Britain) and neutral countries (such as India). The war aroused criticism throughout the world as, in McNamara's words: 'The picture of the world's greatest superpower killing or seriously injuring 1000 non-combatants a week, while trying to pound a tiny, backward nation into submission on issues whose merits are hotly disputed, is not a pretty one.'

If the USA had ever held the moral high ground in the Cold War, then it certainly lost it in Vietnam. The USA had claimed to be leading the fight for freedom in the Cold War, but there were many people in other countries who felt disgust at the American involvement, and particularly at the bombing. From 1968, there were anti-American protests in many Western countries because of US involvement in Vietnam.

The Vietnam War confirmed the US conviction that the Cold War had to be fought through military methods rather than by winning hearts and minds. Vietnam confirmed the US tendency to see victory in the Cold War as dependent on military solutions rather than on economic and social improvement in less-developed nations. This can be seen in Latin America, where the war put paid to the Alliance for Progress as the US government finances became overstretched, and where the USA increased its support for military and militantly anti-Communist regimes. As Kissinger told Thieu in 1972, 'We have fought for four years, we have mortgaged our whole foreign policy for the defence of one country.'

Conclusions

The development of the Cold War was highly significant for the Vietnamese in the 1940s and 1950s. Their war for independence became subsumed in the Cold War struggle. After Eisenhower set up the 'independent' state of South Vietnam, the war in Vietnam began to affect the Cold War, damaging US relations with China and Latin America in particular. However, the exhaustion of the USA due to Vietnam, coupled with Sino-Soviet tensions, contributed to a relaxation of Cold War tensions and then to the end of the Cold War. The exhaustion and preoccupation of the USA contributed to increased Soviet adventurism, especially in Afghanistan after 1979. This helped bring about the fall of the USSR and the end of the Cold War. There it could be argued that the Vietnam War had a beneficial impact on the development of the Cold War.

In conclusion then, the development of the Cold War was highly significant in Vietnam in the 1940s and 1950s, and Vietnam was highly significant in the development of the Cold War in the 1960s and 1970s.

← **How important was Vietnam in the Cold War?**

SUMMARY DIAGRAM

The role of Vietnam in the development of the Cold War

Chapter summary

US involvement in the Vietnam War

Vietnamese nationalists such as the Communist Ho Chi Minh fought for Vietnamese independence against Japan (1941–5), France (1945–54) and the USA (1954–73).

President Truman decided to support the French against the Vietnamese Communists, because France was an anti-Communist ally, and because of the Soviet and Chinese Communist threat, McCarthyism and the Korean War. Truman invested US money and prestige in Vietnam and initially Eisenhower did the same.

When the French agreed to leave Vietnam, Eisenhower felt freed from the taint of French colonialism and defied the Geneva Accords, creating an 'independent' non-Communist South Vietnamese state under Diem. Despite doubts about Diem, whose regime was unpopular and destabilized by Communists, Eisenhower greatly increased the American commitment to Vietnam. Eisenhower's nation building in Vietnam was motivated by containment, the domino theory, and his desire to rollback Communism.

Like Eisenhower, Kennedy continued the involvement because of his belief in containment and the domino theory. Also, Kennedy emphasized the importance of the 'Third World', and had to compensate for failures in Cuba and Laos. His advisers urged escalation, and he was a prisoner of his own campaign rhetoric and his anxiety to prove himself and to get re-elected. The Saigon regime was still not winning, so Kennedy increased the number of 'advisers' to nearly 20,000, many of whom were actually engaged in combat. The Kennedy administration's involvement in the coup against Diem further increased the American commitment. Some people believe that Kennedy would have got out of Vietnam had he lived, but that is a dubious assertion. Successive presidents were caught in the commitment trap. Eisenhower, Kennedy and Johnson knew that they could not win, but felt they dared not get out.

Johnson continued the US involvement because he was a typical Cold Warrior and, like his predecessors, he was worried about his own and his party's electoral prospects. He felt emotionally and constitutionally bound to continue with Kennedy's policies and advisers. As the USA was still not winning in Vietnam, and US personnel were in danger, Johnson followed the advice of his cabinet and the military and escalated. He bombed the North and sent in ground troops.

The Americans failed to defeat the Communists because neither they nor the Saigon regime could win the hearts and minds of the South Vietnamese people. ARVN frequently performed badly and the Communists were more popular and more determined. The US forces in Vietnam were disunited. Their 'comfortable' war disoriented the soldiers, who found the conditions particularly demoralizing. US war aims were not particularly inspiring, and US methods (supporting the Saigon regime and bombing) were unsuccessful. During 1967–8, the Johnson administration lost confidence with the exit of McNamara, the Tet Offensive, increasing protests and financial and economic problems.

Despite his Cold Warrior record, Nixon decided to get out of Vietnam because of the Tet Offensive, the Sino-Soviet split, US divisions, and his hopes for re-election. He got out through diplomatic concessions, *détente* and bombing. There were mass protests against that bombing and against Nixon's apparent extension of the war to Cambodia and Laos.

Although Nixon got American troops out of Vietnam, it took four long years to force Hanoi to agree to allow Thieu to remain in power. Nixon did not really gain 'peace with honor', as he had to agree to allow North Vietnamese forces to remain in South Vietnam. Furthermore, South Vietnam fell to Communism within two years of the 'peace'. The war probably cost Nixon the presidency, contributing to Watergate and his downfall.

The development of the Cold War was highly significant for Vietnam in the Truman and Eisenhower years. It was the Cold War context that got the USA involved in Vietnam. As that involvement increased, Vietnam began to have an impact on the Cold War, delaying *détente* at first, making the USA weaker and the USSR more adventurous. Ultimately, though, it contributed to *détente* and to the end of the Cold War.

Examination advice

How to answer 'compare and contrast' questions

For <u>compare and contrast</u> questions, you are asked to identify both similarities and differences. Better essays tend to approach the question thematically. It is best not to write half of the essay as a collection of similarities and half as differences. Finally, straight narrative should be avoided.

Example

<u>Compare and contrast</u> Lyndon Johnson's policies in Vietnam with Richard Nixon's.

1. It helps to put your answer into context. Do be sure to mention that Johnson was president from 1963 to 1969 and Nixon from 1969 to 1974. You will find that in some cases there were stark differences between the two presidents' policies while in others very close similarities. Answers that receive higher marks often will explain why there were differences and similarities instead of just stating what these were.
2. When answering a 'compare and contrast' question like this one, you should create a chart that illustrates the similarities and differences between these two presidents' policies. Take five minutes to do this before writing your essay. An example is given below.

Policies	Johnson	Nixon
Goals	Support South Vietnam and prevent unification with the North	Provide the means for South Vietnam to be able to defend itself
Ground war	Sent in first regular combat troops in March 1965. Escalated the war. By 1968 there were more than 500,000 US soldiers in South Vietnam	Began to draw down numbers of US soldiers. Promoted 'Vietnamization' plan. Invaded Cambodia in 1970
Air war	Relentless bombing of North and South Vietnam. Operation Rolling Thunder	Continued bombing campaigns including 1972 Christmas bombing in the North
Support for South Vietnamese politicians	Continued to support the numerous South Vietnamese presidents who took power in Saigon	Supported Thieu but eventually cut him out of peace negotiations
Peace talks	Secret but fruitless talks held in Paris with North Vietnamese	Further negotiations with North Vietnamese. Eventually resulted in Paris Peace Accords of January 1973

3. In your introduction, clearly state how the two presidents' policies were similar and different and why. You may wish to focus on how Johnson oversaw a marked escalation of war with its attendant rising costs and casualties. When Nixon came to power, he claimed he was going to end the war quickly. This did not happen. What were the strengths and weaknesses of each president's policies? How did the Cold War have an impact on decisions taken?

An example of a good introductory paragraph for this question is given below.

> The greatest contrast in the Vietnam policies of presidents Johnson (1963–9) and Nixon (1969–74), lay in their aims. While Johnson escalated the military involvement up until the final months of his presidency, aiming for victory, or at least to avoid defeat, Nixon's aim was to get out, to get 'peace with honour'. Johnson and Nixon used similar methods in pursuit of their aims, including heavy aerial bombing, ground offensives and support for the Saigon regime, but there were significant contrasts. These included Nixon's policy of extension of the bombing to Laos and Cambodia, of Vietnamization, and of significant concessions to the Communists in order to gain peace.

4. In the body of the essay, you need to discuss each of the points you raised in the introduction. Devote at least a paragraph to each one. It would be a good idea to order these in terms of which ones you think are most important. Be sure to make the connection between the points you raise and the major thrust of your argument. An example of how one of the points could be addressed is given below.

> Both presidents used heavy aerial bombardment. Johnson began this in 1964 in retaliation for perceived Communist attacks on US ships in the Gulf of Tonkin. He escalated the bombing to such an extent that it was known as 'Rolling Thunder' by early 1965. Johnson's aims were to damage North Vietnamese morale, halt the supplies coming down the Ho Chi Minh trail, and to hamper guerrilla operations in the South. Nixon developed that policy in several ways. He extended the bombing to the Ho Chi Minh trail in Cambodia and Laos and escalated the bombardment of the North, especially Hanoi and Haiphong. He used the bombing, as at Christmas 1972, to disguise a

US retreat from power and to compensate for the withdrawal of US troops. So, while both presidents relied heavily on the bombing, there were differences in their targets and in the motives behind their policy. As for the results of their bombing policy, neither Johnson nor Nixon defeated the Communists but it could be argued that Nixon's bombing enabled Thieu to stay in power after 1973, which gave some semblance of 'peace with honour'.

5. In your conclusion, you should summarize your findings. This is your opportunity to support your thesis. Remember not to bring up any evidence that you did not discuss in the body of your essay. An example of a good concluding paragraph is given below.

While both presidents aimed to counter Communism, Johnson's great aim in Vietnam was military victory, while Nixon's was to exit with some semblance of 'honour'. Their methods were similar in some ways (bombing, ground offensives and support for the government in Saigon), but different in that Nixon extended the bombing to Laos and Cambodia, gave ARVN greater responsibility, and gave Hanoi concessions that Johnson could not bring himself to give. Neither really achieved their aims and the methods of both were abhorrent to many Americans, so that ultimate failure is clearly the main similarity in their policies.

6. Now try writing a complete answer to the question following the advice above.

 Examination practice

Below are two exam-style questions for you to practise on this topic.

1   Why was the USA unable to defeat North Vietnam?
    (For guidance on how to answer 'why' questions, see page 190.)

2   Assess the effectiveness of Nixon's Vietnamization strategy.
    (For guidance on how to answer 'assess' questions, see page 39.)

CHAPTER 6

The Cuban Revolution

This chapter introduces the study of the Cold War in Cuba, which is explored further in Chapter 8. It looks at the background to Fidel Castro's Cuban Revolution of 1959, at how Castro came to power, and at the USA's role and reaction to events in Cuba up to 1959. You need to consider the following questions throughout this chapter:

✪ To what extent was Castro's Cuban Revolution shaped by Cuban traditions rather than by Communism?

✪ How did Castro gain power?

✪ What was the significance of Castro's accession to power in Cuba?

① Cuba before 1959

▶ Key question: To what extent was Castro's Cuban Revolution shaped by Cuban traditions rather than by Communism?

 **KEY TERM**

Marxist–Leninist
Someone who follows the Communist ideology of Karl Marx and Vladimir Lenin.

Fidel Castro came to power in Cuba in the winter of 1958–9 by overthrowing Fulgencio Batista (see page 139). Two years later he declared himself to be a **Marxist–Leninist** and under him Cuba was generally considered to be a Soviet satellite state. That eventual outcome has led some commentators to see Castro's overthrow of Batista as a Communist revolution, but it is more accurate to see that overthrow as very much in the Cuban tradition.

Was Castro's revolution in the Cuban violent tradition?

→ The Cuban violent tradition

Born out of the violence of Spanish conquest, colonial Cuba suffered from piratical intrusions and violently resisted authority in revolutionary wars of independence in the nineteenth century. In the first half of the twentieth century, the pattern of internal rebellion and external intervention (this time by the USA) continued. A favourite children's game was revolution, complete with line-ups and shootings of the enemy. Ironically, the Cuban Communist Party rejected this Cuban tradition of violence, but the anti-Batista revolution that brought Castro to power in 1959 was very much within it.

Was Castro's revolution in the Cuban nationalist tradition?

→ The Cuban nationalist tradition

Cuban nationalism was clearly demonstrated in revolts against Spanish colonial rule in 1868–78 and 1895–8. While there was considerable anti-Spanish feeling, there was a strong admiration and affection for the USA and a tradition of looking to the USA for aid and refuge. After independence,

Cuban governments were generally pro-US, but the tradition of resentment of the USA was even stronger than the tradition of affection.

Resentment of the USA

In the late nineteenth century, the USA considered the government of Cuba to be a matter of US national security because of geographical proximity (see the map on page 147) and the importance of the Caribbean to the Panama Canal and to US trade. The USA even tried to buy Cuba from Spain on several occasions, which worried Cuban nationalists such as José Martí. Born in Havana in 1853 to Spanish immigrants, Martí devoted much of his short life to the cause of Cuban independence and remains a much-revered figure in Cuba even today, especially as his concerns about education and US imperialism remain current. A critic of capitalism, but also of Marx, he died fighting for independence against Spain in 1895.

In 1898, the USA declared war on Spain and intervened in the Cuban War of Independence. The US Navy blockaded Cuba and US forces defeated the Spanish troops. Most Cuban rebels welcomed the intervention, but subsequent US behaviour and interventions changed the Cuban perspective. Twentieth-century Americans usually viewed that US intervention as an example of an unselfish assistance to the victims of colonialism. However, many Cubans came to believe that 1898 was the beginning of a long series of US attempts to dominate their island. Ominously, the USA negotiated with Spain for Cuba's 'independence' and excluded the Cubans from the process. The USA then occupied Cuba from 1898 to 1902.

American occupation

The aims of the American occupation were to maintain political stability, to rebuild the economic infrastructure in order to attract US investment, and to keep Cuba securely within the US sphere of influence. Occupied Cuba was governed effectively and humanely. Famine and disease were virtually wiped out and education, the judicial system and communications were greatly improved. However, the USA gained a stranglehold on the Cuban economy: US companies controlled most of the sugar and tobacco industries. By the end of the occupation, US domination was increasingly resented.

The Platt Amendment

The USA was keen to direct Cuba toward stable self-government and in 1900, 31 elected Cuban delegates convened to draw up a constitution for Cuba. The USA insisted that what became known as the **Platt Amendment** be added to the Cuban constitution. This amendment gave the USA the right to intervene in Cuba for 'the maintenance of a government adequate for the protection of life, property and individual liberties'. The USA also retained control over Cuban foreign policy and obtained the land on which to build the naval base that still exists today at Guantánamo Bay. This was clearly not real independence. Furthermore, the provision for intervention suggested that the Cubans were incapable of self-government.

 **KEY TERM**

Platt Amendment US amendment to the Cuban constitution, named after US Senator Orville Platt who proposed it. It gave the USA the right to intervene in Cuba.

The Platt Amendment was narrowly approved by the Cuban assembly, 15–14. Those who voted for it knew that the USA would not grant Cuba any independence without its insertion in the constitution. They believed that even restricted independence was preferable to continued US occupation. The amendment offended (and still offends) Cuban nationalism but it also facilitated a tradition of Cuban governments looking to the USA for help against internal opposition, supposedly for the maintenance of 'adequate' government.

Cuba's new democratic constitution did not work well. Elections were often fraudulent and resultant revolts prompted frequent US intervention under the Platt Amendment. In 1906, the Cuban government requested US intervention, to the annoyance of President Theodore Roosevelt, who wished 'that infernal little Cuban Republic' could 'behave'. American governments ran Cuba from 1906 to 1909. There were further interventions in 1912 (to protect US-owned sugar estates from the 'Negro rising') and in 1917–23 (at the request of the Cuban government).

 **KEY TERM**

'Pseudo-Republic'
Castro's term for 'independent' Cuba, 1901–59.

The USA was supportive of the **'pseudo-Republic'**, but the ever-increasing US economic domination, coupled with the economic dislocation of the Depression era, fuelled Cuban nationalism. This was especially intense at the University of Havana, where there were demands for an end to the Platt Amendment. In the 1933 revolution there were verbal attacks on what one middle-class revolutionary called the 'inanimate government named by the US ambassador'.

The Batista governments

During the years in which the pro-American Fulgencio Batista dominated Cuba (1933–44, 1952–9), the anti-American tradition continued. While much was achieved during 1952 and 1959 (law and order were restored, the economy was diversified and 'Cubanized', and the Cuban standard of living rose), American domination of the island was increasingly resented. Batista had close ties to the US government and US organized crime (the Cuban capital, Havana, had long been a haven for gamblers, drug dealers and prostitutes). The Americans continued to dominate the Cuban economy and to possess the strategically important port at Guantánamo Bay. In 1960, a former US ambassador to Cuba said that under Batista, 'the American ambassador was the second most important man in Cuba; sometimes even more important than the president'.

Fidel Castro's attacks on the Batista regime between 1952 and 1959 owed much to the Cuban anti-American tradition. Once Castro was in power, his anti-Americanism became ever more pronounced. Historian Richard Gott (2004) described Castro's Cuba as 'a Communist country where nationalism was more significant than socialism, where … Martí proved more influential than … Marx'.

The Cuban radical tradition

There was a strong tradition of **left-wing radicalism** in Cuba. In the early twentieth century, Cuban workers were inspired by and co-operated with radical left-wing groups such as socialists and Communists. The Cuban Communists were well organized but never very influential. They were distrusted by other leftists because they:

- were hostile toward revolution (they feared it would lead to US intervention)
- rejected **sabotage and subversion** as a means of getting rid of undesirable governments
- had frequently collaborated with Batista
- were perceived as too pro-working class by the Cuban middle-class.

Another Cuban characteristic was student radicalism at the University of Havana, where a nationalistic revival erupted in the 1920s. Student radicals such as Fidel Castro and his brother Raúl demanded nationalization of the sugar industry and the repeal of the Platt Amendment. Raúl joined the youth wing of the Communist Party, visited Romania and Czechoslovakia, and made Soviet contacts that would be used when his brother took power after 1959. Like many leftists in Cuba and in Latin America, Fidel Castro advocated a redistribution of wealth but was not a member of the Communist party and did not get on particularly well with the Communists.

Fidel Castro's anti-Batista revolution was not a Communist revolution. Instead, it was in the Cuban traditions of violence, coups, nationalism, ambivalence toward the USA, and left-wing and student radicalism, that all help to explain Castro's rise to power.

> ← Was Castro's revolution in the Cuban radical tradition?

🔑 KEY TERM

Left-wing radicalism Enthusiastic leftists who believe in a more equal distribution of wealth and political power.

Sabotage and subversion Destruction of property, designed to damage and undermine Batista's regime.

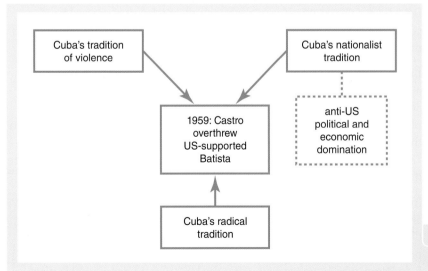

SUMMARY DIAGRAM

Cuba before 1959

Castro before 1959

> ▶ **Key question:** *How did Castro gain power?*

Why did Fidel Castro become a revolutionary?

→ Castro before 1953

Fidel Castro was born in Birán in Cuba in 1926. His father Angel Castro was a Spanish immigrant, his mother was Angel's housekeeper and cook and half his age. They married some years after Fidel's birth. At a time when two-thirds of Cuban agricultural land was under US ownership, Angel Castro owned a reasonably large farm in Cuba, but he and his family were considered 'new rich' and rejected by the traditional Cuban élite.

Angel Castro fought for the Spanish against Martí and the Cuban nationalists. He hated the USA because he thought it had cheated the Spaniards out of victory over the Cuban rebels. The area around Angel Castro's farm was dominated by American companies such as United Fruit (see page 76), whose employees had a polo club, swimming pools and shops selling American goods. The company even had a small licensed army of 20 soldiers.

Fidel Castro studied law at the University of Havana in the 1940s. He was both academically gifted and a superb athlete. His baseball skills so impressed American talent scouts that the New York Giants offered him a professional contract with a $5000 signing-on fee in 1949. Their negotiators said, 'We couldn't believe he turned us down. Nobody from Latin America had said *no* before.' It was politics that was Castro's great love. University politics were characterized by fists, guns and kidnappings. A student claimed Fidel Castro was involved in a gun attack on another student and he was suspected of involvement in the assassination of a government minister and university lecturer who himself had a history of violence.

Like his hero José Martí, Castro was an enthusiastic Cuban nationalist but also interested in Latin American politics. In 1947 he joined a force of 1200 assembled by future Dominican Republic president Juan Bosch in order to overthrow the US-backed Dominican Republic dictator Rafael Trujillo. When the Cuban navy boarded their ship, Castro jumped overboard and swam 10 miles through shark-infested waters to his family home in order to escape them.

In 1948, a Pan-American Conference was held in Bogotá, Colombia. It aimed to develop the old Pan-American Union of American States into the OAS. Argentine and Cuban students, one of whom was Castro, planned a protest at the conference. Their fares were paid by the Argentine dictator Juan Perón, who hoped to embarrass the USA. Castro distributed leaflets attacking US colonialism. In the riots (the ***bogotazo***) that followed the

KEY TERM

Bogotazo A massive popular uprising in 1948 in Bogotá, Colombia, over the assassination of a populist politician, Jorge Eliécer Gaitán.

assassination of a popular liberal politician, an estimated 3000 people died. US Secretary of State George Marshall and other foreign ministers blamed the Communists. Subsequent accounts claimed Castro was important in inciting the riots while calling for a Communist revolution, but these accounts are not persuasive. The *bogotazo* convinced Castro of the potential of the masses in revolt.

Castro graduated in 1950 and began to practise law. Not particularly interested in his legal career, he had few clients and little income. Politics remained his passion and he published many articles, demanding 'justice for the workers', Puerto Rican independence and opposition to 'the tyrants of [Latin] America'. Historian Hugh Thomas (2001) described a complex character: 'Castro was now a politician without a platform as well as a lawyer without clients ... He was nearing 30, his father was still vaguely supporting him, his marriage was not very successful ... Something had to be done if the chance of a political career was not to slip through his fingers.' Thomas emphasized Castro's love of risk-taking and his involvement in violence, and quoted university contemporaries who saw him as 'a power-hungry person, completely unprincipled, who would throw in his lot with any group he felt could help his political career ... Obviously, power meant much to him.' Thomas also recognized, but perhaps underestimated, Castro's patriotic ardour. For a variety of reasons then, Castro decided on violent revolution as the only way to achieve change and to end Cuba's political corruption and economic dependence upon the USA.

Castro's unsuccessful revolt of 1953

In 1953, Castro planned an attack on two barracks (in order to capture armaments) and on several public buildings. He hoped the attacks might trigger a popular rising against the Batista regime, but they stood little chance of success (the Cuban Communist Party described his attacks as an ill-organized **putsch**). Castro personally led the attack on the Moncada barracks, where he was outnumbered 10 to 1 by soldiers with far better weapons. Castro had 150 followers, none of whom were Communist. Few were killed in the attack, but around 80 were captured. Batista's unpopularity was increased by his treatment of Castro's followers. Many were tortured (eyes gouged out, genitals ripped off) and then killed. Those like Castro who evaded capture for a few days were brought to trial.

Castro's trial

The trials gained Castro greater fame and support. He defended himself, his followers and the other accused with notable effectiveness. When asked who was behind the rebellion, he said, 'The intellectual author of this revolution is José Martí, the apostle of our independence.' Arguing that his revolt was justified, he said, 'Condemn me. It does not matter. History will absolve me.' He wrote his speech (see Source A) in prison and smuggled it out in

← What was the significance of Castro's 1953 rising?

 **KEY TERM**

Putsch Attempted revolution.

matchboxes. Widely distributed, it was an effective manifesto for his revolution. In it, he claimed that if successful he would:

- 'return power to the people'
- redistribute land
- introduce worker profit-sharing and pensions
- attack corruption
- improve education
- nationalize public utilities
- introduce rent controls
- show solidarity with the 'democratic peoples' of Latin America
- diversify the economy.

SOURCE A

An extract from Castro's speech at his trial in 1953, in which he outlined his plans if his revolt had succeeded.

[I would have] returned power to the people … given … ownership of the land to all tenants and subtenant farmers, lessees, sharecroppers and squatters … granted workers and employees the right to share 30 per cent of the profits of all the large … enterprises … ordered the confiscation of all … holdings … that rightfully belong to the Cuban people. Half of the property recovered would be used to subsidize retirement funds for workers and the other half would be used for hospitals, asylums and charitable organizations … The problem of the land, the problem of industrialization, the problem of housing, the problem of unemployment, the problem of education and the problem of the people's health: these are the six problems we would take immediate steps to solve, along with the restoration of civil liberties and political democracy … Condemn me. It does not matter. History will absolve me.

?

Suggest reasons why Castro's speech in Source A might win him popular support.

> **What was the significance of Castro's stay in Mexico?**

Castro in Mexico

Due to family connections to Batista and to Batista's overconfidence, Castro was released from prison. A combination of factors sent him into exile. First, the general atmosphere in Cuba was somewhat alien on his release from jail. Batista's amnesty had raised hopes of a more moderate regime, and many Cubans were inclined to give the dictator another chance, especially as he promised to hold elections. Second, neither Castro nor his followers could forget their 68 murdered comrades and finally Castro's own life was probably in danger. It was rumoured that a car riddled with bullets was ready for his body to be 'found' in after he had been killed 'fighting the police'. So, Fidel Castro and his brother Raúl fled to Mexico, a country enamoured of its own revolution (1910–20), and to which earlier generations of Cuban rebels had fled.

One of the most important things to emerge from the stay in Mexico was Fidel Castro's meeting with the young Argentine Marxist and doctor, Ernesto Guevara, nicknamed 'Che' ('Buddy'). Born in Argentina in 1928 to progressive middle-class parents, Guevara had toured Latin America while a medical student and been horrified by the poverty and prejudice he saw in the **Andes**. In Guatemala in 1953–4, he witnessed the US-backed overthrow of Árbenz, which left him with a deep and lasting distrust of the USA that he shared with Castro. Their mutual chemistry was immediate and had a lasting impact on Cuba. Guevara gave Castro extra ideas about the revolutionary potential of Latin America; Castro gave Guevara the opportunity to participate in a Cuban Revolution.

KEY TERM

Andes Mountain range in Latin America. Andean states include Peru and Bolivia.

SOURCE B

The iconic image of Che Guevara found on T-shirts and posters all over the world.

Why do you suppose this image of Che Guevara in Source B has become one of the most instantly recognizable images in the world? Research the circumstances in which the photo this image was based on was taken and find out how many of your acquaintances recognize the picture, but also know who Che Guevara was.

How Batista was overthrown

Who or what was the most important reason for Batista's overthrow?

While Castro was in Mexico, protests and strikes started up in Cuba, which prompted Batista's special police to revive the torture and cruelty that followed the 1953 *putsch*. Determined to overthrow the Batista regime, Castro concentrated on organizing military training for his men in Mexico, where one of his military instructors persuaded him that guerrilla war would be more effective than frontal attacks. During this exile, Castro and the Cuban Communist Party exchanged bitter verbal attacks.

In 1956, Castro and 81 followers landed in Cuba. By January 1959, Castro and the revolutionaries had overthrown Batista for reasons explained below.

Castro's leadership

While Batista was a corrupt, unpopular and increasingly lazy ruler, Fidel Castro was determined, fearless, charismatic and resourceful. While in exile in Mexico in 1955, he trained his followers well and undertook a fundraising tour of the USA. The $9000 he collected would play a very important role in funding the planned overthrow of Batista.

In 1956, Castro and his 82 guerrillas sailed from Mexico to Cuba in the *Granma*, an aptly named old boat. Castro always exploited Cuban nationalist traditions with great effectiveness, presenting himself as Martí's heir. He aimed to land exactly where Martí had landed 60 years earlier, but *Granma* hit terrible storms, took on water, and ran aground in some mangrove swamps. 'It wasn't a landing, it was a shipwreck,' said one guerrilla. The rebels ploughed their way through the thick undergrowth of a swamp crawling with millions of tiny crabs, then moved across sugarcane fields toward the 90-mile long and 30-mile wide Sierra Maestra, where, like many Cuban revolutionaries before them, they would be hidden and protected by a thick rainforest. Batista's forces chased them across the fields, in one of which Castro lay hidden and barely moving for five days. Desperate for water, the rebels sucked sugarcane stalks, which made them even thirstier. One rebel drank his own urine. Around 21 guerrillas survived the chase. Subsequent claims that the number was 12 were no doubt intended to associate Castro and his followers with Jesus and his disciples. Yet again and against all the odds Castro had survived, which helped create his image as a heroic and immortal figure.

Effective guerrilla warfare

Although their numbers were low, Castro's guerrillas were highly effective. They would launch an attack on Batista's forces and then disappear into the forest, where sympathetic mountain farmers often helped them. The guerrillas sabotaged the sugarcane fields, which were the main source of income of the government and the country. A flyer was distributed instructing sugar workers how to set fire to the cane. One suggestion was to tie a rat to a gasoline-soaked sponge and then to set the sponge on fire so that the rat would run into the sugarcane fields. Castro set a good example by ensuring the early destruction of his own family's fields, which permanently damaged his relationship with his mother.

Castro's guerrillas won over many of the poor, paying for their food when possible, and declaring 'liberated areas' in which the peasants were given land and livestock confiscated from wealthy landowners. This was in great contrast to the behaviour of Batista's army, which terrorized the peasantry as they searched for insurgents. As time went on, the people in the mountains began to realize that Castro was there to stay and that they had less to gain from co-operation with Batista and his forces.

The revolutionaries worked successfully to create an infrastructure in liberated territories, building rudimentary hospitals, schools, factories producing cigars and ammunition, and a training centre for new recruits. When necessary, Castro's guerrillas were merciless. One scout took $10,000 from Batista's army to lead the guerrillas into an ambush. Che Guevara recorded in his diary that this made everyone 'uncomfortable … I ended the problem giving him a shot with a .32 pistol in the right side of the brain, with exit orifice in the right temporal. He gasped a little while and was dead.' Guevara said the peasants were often suspicious, afraid, and willing to accept rewards to betray the revolutionaries: 'The execution of antisocial individuals who profited from the situation of force established in the country was, unhappily, not rare in the Sierra Maestra.'

Propaganda

Castro was a superb propagandist. He knew from nineteenth-century examples that it was good to get the American press onside, and he did this with the *New York Times* (see Source C). He did not want its reporter Herbert Matthews to know there were only 18 guerrillas at his headquarters, so Raúl moved the band around and told them to make as much noise as possible. A messenger interrupted one interview with news of a second column of guerrillas that existed only in the guerrillas' imagination. Che Guevara wrote of the early days in the Sierra Maestra: 'At that time the presence of a foreign journalist, American for preference, was more important for us than a military victory.'

Matthews' reports reassured Cubans that Castro was still alive, gave Americans an attractive picture of a young idealist struggling against a corrupt dictatorship, and played an important part in the US decision to halt aid to Batista.

SOURCE C

An extract from Herbert Matthews' article in the *New York Times*, February 1957.

Fidel himself strode in. Taking him, as one would at first, by physique and personality, this was quite a man – a powerful six-footer [1.8 m], olive-skinned, full-faced, with a straggly beard. He was dressed in an olive gray fatigue uniform and carried a rifle with a telescopic sight, of which he was very proud … The personality of the man is overpowering. It was easy to see that his men adored him and also to see why he has caught the imagination of the youth of Cuba all over the island. Here was an educated, dedicated fanatic, a man of ideals, of courage and of remarkable qualities of leadership … Senor Castro speaks some English, but he preferred to talk in Spanish, which he did with extraordinary eloquence … He has strong ideas of liberty, democracy, social justice, the need to restore the Constitution, to hold elections. He has strong ideas on economy, too, but an economist would consider them weak … [His] movement talks of nationalism, anti-colonialism, anti-imperialism. I asked Senor Castro about that. He answered, 'You can be sure we have no animosity toward the United States and the American people.'

Using quotations from Source C to prove your point, how far would you agree that Matthews was depicting Castro in highly favourable terms?

Other revolutionaries

After Castro emerged as the leader of Cuba, a tendency developed to look back on the revolution as being solely due to him. However, in the time-honoured Cuban tradition of violence and rebellion, others had been similarly organizing against Batista. For some years, the contribution of the **urban revolutionaries** was overlooked, but they actually played an equally important part in the overthrow of Batista. After the *Granma* landed, much of the urban sabotage that helped bring about the fall of Batista was done by revolutionaries independent of Castro's movement although doubtless encouraged by his activities. Also extremely important was Castro's associate, the schoolteacher Frank País, who had remained in Cuba while Castro was in exile. Despite having had no military training, País proved to be an exceptionally talented military leader. While Castro landed, País initiated a simultaneous rising against Batista in Santiago. He organized morale-boosting commando raids on the customs house, police headquarters and harbour headquarters. He captured Santiago's public buildings and brought the city's official life to a standstill. He urged Castro to broaden the support of the movement, so Castro targeted middle-class liberals, promising free elections and compensation for landowners who would suffer from any future redistribution of wealth.

The 'End of Fidel' offensive

In May 1958, Batista mobilized 10,000 soldiers for a *Fin de Fidel* ('End of Fidel') offensive. Castro had only 321 men, poorly armed and short of ammunition, while his brother had 150 on the second front. However, the rebels had advantages. The mountains, forests and gorges were as yet unmapped, so Batista's men struggled to find Castro's guerrillas. The two generals in charge of the operation loathed each other, and Castro sensed that one might have been sympathetic to the rebel cause. Batista's officers were chosen for their association with the dictator rather than for any military ability. Their army had no experience of combat, or of the guerrilla warfare that Castro's men used in order to avoid pitched battles against superior numbers. The guerrilla tactics were flexible and effective. They drew Batista's soldiers into ambushes, especially in narrow gaps, and hid high explosive mines in their path. The guerrillas convinced Batista's men that they were everywhere and in great numbers, which demoralized the dictator's army, two-thirds of whom were raw recruits. Desertion rates were high (30 out of 80 on 24 July at El Cerro) and morale was not improved when Batista's air force dropped napalm on his own men. After the USA had suspended military aid to Batista in the spring of 1958, the loyalty of Batista's troops decreased. The rank and file were attracted by Castro's promises and propaganda. In sharp and deliberate contrast to Batista, Castro treated prisoners well. Some were even sent back to their fighting units, which while humane, also served to demonstrate contempt of their fighting potential. Although many civilians suffered from the bombing of the mountains,

Castro's units survived. In the end, the combination of bad weather and the great number of dead and wounded (around 1000), caused Batista to end the offensive in August 1958.

Batista's loss of support

While Castro was based in the east, Che Guevara and his guerrillas moved toward the centre of the island. They lost all their vehicles to air attacks or fuel shortages, but heroically travelled hundreds of miles on foot across swamps and raging torrents until they arrived at their destination, starving and in rags. They severed Cuba's sole east–west road and the railway, which caused massive problems for the Cuban government and economy. Guevara's brilliant military leadership played a very important part in the rebels' eventual success, as in December 1958, when he and 300 rebels besieged and took Santa Clara, a strategically important city with a 150,000 population. There they captured a full garrison of 2500 demoralized soldiers, surrounding and taking a train that supplied the garrison with weaponry.

An estimated 30,000 acts of sabotage against sugar-processing plants, large landed estates, banks and company headquarters, helped bring the Cuban economy to its knees. After Batista's coup in 1952, many Cubans had felt that they could put up with him if he restored law and order. However, corruption and mob rule had increased under him, while the standard of living fell. Unemployment had risen from 8.9 per cent to 18 per cent in 1958 alone and falling sugar prices hit many pockets. Batista's continued rule depended on control of the army, and keeping the middle and upper classes and the USA relatively happy. Under pressure from the revolutionaries, Batista's regime was clearly crumbling and middle-class Cubans began to turn against him.

In his 1959 trip to the USA, Castro visited Princeton University, where he attributed the success of the revolution to Batista and the 'fear and hatred' his secret police engendered (and also to the fact that the rebels' had not preached class war' by declaring themselves to be Communist). Suspects, including young students, were publicly executed and left hanging in the streets as a warning to would-be revolutionaries. Batista's torture and murder of revolutionaries, both real and suspected, made increasing numbers of Cubans see the rebels as liberators. The agencies responsible for the torture were the SIM (Military Intelligence Service), established with the help of the FBI, and the BRAC (Bureau for the Suppression of Communist Subversives), rumoured to have been the offspring of the CIA. Castro had never had good relations with the Cuban Communist Party, but Batista's insistence that the rebels were Communists led to a police crackdown on the party that helped push them into joining Castro. In July 1958, the Communists and other Cuban opposition groups recognized Castro as the sole leader of the revolution.

As Castro looked increasingly likely to win, more men joined him. In late 1958, the Castro brothers and their 3000 men captured Santiago with its 5000 troops without having to fire a shot. This was a clear demonstration that Batista's regime had collapsed, and on 1 January 1959 Batista resigned and fled to the Dominican Republic. He took Cuba's gold reserves with him, but left incriminating documents that revealed the extent of his corruption, crimes and close co-operation with the USA.

The contribution of the USA

The contribution of the USA to Castro's victory should not be overlooked. Castro had some moral support in the USA. The *New York Times* was favourable, as were some members of the CIA. By late 1958, the CIA recognized that Batista was losing the struggle, and some historians have suggested that the CIA gave Castro arms. It has also been claimed that the Mafia helped him, believing that this would help to safeguard their lucrative business interests in Cuba if he were victorious. Cuban exiles in the USA certainly provided armaments.

? Using Sources D and E, sum up the reasons Kennedy gives for Castro's victory in 1959. Which reason do you think he considers most important?

SOURCE D

In the presidential election campaign of 1960, the Democrat John Kennedy faced the Republican Richard Nixon. During the campaign, Kennedy criticized the Eisenhower administration for supporting Batista.

Fulgencio Batista murdered 20,000 Cubans in seven years … and he turned democratic Cuba into a complete police state – destroying every individual liberty. Yet our aid to his regime, and the ineptness of our policies, enabled Batista to invoke the name of the United States in support of his reign of terror. Administration spokesmen publicly praised Batista – hailed him as a staunch ally and a good friend – at a time when Batista was murdering thousands, destroying the last vestiges of freedom, and stealing hundreds of millions of dollars from the Cuban people, and we failed to press for free elections.

SOURCE E

In an article in the *New Republic*, Jean Daniel, an Algerian–French freelance journalist quoted President Kennedy in 1963.

I believe that there is no country in the world … where economic colonization, humiliation and exploitation were worse than in Cuba, in part owing to my country's policies during the Batista regime. I believe that we created, built and manufactured the Castro movement … without realizing it … I can assure you that I have understood the Cubans. I approved the proclamation which Fidel Castro made in the Sierra Maestra, when he justifiably called for justice and especially yearned to rid Cuba of corruption. I will go even further: to some extent it is as though Batista was the incarnation of a number of sins on the part of the United States … In the matter of the Batista regime, I am in agreement with the first Cuban revolutionaries.

Even more importantly, the Eisenhower administration did little to support Batista in the crucial period of his overthrow, even though the USA had appreciated his anti-Communist stance in the Cold War. According to historian Hugh Thomas (2001), 'the most important decision of the war was taken, symptomatically in Washington', when in 1958 the USA stopped the sale of weapons to Batista.

It could be tentatively argued that the most important American contribution was inadvertent in that Castro quickly and publicly harnessed the traditional anti-American feeling among some Cubans when, within hours of his victory, he said in January 1959, 'This time it will not be like 1898, when the North Americans came and made themselves masters of our country.' However, in the old ambivalent tradition, he dined that evening with the American consul.

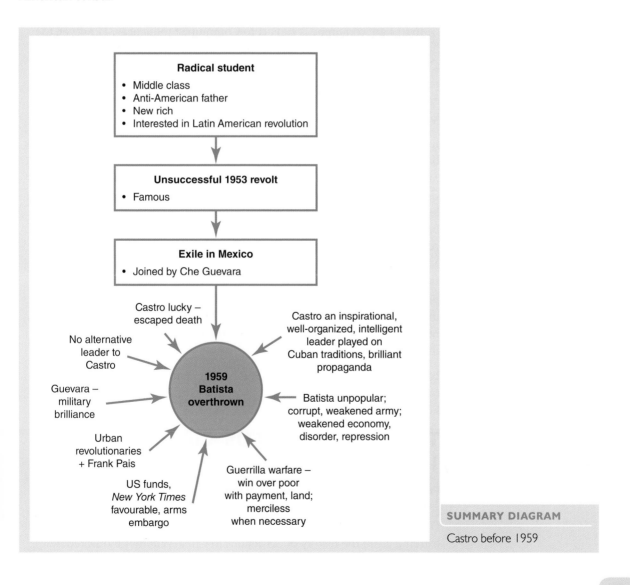

SUMMARY DIAGRAM

Castro before 1959

Eisenhower, Cuba and Castro

> ▶ **Key question:** What was the significance of Castro's accession to power in Cuba?

Was American hostility to Castro inevitable?

The initial American reaction

The initial US reaction to Castro's second attempt to overthrow Batista was mixed. In 1958, an expert on Cuba in the State Department, William Wieland, wrote: 'I know that Batista is considered by many as a son of a bitch … but American interests come first … at least he is our son of a bitch, he isn't playing ball with the Communists … On the other hand, Fidel Castro is surrounded by commies. I don't know whether he is himself a Communist … [but] I am certain he is subject to Communist influences.' However, the influential *New York Times* ran a series of almost adulatory articles about Castro when he was in the Sierra Maestra, and although the USA had previously equipped Batista's army and air force, it now placed an arms embargo on Cuba, which greatly helped Castro's accession to power in January 1959.

Initially, American liberals liked Castro. He seemed preferable to the dictator Batista and in April 1959 was invited to visit the USA, where he addressed a huge audience at Harvard. However, the CIA considered Castro a potential Communist, so Eisenhower was cautious. When Castro visited Washington, Eisenhower went off to play golf. By late 1959, even American liberals were uneasy about the prominence of Communists in Castro's government. Alienated by Castro's confiscation of American property, which began in May 1959, American businessmen bemoaned the 'loss' of Cuba. A handful of radicals such as sociologist C. Wright Mills pointed out the problems in pre-Castro Cuba. Mills' book *Listen, Yankee!* criticized American imperialism in the Caribbean. However, his pleas for 'Hands off Cuba!' and 'a completely new USA approach to the problems of the hungry world' were ignored by the US government.

Basically, given Castro's political and economic nationalism, and the traditional US domination of Cuba's politics and economy, US–Cuban hostility was probably inevitable.

When and why did US–Cuban hostility develop?

The deterioration of US–Cuban relations, 1959–61

From the first, Castro was critical of the USA, and as time went on, his speeches became more and more anti-American. Historian Hugh Brogan (1996) described Castro as 'bigotedly hostile' to the USA, which seems a little extreme given the history of US actions in Cuba. Whether motivated by bigotry or by a desire for Cuban control over the Cuban economy, or by both,

SOURCE F

A map of Cuba.

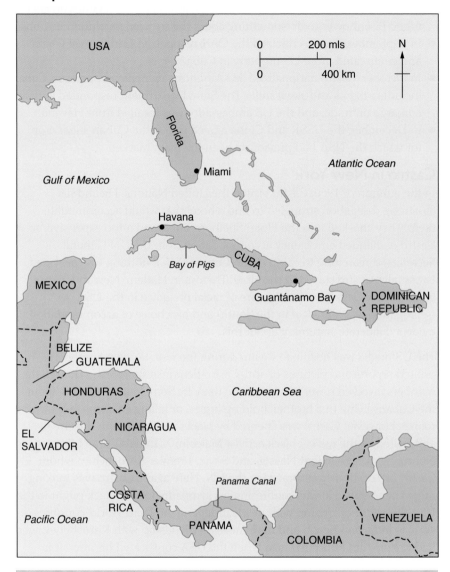

Using Source F, suggest reasons why the USA was always concerned about Cuba.

Castro's expropriations hit US businesses and investors. He sought to end the American stranglehold over the Cuban economy and throughout 1960 the relationship deteriorated:

- In February Castro signed a trade agreement with the USSR.
- In March Eisenhower decided Castro would have to go and approved a covert CIA operation to overthrow him.
- In July the USA halted American purchases of Cuban sugar.
- In August Castro nationalized US-owned businesses and Eisenhower began to mobilize hemispheric opposition to Castro. In the Caracas Declaration of 1954, the OAS had committed itself to oppose Communism

in Latin America, and although the OAS publicly opposed the idea of any US intervention in Cuba (Castro was very popular among ordinary people in Latin America) some anti-Communist Latin American regimes privately urged Eisenhower to do something about the socialist revolution in Cuba.

- In September, Castro criticized the OAS, recognized Communist China, and confiscated more US property in Cuba.
- In October, Castro nationalized 382 American-owned companies in Cuba, including banks and sugar mills. The State Department responded with an embargo on trade, and the US ambassador was recalled from Havana.
- In December, the USSR and China agreed to buy the Cuban sugar crop, for which the USA had previously been the main market.

Castro in New York

In the autumn of 1960, Castro visited the United Nations. He and his 85-strong delegation struggled to find a hotel that would accommodate them. They checked into the Hotel Shelburn but found it too expensive, so Castro demanded emergency accommodation from the UN General Secretary, threatening to camp out in Central Park if nothing was provided. Eventually, Castro stayed in the Hotel Theresa in Harlem, New York City's black ghetto. Castro was well aware of racial prejudice in the USA (segregation was still legal in the South) and his choice of accommodation made a deliberate statement about this.

The US media was hostile to Castro during the visit. Some newspapers printed reports and pictures of anti-Castro demonstrations even though the numbers involved never reached more than 25. Some purveyed tales about the Cubans living in a brothel, holding orgies, or killing chickens in their rooms. However, Castro was cheered by blacks and Latinos in the streets, and visited by the radical black activist Malcolm X, India's Prime Minister Nehru, Egypt's President Nasser, and Soviet Premier Khrushchev, whom Castro ostentatiously embraced at the UN. Here again, Castro was making more statements. He was confirming his sympathy for the black plight in the USA, his sense of kinship with newly independent 'Third World' countries such as India and Egypt, and his increasing friendship with Khrushchev, who had to help him return to Cuba when the USA confiscated his aircraft in retaliation for his confiscation of US property in Cuba.

SOURCE G

An extract from an article by the chief correspondent of the popular German newspaper, *Suddeutsche Zeitung*, Hans Ulrich Kempski, about Castro's visit to New York City in 1960.

Attributes such as murderer, hangman or butcher, applied to Khrushchev on placards and press articles, sounded well-nigh respectable in comparison with the outpourings of hate that any public mention of Castro's name provoked. Whereas, the previous year, he had been wildly cheered for five whole days in New York, he was now reviled as a hairy rat, a hobo and ravisher of young girls, whose greatest pleasure was to hold a knife to any American's bare throat.

How far would you trust this description in Source G of Castro's 'welcome' in New York?

Castro and Communism

← **Was Castro a Communist in the Eisenhower years?**

During Eisenhower's presidency, it was difficult to decide or prove whether Castro was a Communist. In the early days of the Castro regime, the US ambassador told Eisenhower that he was not a Communist and was likely to be neutral in the Cold War. In March 1960, the CIA also agreed that Cuba was not a Communist country. However, as Castro's relations with the USA deteriorated and his relations with the USSR improved, 'the Cold War mentality made it inevitable that Washington would smell a plot by the Soviet Union to extend its influence in a manner highly dangerous to US security', according to historian Hugh Brogan (1996).

There is no doubt that by the end of Eisenhower's presidency, the USA considered Castro a great problem. In January 1961, one of Eisenhower's last acts as president was to cut off diplomatic relations with Castro. The USA felt that its worst fears about the arrival of Communism in a Latin American country had been confirmed. However, as yet, Castro had not declared himself a Communist, and it could be argued that he was a problem that Eisenhower, through his continued support of the dictator Batista, his failure to recognize Cuban economic and political nationalism and grievances, and his increasing hostility to Castro, had done little to pre-empt and prevent. As was seen in Chapter 4, Eisenhower's Latin American policy was unimaginative and unimpressive and, it could be argued, this was particularly the case in Cuba.

Why Castro feared the USA in 1960	Why the USA feared Castro in 1960
• Castro resented US economic domination • The US soon turned against Castro's revolutionary government and plotted an invasion • The US had supported Batista for years, and had frequently intervened in Cuba • The US owned the naval base at Guantánamo Bay on the island of Cuba	• Castro nationalized and expropriated US-owned businesses and property • A Communist Cuba, physically close to the USA and its shipping routes to the Panama Canal, threatened US strategic interests • Castro made trade deals with the USSR • The USA concluded from his expropriation and deals with the USSR that Castro was a Communist • Castro might encourage other Latin American nations to go Communist

SUMMARY DIAGRAM

Eisenhower, Cuba and Castro

Chapter summary

The Cuban Revolution

The Cuban Revolution was shaped by the Cuban traditions of violence, nationalism, resentment of the USA, and left-wing radicalism, rather than by Communism. Fidel Castro was well versed in all these traditions. Despite qualifying as a lawyer, he was fascinated by both Cuban and Latin American politics. His first revolt against the dictator Batista in 1953 was a failure, although he gained fame and acclaim in his 'History will absolve me' speech at his trial. After Batista unwisely released him from jail, Castro went to Mexico and began to prepare for a second attack. In Mexico, he met and grew close to Che Guevara. Both resented US imperialism and sought greater economic equality for Latin Americans.

In 1959 Castro led the overthrow of Batista. There were many reasons for his success. Batista was corrupt, unpopular and lazy, while Castro was determined, charismatic, a skilled propagandist and a very able military leader. Castro played effectively on Cuban nationalism and waged effective guerrilla warfare. His policies appealed to the poor, but he was ruthless when necessary. Other revolutionaries, including some who had little connection to Castro, made significant contributions. Along with the urban revolutionaries, Guevara and Frank País were important. Batista's armies struggled against the guerrillas and began to lose heart. As Batista was clearly unable to defeat his opponents, he lost more and more support, and fled in January 1959.

The USA contributed to Castro's victory in several ways. The *New York Times* gave him a favourable press, and the Eisenhower administration put an arms embargo on Batista in 1958. In general, the initial US reaction to Castro was quite positive, although fears that he might have Communist sympathies appeared to be confirmed when it became clear that Castro was unwilling to tolerate US economic domination.

Given Castro's political and economic nationalism, US–Cuban antagonism was probably inevitable, although in Cuba as in the rest of Latin America, Eisenhower could be considered unimaginative and unimpressive in his policies.

 # Examination advice

How to answer 'evaluate' questions

For questions that contain the command term <u>evaluate</u>, you are asked to make judgements. You should judge the available evidence and identify and discuss the most convincing elements of the argument, in addition to explaining the limitations of other elements.

Example

<u>Evaluate</u> the impact of guerrilla warfare during the Cuban Revolution, 1956–9.

1. For this question you should aim to make a judgement about the degree to which guerrilla warfare movement had an impact on the Cuban Revolution. In order to do this you will need to evaluate why guerrilla war was used and what it actually accomplished. Stronger answers will also discuss other factors that helped shape the successful overthrow of the Batista regime. Do pay attention to the dates provided. You will need to

make reference to the whole time frame. In other words, do not focus solely on one specific year.

2. Before writing the answer you should write out an outline – allow around five minutes to do this. For this question, you could include evidence such as examples of guerrilla warfare and their effectiveness (put these in chronological order):

- *1956: small force landed on southern coast. Disastrous beginning. Most of 82 men killed*
- *Castro went to Sierra Maestra mountains. Slowly regrouped and recruited.*
- *1956–8: created infrastructure in mountains. Put in land reform in liberated territories. Some health care. Designed to win over support of peasants.*
- *Began guerrilla campaign. Small irritating attacks. Captured weapons.*
- *May 1958: Beginning of Fin de Fidel Offensive. 10,000 government soldiers sent in to find and destroy Castro. Batista unable to put an end to Castro because mountains were mostly impenetrable. Army became demoralized.*
- *Castro continued to fight and carry out small attacks on government soldiers. High desertion rate among government forces.*
- *Che Guevara led guerrillas under his command to central city of Santa Clara. Key victory.*
- *30,000 acts of sabotage to bring Cuban economy to its knees.*
- *Late 1958: Castro brothers captured Santiago in east.*
- *1 January 1959. Batista fled.*

Other factors:

- *Castro successfully employed propaganda. Created support in US through New York Times reporter, Herbert Matthews.*
- *Urban guerrillas not affiliated with Castro also kept up their campaigns against Batista.*
- *USA put arms embargo on Batista government in 1958.*
- *Castro won support among many Cubans by keeping his struggle non-ideological.*
- *Unpopularity of the Batista regime.*

3. In your introduction, you should briefly define <u>guerrilla warfare</u> and <u>impact</u> (social, political, strategic, economic). You will also need to state your thesis. This might be: 'Guerrilla warfare was the deciding factor in the overthrow of the Cuban dictator in 1959. However, there were other

important factors, as well, including the role of the US government and the US press.' Do not waste time by restating the question.

An example of a good introductory paragraph for this question is given below.

In his campaign to overthrow the Cuban dictator Fulgencio Batista from 1956 to 1959, Fidel Castro relied on guerrilla warfare to counter the much stronger Cuban armed forces. His strategy of slowly wearing down his opponents by use of small-scale but effective attacks was ultimately successful. As Batista's forces lost morale and deserted in increasing numbers, Castro and his guerrilla commanders took the battle from the mountains to two of the largest cities, Santiago de Cuba and Santa Clara in 1958. While this strategy worked, Castro was also able to use foreign media to counter Batista's claims that the guerrillas were a spent force. This, combined with the US decision to cut off arms to their former ally, helped the Castro forces attract more recruits and more support in the urban areas. Castro was able to impact the Cuban economy by carrying out thousands of attacks on the infrastructure of the country; this hastened the collapse of Batista's increasingly unpopular regime and it is that unpopularity that Castro said was the most important factor in the success of the Cuban Revolution.

4. In the body of your essay, devote at least one paragraph to each of the topics you raised in your introduction. This is your opportunity to support your thesis with appropriate evidence. Be sure to explicitly state how your supporting evidence ties into the question asked. If there is any counter-evidence, explain how and why it is of less importance than what you have chosen to focus on.

5. A well-constructed essay will end with a conclusion. Here you will tie together your essay by stating your conclusions. These concluding statements should support your thesis. Remember, do not bring any new ideas up here.

6. Now try writing a complete answer to the question following the advice above.

 Examination practice

Below is another exam-style question for you to practise on this topic.

Analyse the key factors that led Castro to undertake his revolution in 1959. (For guidance on how to answer 'analyse' questions, see page 90.)

CHAPTER 7

From Kennedy to Carter: US foreign policy in Latin America 1961–81

This chapter covers US relations with Latin America from 1961 to 1981, looking at the USA's attempts to improve relations under Kennedy and Carter, at US interventions under Johnson and Nixon, and at how these policies were affected by, and affected, the Cold War. You need to consider the following questions throughout this chapter:

✪ How successful were Kennedy's Latin American policies?

✪ What were the implications of Johnson's policies for Latin America?

✪ Was the USA losing control of the Western hemisphere in the mid-1970s?

✪ What implications did President Carter's policies have for Latin America?

1 President Kennedy and Latin America

▶ **Key question:** *How successful were Kennedy's Latin American policies?*

In the 1960 presidential election, the Democrat John F. Kennedy faced Vice President Richard Nixon. Exhibiting a youthful and new dynamism that contrasted sharply with the grandfatherly Eisenhower, Kennedy attacked the Eisenhower administration for laxity in waging the Cold War. He claimed that Eisenhower had left the USA behind the USSR in the arms race and had lost prestige in Africa, Asia and 'the most important area in the world', Latin America.

In his inaugural address, Kennedy promised to wage the Cold War with greater vigour, to 'pay any price, bear any burden, meet any hardship, support any friend, oppose any foe to assure the survival and success of liberty'. He told Congress that he was particularly interested in winning over the 'Third World', 'the great battleground for the defense and expansion of freedom'. He said he wanted these 'lands of the rising peoples' to start looking at what the USA rather than the USSR or China was doing. He told his ambassador to Peru that Latin America 'requires our best efforts'.

How successful was
the Alliance for
Progress?

→ # Kennedy and the Alliance for Progress

In November 1961, Kennedy announced an ambitious new plan to Latin American diplomats. He promised $20 billion from public and private money to help Latin America bring about essential social change. There was continuity between Kennedy's Alliance for Progress and Eisenhower's promise of $500 million to aid Latin American development (see page 86), but Kennedy's policy was far more ambitious than those of his predecessors (see table). He called for more 'homes, work … health and schools', and emphasized that land and tax reform and democratic governments were equally essential for progress. He felt that the time for greater Western-style democracy was opportune, as 10 Latin American dictatorships had been toppled between 1956 and 1960, and many considered Rómulo Betancourt's Venezuelan government to be a model of progressive democracy.

President and years in office	Percentage
Truman (1945–53)	3 per cent
Eisenhower (1953–61)	9 per cent
Kennedy (1961–3)	18 per cent

Percentage of the USA's foreign aid budget given to Latin America

Kennedy asked the OAS (see page 28) to hold a meeting to establish the institutional and organizational framework of the Alliance and at Punta del Este in Uruguay in August 1961, he promised $10 billion in public and private money to the Western hemisphere in the next decade. In return, the Latin Americans had to promise economic and social reforms, such as the redistribution of land and the tax burden. All OAS members except Cuba (Che Guevara denounced the Alliance as an 'instrument of economic imperialism') agreed to participate in the Alliance.

Alliance for Progress: successes

There are many examples of the Alliance helping Latin American development. The governments of Peru and Brazil administered housing programmes supported by the Alliance. When Kennedy offered Chile's President Jorge Alessandri $1 billion or more annually if Chile agreed to participate in Alliance programmes, Alessandri responded with enthusiasm to the Alliance's call for advances in education, housing and land reform. He increased the number of public schools and university students and persuaded the Chilean Congress to give tax exemptions on new housing construction. Forty thousand new units were built, some financed by the Chilean government, others by private capital. Alessandri also persuaded Congress to authorize government expropriation of fallow farmland, which was redistributed to small farmers. When the Christian Democrat Eduardo Frei Montalva, of whom the USA approved, won the Chilean presidential election in 1964, US economic assistance rocketed to 15 per cent of the Chilean national budget.

The Alliance also had some positive spin-offs for US diplomacy. In a December 1961 visit to Venezuela and Colombia, Kennedy emphasized his 'good neighbor' policy (see page 10) and the Alliance for Progress. Crowds in both countries cheered the young Catholic president with the glamorous wife and the promises of aid (see Source A). Disarmingly frank, Kennedy admitted to the leaders of Colombia, 'We in the USA have made many mistakes in our relations with Latin America.'

SOURCE A

President John F. Kennedy opening a school in Bogotá, Colombia, December 1961.

What can you infer about Kennedy and the Alliance for Progress from Source A?

Alliance for Progress: mixed results

Colombia was a showcase of the Alliance for Progress, and there were valuable achievements, such as newly built schools. However, the Alliance could not offset severe economic difficulties caused by low coffee prices, unemployment and lack of industrial development, and it increased Colombia's economic dependence on the USA, which aroused some resentment.

Some Alliance for Progress projects were seen as arrogant. Latin American educators resented being told that the US educational system should replace their more rigorous, but less democratic system. Some projects were seen as impractical. New housing units were sometimes built so far from the city centres where the head of the family worked that many families abandoned their new homes and moved closer to the workplace.

Alliance for Progress: failures

By the time Kennedy died in November 1963, Alliance officials claimed that 35 million Latin Americans had benefited, but the hoped-for growth and reforms had not really materialized. The Alliance was not particularly effective between 1961 and 1966, for several reasons.

Overambitious

Kennedy recognized that the Alliance was very ambitious, publicly describing Latin America's problems as 'staggering'. The US ambassador in Mexico said, 'The obstacles to change vary from country to country, but they are all deep-seated and each will be extremely difficult to remove.' A State Department expert said the USA was asking Latin America to become like the USA within a few years and against the interests of the rich and powerful, who naturally opposed land redistribution and taxes designed to reduce economic inequality. Furthermore, corruption was endemic among the Latin American élites, which meant that US aid did not always reach the places it was intended to reach.

One aim of the Alliance was more democracy in Latin America, but many Latin American nations lacked the necessary political stability. The 1960s was a decade of multiple overthrows of democratically elected presidents by the military: Frondizi in Argentina in 1962; Prado in Peru and Bosch in the Dominican Republic in 1962; Fuentes in Guatemala, Arosemena in Ecuador and Morales in Honduras in 1963; Goulart in Brazil and Estenssoro in Bolivia in 1964; Illia in Argentina in 1966. Ironically, when Argentina's President Arturo Frondizi was ousted in a military coup in 1962, some observers speculated that a Washington-sponsored austerity programme to stabilize the economy had helped provoke the coup.

Too American

One Alliance co-ordinator said the programme offended Latin American nationalism: 'it looks foreign and imported ... a "Made in the USA" product'. Many major Latin American nations, such as Argentina, Brazil and Mexico, were reluctant to submit their development programmes to US scrutiny. Latin Americans resented the fact that 60 per cent of any US aid was 'tied', which meant that they had to buy American products that were usually more expensive than those made in Germany or Japan. Furthermore, from 1961 to 1969, only $4.8 billion was actually dispersed. The remainder of the $10 billion pledged for the decade was kept in the USA to defray Latin American debts. Naturally, the US Congress was resistant to giving away large quantities of taxpayers' money to Latin Americans. Furthermore, the American president of the Chase Manhattan Bank admitted in 1964 that the Alliance was failing 'because private [US] investors have been reluctant to put their funds to work'.

Divisions in Washington

There were problems with bureaucratic in-fighting in Washington. Kennedy's friend Arthur Schlesinger warned him that the State Department's Latin American experts, 'keenly resented the intervention of outsiders', were 'predominantly out of sympathy with the Alliance' and constituted 'a sullen knot of resistance to fresh approaches'. The State Department's lack of enthusiasm hampered the productivity of the Alliance in its first two years. The Kennedy administration did not learn from the lessons and preparatory work of the Brazilian OPA (see page 85) and the Brazilian ambassador to the USA, Roberto Campos, said the programme was 'highly bureaucratized, extremely timid, and overly conservative. There was a gap between … generous intention and the reticent performance of the administrative machinery.'

US economic interests

Sometimes, US economic interests led the USA to work against the aims of its own Alliance. Che Guevara spoke of the 'intrinsic contradictions' of the Alliance: 'By encouraging the forces of change and the desire of the masses, you might set loose forces beyond your control, ending in a revolution that would be your enemy.' There were frequent examples that proved Guevara's point, as when Kennedy opposed a Honduran reform that confiscated the fallow land that belonged to the US companies Standard Oil and United Fruit. Similarly, US anxiety about the leftist Brazilian leader João Goulart increased in 1962, when the provincial government of Rio Grande do Sul expropriated land belonging to a subsidiary of an American corporation, International Telephone and Telegraph Company. Kennedy ordered the State Department to press Goulart to force a reversal. Goulart did so but became increasingly critical of multinational corporations and what he described as US imperialism. While agreeing to release $129 million worth of Alliance funding for Brazil, Kennedy covertly authorized the CIA to spend $5 million fighting anti-Goulart politicians in elections throughout Brazil and let the Brazilian military know that the USA would support a coup against Goulart if he was clearly 'giving the damn country away to the Communists'. The military overthrew Goulart in 1964.

US political interests

Sometimes US political interests clashed with Alliance aims. Theodore Sorensen later said that his friend Kennedy learned 'that the military often represented more competence in administration and more sympathy with the USA than any other group'. Although one of the aims of the Alliance was to promote democracy, the Kennedy administration usually failed to help democratically elected Latin American leaders as could be seen in Peru and Argentina.

Peru

The USA broke off diplomatic relations and suspended economic aid after a military coup in Peru in 1962 overthrew the democratically elected Victor Raúl Haya de la Torre, but then quickly resumed relations with the new junta.

Argentina

President Frondizi of Argentina had courted the USA because of its influence in the world market, its role in the **IMF**, and its funding of Alliance for Progress programmes that helped his government maintain fiscal solvency. Frondizi took decisive steps toward economic reform, but the USA found him insufficiently supportive of its Cold War policies and was not unhappy when a military junta overthrew him. The US inaction at his overthrow owed much to the fact that the new government spoke out against Fidel Castro. Whatever the motivation of the USA, Argentine democracy was destroyed and, typically, Argentine right-wing governments continued to receive US financial aid.

The US anti-Communist crusade

The Alliance was part of Kennedy's anti-Castro campaign, which was why it made sense to the USA to combine the Alliance with the training of soldiers and police officers (see page 161). However, many Latin Americans found the military emphasis alien to the ethos of the Alliance. Some Latin Americans believed the Alliance was simply an American tool for combating Communism and re-named it the 'Fidel Castro Plan'.

The Mann Doctrine

Kennedy's successor, President Johnson, appointed Thomas C. Mann to co-ordinate the Alliance for Progress, but Mann lacked sympathy for Alliance aims. His view was that the USA should be more tolerant of military rule and should emphasize the protection of US investments in Latin America.

SOURCE B

? What is Source B's viewpoint on the Alliance for Progress and how much value would you put upon its conclusions?

From Chilean leader Eduardo Frei Montalvo, 'The Alliance That Lost Its Way', published in the US journal *Foreign Affairs* in 1967.

Has the Alliance achieved [its] objectives? Has it preserved democracy and helped to implement substantial changes? Unfortunately the answer is negative … This does not mean that the Alliance has failed. It has brought about many beneficial changes. Under its auspices there have been advances in education, in public health services, in communal improvement, in the development of rational economic programs, and in better understanding between Latin America and the United States. But these … could have been secured simply with the financial assistance of the United States … The problem is that what was fundamental to the Alliance for Progress – a revolutionary approach to the need to reform – has not been achieved. Less than half of the Latin American countries have started serious programs of agrarian reform. Drastic changes in the tax system are even scarcer, while the number of democratic regimes … has actually declined … The salvation of the Alliance [requires] the people … to participate in it … The Latin American institutions which collaborate with the Alliance do not include trade unions, student federations, peasants leagues, cooperatives, etc. … [Its success also depends on] the discouragement of the arms race.

Key debate: the achievements of the Alliance for Progress

Alliance for Progress: success

Some historians consider the Alliance to have had considerable success. Kennedy's biographer Hugh Brogan (1996) said it was a propaganda triumph that encouraged modernizers and reformers throughout Latin America, and added lustre to Kennedy's reputation. Historian Edwin Williamson (2009) considered it 'far more than a cynical exercise in imperialist self-interest; it represented an attempt to foster in Latin America, through a process of peaceful reform, the democratic values that the USA itself professed to live by'.

Alliance for Progress: failure

In 1962, Kennedy told President Jorge Alessandri of Chile that some people thought the Alliance a failure. Kennedy's biographer Robert Dallek (2003) agreed, citing the State Department admission in 1962 that 'virtually nothing is being done' with regard to the economic improvement of Latin America, and pointing out that talk of promoting democracy and self-determination ('a central principle of the Alliance') could not be squared with secret US interventions in Cuba, Brazil, Peru, Haiti and the Dominican Republic – among others. 'In its brief 18-month life, the Alliance had become an imperfect cover for traditional actions serving perceived US national security,' according to Dallek.

Historian Walter LaFaber (2008) contended that by 1966 the Alliance had 'miserably failed'. It had created rising Latin American expectations that were crushed by the US, which supported military regimes, used Latin America as an export market for US goods, and intervened in the Dominican Republic.

Revisionist historians on the left emphasize that the Alliance for Progress failed to counter the dynamic impact of the Cuban revolution, but right-wing historians criticize it for having undermined free trade and encouraging revolutionary movements.

Stephen Rabe (1999) said Kennedy 'opted for the short-term security that anti-Communist elites, especially military officers, could provide over the benefits of long-term political and social democracy', but perhaps over-generously concluded: 'Kennedy brought high ideals and noble purposes to his Latin American policy. Ironically, however, his unwavering determination to wage Cold War … led him and his administration ultimately to compromise and even mutilate those grand goals for the Western hemisphere.'

Conclusions about the success of the Alliance for Progress

The Alliance for Progress had mixed success. Kennedy was prone to extravagant rhetoric and his declared aims for the Alliance were over-ambitious. If the aim of the Alliance was to counter the Communist threat

T O K

Examine the language used by President Kennedy when he first proposed the Alliance for Progress on 13 March 1961 (this speech is available online, for example, www.fordham.edu/ halsall/mod/ 1961kennedy-afp1.html) and make a list of what you think are the key words he used. Now draw up your own list of words to characterize the results of the programme by the end of the 1960s. How do these two lists compare? (History, Social Science, Ethics, Emotion, Perception, Language, Reason.)

(Kennedy proposed the Alliance a month before the Bay of Pigs invasion, see page 162), it could be argued that it failed, judging by the extent of guerrilla activity in the 1960s. If the aim was to promote democracy, it failed, as there were few democratic governments in Latin America by 1970. If the aim was to ameliorate poverty, there were some small-scale successes. For example, Colombia's leader, Alberto Lleras Camargo, was very enthusiastic about the Alliance, and obtained generous funds for development and reform and although his attempts at land redistribution went badly, there was great economic growth.

SOURCE C

A Colombian postage stamp depicting Kennedy and the Alliance for Progress.

? What can you infer about Latin American views of President Kennedy from Source C?

What were the aims and achievements of the Peace Corps?

Kennedy and the Peace Corps

The idea of using young Americans to help others was not totally new. There had been domestic equivalents under President Franklin Roosevelt, and Truman's Point IV Program (see page 28) had mentioned something similar. There was some enthusiasm for a 'Peace Corps' or a 'Youth Corps' in Congress in the late 1950s, but Eisenhower had dismissed it as a 'juvenile experiment'.

During his presidential election campaign in 1960, Kennedy was impressed by the idealism of University of Michigan students, and in November 1960 he outlined his Peace Corps idea.

Aims and methods of the Peace Corps

Under the Peace Corps, over 100,000 young Americans would serve in developing countries, which Kennedy saw as the next great theatre of the Cold War struggle. Along with helping poor nations to help themselves through teaching and technical aid, Kennedy said 'young men and women, dedicated to freedom' could improve America's international image in the Cold War and counter Communist recruitment. The American public was impressed: by late 1960, Kennedy had received more letters on the Peace

Corps than on any other topic, and polls showed a 71 per cent approval rating.

Kennedy put his brother-in-law Sargent Shriver in charge of the Peace Corps. Shriver was an inspired choice, a tireless, idealistic, charismatic, well-travelled businessman, who attracted quality staff. Kennedy wanted to incorporate the Peace Corps within the Agency for International Development (USAID). Luckily, given the fate of the Alliance for Progress, Shriver and Vice President Lyndon Johnson (the latter 'collared Kennedy … and in the course of the conversation badgered him so much that Kennedy finally said alright') ensured that the president let the Peace Corps stand alone, free to develop in an unrestricted manner.

Between 1961 and 1963, the Peace Corps sent volunteers to 44 developing countries that requested aid. Volunteers who got through the tough training programme (22 per cent of them failed) went off to provide a useful skill and increase mutual understanding with foreign nations.

Achievements of the Peace Corps

The Peace Corps had some failures, some volunteers with too little to do, some who got sent home for bad behaviour, but most were impressive. Future Democrat Senator Paul Tsongas taught mathematics and science in an Ethiopian village and helped build timber footbridges over streams and ditches. Some villagers in Tanzania were so impressed by an African American volunteer that they offered him a wife and a farm in order to encourage him to stay.

Historian James Giglio (1991) described the Peace Corps as one of Kennedy's most innovative programmes, which added lustre to the USA's international image and provided some help for emerging nations. Historian Hugh Brogan (1996) said the Peace Corps was 'a useful educational experiment' that benefited both the USA and the poorer nations. The historian Robert Dallek (2003) noted that a measure of its success was the antagonism generated in Moscow, which claimed it was a propaganda trick to enable the CIA to place agents in Africa, Asia and Latin America. There were some domestic critics of 'Kennedy's Kiddie Korps' ('a lot of kids bouncing around the world in Bermuda shorts'), but the 'kids' helped combat Communist claims about capitalist materialism and selfishness. Another measure of its success was that it has continued for another 50 years, funded by Republican administrations as well as by the Democrats.

> **KEY TERM**
>
> **Canal Zone** Territory within the Republic of Panama, consisting of the Panama Canal and land extending roughly five miles on each side of the waterway.

Kennedy and guerrilla warfare

At the same time as the Alliance for Progress, the Pentagon and the CIA helped train Latin American police and paramilitaries to combat left-wing guerrillas. The Pentagon set up jungle warfare schools in Panama in the **Canal Zone** (see page 9) and at Fort Bragg in North Carolina. USAID brought 500 Latin American policemen to the Canal Zone school, where

> **Why did Kennedy set up jungle warfare schools?**

they were trained in counterintelligence, in how to infiltrate leftist groups and how to control mobs. Nevertheless, by 1966 there were leftist, anti-American guerrillas operating in Bolivia, Colombia, Guatemala, Nicaragua and Venezuela.

How successful were Kennedy's Cuban policies?

? Look at the photograph on the cover of this book. It is Fidel Castro on his April 1959 visit to Washington, when he went to see the Lincoln Memorial. What might you infer from this photograph?

Kennedy and Cuba

Kennedy initially welcomed Castro's revolt against Batista's corrupt dictatorship but became alienated by Castro's anti-Americanism, increasing friendship with the USSR, and 1961 declaration that he was a Marxist–Leninist (see page 196).

The Bay of Pigs invasion

Under Eisenhower, the CIA had planned an invasion of Cuba by discontented Cuban exiles (see page 147). Although warned by many, including Dean Acheson and the British, that the invasion would fail and that it would turn world opinion against the USA, Kennedy supported the invasion plan. He believed that developing countries such as Cuba were the next great arena of the Cold War struggle and hoped they could be won for the USA. The plan had been endorsed by Eisenhower and the CIA. Kennedy assumed that Eisenhower, with all his military expertise, knew what he was doing, and the CIA was at the height of its prestige. Also, Kennedy was a prisoner of his own militantly anti-Communist rhetoric. In his 1960 presidential election campaign, he had promised to do something about Castro, saying that the USA should not allow the USSR to turn Cuba into a base in the Caribbean, and attacking the apparent inactivity of the Eisenhower administration. Had he not continued with Eisenhower's invasion plan, the Republicans would have been highly critical. Finally, using the Cuban exiles seemed like a cheap and easy way of getting rid of Castro.

In April 1961, around 1600 Cuban guerrillas landed at the Bay of Pigs (Playa Girón). Despite the CIA conviction that the invasion would stimulate an anti-Castro rising, it was a disaster. Cuban exiles and US newspapers had forewarned Castro, and although the CIA knew that Castro knew, the invasion still went ahead. The invasion force landed miles away from the mountains to which the CIA had hoped the men could flee if in trouble. Castro was so popular (particularly in the Bay of Pigs where he frequently holidayed) that the force had no chance of support and within two days all were captured by the Cuban army. The CIA and the Cuban exiles were convinced throughout that if the invasion went wrong, Kennedy would send in US forces, but Kennedy had always insisted that US involvement should be minimal.

The CIA and Castro

Humiliated by the failure at the Bay of Pigs, the Kennedy administration urged the CIA to gain revenge on Cuba. Edward Lansdale, who had been in charge of covert operations in Saigon, developed what a subsequent CIA director called the 'nutty schemes' of Operation Mongoose in November 1960. Some of the covert operations were effective, some were not. A CIA memorandum written in 1961 boasted of 800 sabotage operations, 150 arson attacks, and bombs placed at a power station and a railway station. E. Howard Hunt, who had been involved in the overthrow of the Árbenz government in Guatemala in 1954, organized a series of night-time commando raids on Cuba, but they increased Cuban nationalism and encouraged Castro to ask Moscow for military aid.

The CIA approached members of the Mafia (who were keen to re-establish their lucrative prostitution, gambling and drugs operations in Havana) to discuss the assassination of Castro. According to a disgruntled ex-girlfriend, who said Castro had made her abort their child, she was promised $80 million and was to kill Castro with a toxic shellfish pill. However, when they met, she recorded that 'love proved stronger', and she flushed the pill down the bidet. The CIA thought Castro's beard was an essential component of his charisma, so it was suggested that a depilatory powder could be dropped into his shoes that would make it fall out. Other suggestions included poisoning Castro's cigars, offering him a pen with a poisoned tip, contaminating his diving suit with tuberculosis bacteria, and exploding clamshells in the areas where he dived in order to blow his legs off. Lansdale suggested sending a submarine to Cuba that could suddenly light up the sky with firepower that would convince the peasants of Christ's Second Coming. Castro said, 'We believe that the Central Intelligence Agency has absolutely no intelligence at all.' Historians disagree as to whether Kennedy approved of the assassination plots, but it seems likely that he did (see page 98).

Results and significance of the Bay of Pigs invasion

The results and significance of the Bay of Pigs invasion were as follows:

- To Kennedy's surprise the fiasco actually raised his approval rating to 82 per cent. 'It's just like Eisenhower,' he said. 'The worse I do, the more popular I get.'
- Kennedy and the USA were humiliated in the eyes of the world, and sought revenge through CIA plots (see box). Castro gleefully criticized US imperialism. Even America's staunch ally Britain protested that the invasion was illegal by the standards of international law, which the USA had always claimed to support.
- The historian Walter LaFaber (2008) said the unsuccessful invasion arose from a total US failure to understand the popularity of the Cuban Revolution, which was one of the most significant political changes in the Western hemisphere in 50 years.

- Castro's popularity and position within Cuba were secured.
- Fearing another US invasion, Castro moved even closer to the USSR. He had made an economic agreement with the Soviets back in February 1960, and a few months after the invasion announced his Marxism–Leninism. In July 1962 he travelled with Che Guevara to Moscow to seal Soviet–Cuban economic and defence links.
- The Soviet archives indicate that prior to the Cuban Revolution of 1959 the USSR had little interest in the Western hemisphere and that it was the Bay of Pigs that led the Soviet leader Khrushchev to conclude that the USA was not as powerful in its own backyard as he had thought, that Kennedy was a soft touch and rather foolish, and that he could get away with putting missiles in Cuba.
- Kennedy needed some great political success after the Bay of Pigs, which probably encouraged him to increase the commitment in Vietnam (see page 97) and to stand up to Khrushchev in the Cuban Missiles Crisis (see below), especially as Kennedy had publicly warned after the Bay of Pigs that if any Western hemisphere nations failed to withstand Communism, the USA would intervene on the grounds of US national security.

The Cuban Missiles Crisis, 1962

In August 1962, Soviet missiles and technicians arrived in Cuba. The Soviet motives for putting nuclear missiles in Cuba were as follows:

- In summer 1960, Khrushchev had welcomed Castro as a great new force in Latin America, declared the Monroe Doctrine dead, and promised to defend Cuba. In his memoirs, Khrushchev said that he put the missiles in Cuba because they would deter another invasion attempt by the Kennedy administration.
- In 1962, the Soviets had 50 **ICBMs**, the Americans 304. The Soviets had 150 intercontinental bombers, the Americans 1200. The statistics worried Khrushchev, especially as the Kennedy administration repeatedly boasted about its nuclear superiority in autumn 1961. The Soviets could not afford a massive ICBM build-up, so it made sense to put existing **MRBMs** and **IRBMs** on Cuba, which was only 90 miles from the US coast. However, Khrushchev claimed in his memoirs that maintaining the balance of power between the USA and the USSR was only a secondary consideration.
- In his memoirs, Khrushchev pointed out that the USA had missiles pointing at the USSR in Turkey. 'Since the Americans have already surrounded the Soviet Union with a ring of their military bases and various types of missile launchers, we must pay them back in their own coin … so they will know what it feels like to live in the sights of nuclear weapons.'
- Khrushchev felt that Kennedy was a soft touch, and that he could get away with putting the missiles in Cuba, just as Kennedy had let him get away with the building of the **Berlin Wall**.

 **KEY TERM**

ICBM Intercontinental ballistic missile.

MRBM Medium-range ballistic missile.

IRBM Intermediate range ballistic missile.

Berlin Wall Wall built by the Communists in August 1961 to halt the haemorrhage of people from Communist East Berlin to capitalist West Berlin.

- Khrushchev hoped that gaining the advantage in Cuba, through the missiles, would put him in a stronger position with regards to gaining concessions in Berlin.
- Khrushchev wanted some great foreign policy success in order to impress his critics at home and in China.

Kennedy's response

During September 1962 there were rumours in the American press that the Soviets had put offensive nuclear missiles in Cuba. Kennedy warned the USSR that would be intolerable, but he remained confident that the Soviets would not station nuclear missiles outside their own territory – they had never done so before. Then on 14 October an American U2 spy plane photographed the missile sites. Missiles launched from Cuba would be more accurate than any ICBMs sent from the USSR itself, and the great east coast cities of the USA were within range. Kennedy opposed the installation of the missiles because he believed that it was dangerous for US national security if the USA looked weak in the face of Soviet missiles 90 miles off the coast of Florida. Also, it was politically dangerous to allow Khrushchev to get away with this in the way that he had got away with building the Berlin Wall.

On 16 October, Kennedy established his Executive Committee of the National Security Council (Ex Comm), which considered the following five options.

Option 1: doing nothing
This was not really an option, otherwise the arrival of the missiles in Cuba would be seen as a Soviet victory. According to historian Michael Dockrill (2005), Khrushchev 'completely underestimated Kennedy's combative psychology'. The forthcoming congressional mid-term elections also had to be considered: Kennedy and the Democrats did not want to look weak.

Option 2: diplomacy
Using normal diplomatic channels such as the UN would be too slow.

Option 3: force
Some of Kennedy's military men preferred the armed option, whether a 'surgical air strike' or an invasion of Cuba. However, that would lead to the deaths of Soviets, which might then lead to a third world war. The Under Secretary of State George Ball said that he opposed the surgical air strike, having 'concluded from the records of Allied bombing in Europe that if the medical profession should ever adopt the air force definition of *surgical*, anyone undergoing an operation for appendicitis might lose his kidneys and lungs yet find the appendix intact'.

Option 4: Turkish missiles for Cuban missiles
Kennedy's ambassador to the UN, Adlai Stevenson, suggested that the US missiles in Turkey be withdrawn in exchange for the withdrawal of the Soviet missiles in Cuba, but this was rejected by the Kennedy administration.

 **KEY TERM**

Surgical air strike
Bombing aimed at highly specific targets.

Option 5: blockade

George Ball suggested a blockade, in which US naval vessels would stop Soviet vessels attempting to get more men and materials to Cuba. Kennedy did not use the word blockade, but talked of a 'quarantine', which sounded less aggressive. The advantage of the blockade was that it would give Soviet leader Khrushchev time to think again, but as it would also give him time to complete the installation of the missiles, American planes and troops were kept on red alert. A further disadvantage of the blockade was that if the Soviets chose to defy it, a full-scale Soviet–American war might erupt.

The Kennedy administration kept the crisis secret for over a week, then on 22 October Kennedy told the American people the Soviets were building bases in Cuba 'to provide a nuclear strike capacity against the Western hemisphere' and announced the 'quarantine'. He said that the 1930s had taught Americans not to appease aggressors and that any nuclear missile launched from Cuba would be interpreted as a Soviet attack on the USA and result in US retaliation against the USSR. He said that the missiles would have to be removed.

The situation was unbelievably tense. The USA had B-52 bombers on red alert, and 156 ICBMs primed ready to go. The world watched the development of events with horror. On 23 October, Kennedy obtained Latin American support when the OAS agreed to the blockade by 19 votes to nil.

Initially, the blockade line around Cuba was 800 miles, but Kennedy decreased it to 500 miles in order to give Khrushchev more time to think. On 24 October, two Soviet ships and a Soviet submarine were near the 500-mile blockade line but then, with the world apparently on the verge of nuclear annihilation, Khrushchev backed down.

While Kennedy prepared a possible invasion of Cuba, Khrushchev sent him a message on 26 October, offering to get the missiles out if Kennedy stopped the blockade and promised not to invade the island. On 27 October a second Soviet message added another demand, the removal of US missiles from Turkey. Kennedy ignored the second offer, and accepted the first. He told the Soviets that if they did not reply there would be an American invasion of Cuba on the 29th. Radio Moscow broadcast Khrushchev's promise to dismantle the missiles, and the Voice of America radio station broadcast the US acceptance of the offer.

Why did Khrushchev back down?

Khrushchev backed down because he knew that the US had its forces on full alert, and had nuclear and naval superiority. Also, he had obtained Kennedy's promise not to invade Cuba, and a secret US promise to withdraw its missiles from Turkey.

The results and significance of the Cuban Missiles Crisis

- The crisis demonstrated how a small country such as Cuba could end up as a pawn in the Cold War. Khrushchev decided to withdraw the missiles without consulting Castro, who was furious, and refused to return the Soviet bombers until November.
- The Soviet leader Khrushchev claimed that he had saved world peace. However, the West considered the crisis the triumph for Kennedy, and Khrushchev's fall from power not long after (October 1964) suggests the Soviets agreed.
- Both the USA and the USSR were frightened by the crisis, which led to something of a thaw in the Cold War:
  - In June 1963 a **hotline** was installed between the Kremlin and the White House so that in future crises the Soviet leader and the American president could communicate directly by telephone.
  - In August 1963, a Soviet–American Partial Nuclear Test Ban Treaty was signed, the first such treaty of its kind.
- Some Americans believed the crisis demonstrated the so-called 'imperial presidency' in the USA.
- The crisis probably led to American overconfidence and to the increased involvement in Vietnam.
- The USA grew more determined that there should be no more Communist nations in the Western hemisphere – hence the Johnson Doctrine in 1965 (see page 171).
- The crisis led to a more multipolar world in which new centres of power other than Moscow and Washington developed. Whereas previously the world had seemed to move on a Washington–Moscow axis, the Cuban Missiles Crisis led to tensions between the Americans and their allies and between the Soviets and their fellow Communists. The Chinese called Khrushchev a fool for putting the missiles in Cuba, and a coward for removing them, which widened the Sino-Soviet split. The Americans had problems with several allies. France and Canada were highly sensitive about what they perceived to be US attempts at domination and American slights to their honour. French President Charles de Gaulle resented the fact that Kennedy had not consulted with him during the Cuban Missiles Crisis. He talked about 'annihilation without representation' and withdrew from NATO in 1966. Canada's Prime Minister John Diefenbaker was similarly upset when Kennedy, without consulting him, issued a statement saying the USA had Canada's full support. However, their relations had been uneasy before the Cuban Missiles Crisis. Diefenbaker resented Kennedy publicly mispronouncing his name, criticizing his French, and appealing to the Canadian Parliament to join the OAS, membership of which Diefenbaker had already specifically rejected. Robert Kennedy said that his brother 'hated' the Canadian leader and after their first meeting, Kennedy had said he never wanted 'to see that boring son of a bitch again'.

🔑 KEY TERM

Hotline Direct telephone line between the White House and the Kremlin.

Imperial presidency Continuous Cold War emergencies increased presidential authority, and some contemporaries felt the president was becoming dangerously powerful.

- In 1992, historians gained access to Soviet sources for the first time and it was revealed that the nuclear warheads were already in place in Cuba, which Ex Comm had not known in 1962. When Kennedy's Secretary of Defense Robert McNamara learned of this in 1992, he said, 'This is horrifying. It meant that had a US invasion been carried out … there was a 99 percent probability that nuclear war would have been initiated. The actions of all three parties were shaped by misjudgment, miscalculations, and misinformation.'

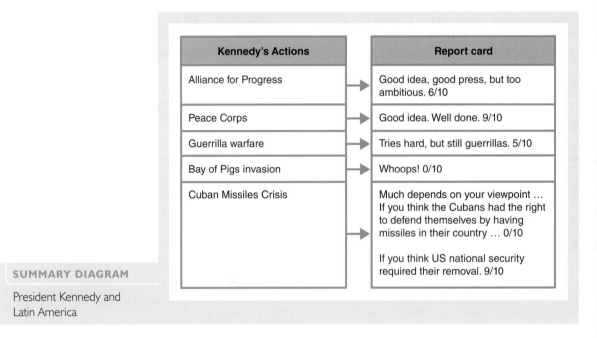

Kennedy's Actions	Report card
Alliance for Progress	Good idea, good press, but too ambitious. 6/10
Peace Corps	Good idea. Well done. 9/10
Guerrilla warfare	Tries hard, but still guerrillas. 5/10
Bay of Pigs invasion	Whoops! 0/10
Cuban Missiles Crisis	Much depends on your viewpoint … If you think the Cubans had the right to defend themselves by having missiles in their country … 0/10 If you think US national security required their removal. 9/10

SUMMARY DIAGRAM

President Kennedy and Latin America

2 President Johnson and Latin America

▶ **Key question:** *What were the implications of Johnson's policies for Latin America?*

After Kennedy's assassination in November 1963, Vice President Lyndon Johnson became president. Johnson's main preoccupation was the Vietnam War (see pages 99, 102–4 and 111–14), but his policies also had implications for Latin America. Under Johnson, the Alliance for Progress was downgraded and the Dominican Republic invaded.

Johnson and the Alliance for Progress

← How and why did the Alliance for Progress decline under Johnson?

According to historian Walter LaFaber (2008), by the time Johnson became president, the Alliance for Progress was already 'crumbling, the victim of the false assumption that enough money and bureaucratic technicians could tinker with and adjust the dynamic nationalisms of an economically unbalanced Latin America to the policy objectives of a prosperous, satisfied, and expanding USA'. Kennedy's vision of economic, social and democratic advancement had failed to materialize. Johnson downgraded the Alliance for Progress because of his emphasis on Latin American political stability and because of advice from the Treasury (the Vietnam War and, to a lesser extent, the Great Society, were very expensive).

Alliance for Progress, political stability and Brazil

The Johnson administration's priority in Latin America was political stability, and the administration felt that this was best achieved not through the Alliance for Progress, but through US opposition to radicalism and the protection of US investments. Military governments were frequently stable and preferable to liberal governments that threatened American companies (by expropriation or by making them more accountable and responsible). The first military coup that the Johnson administration encouraged was that in Brazil in 1964.

During 1963, Brazil's President João Goulart (see page 157) had moved to the left with his land reforms and increasing verbal attacks on multinational corporations and US imperialism. Brazilian army officers were conspiring against him, supported by the US State Department, which had spent nearly $20 million to prevent his election. By mid-1963 many Brazilian Catholics had found him insufficiently anti-Communist. A Catholic nun, Sister Ana de Lourdes, held an anti-Communist parade consisting of what supporters claimed to be 800,000 women in São Paolo (see Source D). In spring 1964, Goulart was overthrown and a military dictatorship was installed. The USA gave this new regime $1.5 billion in economic and military aid, which constituted around a quarter of all US funding for Latin America. Brazil became pro-American, anti-Communist and one of the most stable (and repressive) governments in Latin America.

SOURCE D

The proclamation of Sister Ana de Lourdes and the other leaders of the 'March of the Family for God and Liberty' in São Paulo in 1964.

This nation which God gave us, immense and marvellous as it is, faces extreme danger. We have allowed men of limitless ambition, without Christian faith or scruples, to bring our people misery, [by] destroying our economy, disturbing our social peace, and to create hate and despair. They have infiltrated our nation, our government administration, our armed forces and even our Churches with servants of totalitarianism, foreign to us and all consuming … Mother of God preserve us from the fate and suffering of the martyred women of Cuba, Poland, Hungary and other enslaved nations!

In what ways might Source D have been appealing to some Brazilians? To what extent would you trust this source's contention that Communists ('servants of totalitarianism') were an 'extreme danger' to Brazil?

The Treasury and the Alliance for Progress

Johnson hoped for increased US investment in social programmes (especially health and education) in Latin America, but the Vietnam War and the Great Society were highly expensive. Anxious about the US trade deficit, the Treasury insisted that any aid given to Latin American countries required the recipients to purchase US goods with the money, even if other nations produced the goods more cheaply. This prompted the Colombian president to say in 1968, 'Colombia has received two programme loans under the Alliance. I don't know if we can survive a third.'

Alliance for Progress and the Panama Canal

The receipt of Alliance for Progress loans was no guarantee of improved relations with Latin American countries, as demonstrated by events in Panama in 1964. Panama was one of the countries that received the initial large-scale loans to help build houses, but when American students repeatedly raised the US flag in front of their Canal Zone School and Panamanian students tried to remove the flag, riots broke out; 20 Panamanians and four Americans died. American troops moved in to restore peace. Panama's foreign minister denounced this as 'ruthless aggression' against a 'defenceless civilian population'. The Johnson administration blamed the riots on Communists (see Source E), but they were caused by Panamanian nationalism. In response, Johnson began the 14-year negotiations through which Panama would eventually become sovereign in the Canal Zone.

SOURCE E

?
Using quotations from Source E to prove your point, how would you describe Russell's attitude to Panama and Panamanians?

A transcript of a telephone conversation between President Johnson and Senator Richard Russell of Georgia, January 1964.

Johnson: Dick, I want to talk to you off the record a minute about this Panama situation. What do you think?

Russell: Mr President, [if I were you] I would say this is a most regrettable incident … However, the Panama Canal Zone is the property of the United States, the Canal was built with American ingenuity and blood, sweat and sacrifices. It is a vital necessity for the economy and the defense of every nation in this hemisphere … Under no circumstances would you permit the threat of interruption by any subversive [Communist] group … Those people down there … We brought them out of the jungles. If we wasn't [sic.] there, they wouldn't have anything. They'd be living out there half naked in the swamps. It's the Panama Canal. We can't risk having it sabotaged or taken over by any Communist group.

Johnson's intervention in the Dominican Republic, 1965

← **Why and with what results did Johnson intervene in the Dominican Republic?**

The Dominican Republic's 3.3 million people were among the poorest in Latin America. The US government had been, in effect, in control of the Dominican Republic in the early twentieth century, but then stepped aside for Rafael Leónidas Trujillo Molina (1891–1961), who established what proved to be a long-lasting dictatorship when he assumed control of the US-trained security forces. President Roosevelt described him as a 'son of a bitch', but 'our son of a bitch'.

Despite Trujillo's brutality (in 1937 he ordered the execution of around 25,000 Haitians living in the Dominican Republic), he was a close anti-Communist ally of the USA in the 1950s. In 1961, he was assassinated, and historians disagree over the US complicity in his death. Allowing and/or colluding in the assassination of a loyal anti-Communist ally might seem quite strange, but Trujillo had become something of an embarrassment and on occasion was inclined toward independence. After the assassination of Trujillo, the reformist Juan Bosch was elected president with 60 per cent of the vote. Like Kennedy, Johnson disliked Bosch, who was ousted by an army coup within 10 months. The new conservative junta was headed by Donald Reid Cabral, to whom the USA loaned $5 million for the presidential election of 1965. At this point, Bosch supporters rose in rebellion.

> **An old Latin American joke**
> *Question*: Why are there no *coup d'états* in the USA?
> *Answer*: Because there is no US embassy there.

Why Johnson intervened in the Dominican Republic

The USA sent around 30,000 men to crush the rebellion of Bosch's supporters, claiming that it was protecting Americans living in the Dominican Republic. That assertion was probably an attempt to hide the US violation of the OAS charter, which prohibited external intervention in another state. Johnson later gave another and probably more truthful reason, in what became known as the Johnson Doctrine. 'People trained outside the Dominican Republic are seeking to gain control,' he claimed. 'American nations cannot, must not, and will not permit the establishment of another Communist government in the Western hemisphere.' He said change 'should come through peaceful process' and promised that the USA would defend 'every free country of this hemisphere'.

Was the Dominican Republic really threatened by Communism? Historians think not. According to the revisionist historian Walter LaFaber (2008), it proved impossible for the CIA to find any Communists, so Johnson ordered the FBI, 'Find me some Communists in the Dominican Republic.' Historian

Michael Grow (2008) suggested that as in many other US interventions in Latin America, Johnson's prime motivation was to demonstrate the strength of the USA – and its president. Grow cited Johnson's loud lament, 'What can we do in Vietnam if we can't clean up the Dominican Republic?'

The significance of the US intervention

Within the USA, the intervention aroused considerable disquiet, especially when the press publicized Bosch's complaint that 'this was a democratic revolution smashed by the leading democracy of the world'. Although Johnson managed to get a vote of support from the OAS, the Latin Americans spoke privately of their resentment of Yankee contempt for them and use of the '**big stick**'. They were certainly right about the contempt: Johnson famously said, 'The OAS could not pour piss out of the boot if the instructions were written on the heel.'

Another result of the intervention was its contribution to Senator William Fulbright's loss of faith in the president and in US foreign policy (see Source F). Chairman of the influential Senate Foreign Relations Committee from 1959 to 1974, Fulbright publicly asserted that the administration had misled the nation about the dangers of Communism in the Dominican Republic. He then went on to hound Johnson over the Vietnam War.

? In Source F, how does Fulbright account for US actions in the Dominican Republic, and what does he see as the significance of those actions?

SOURCE F

Senator William Fulbright opposed the Bay of Pigs invasion, advocated economic assistance to Latin America and questioned US support for dictators. This extract is from his book *The Arrogance of Power*, published in 1966.

Caught between genuine sympathy for social reform on the one hand and an intense fear of revolution on the Cuban model on the other, we have thus far been unwilling, or unable, to follow a consistent course. On the one hand, we have made ourselves a friend of certain progressive democratic governments and have joined with Latin America in the Alliance for Progress, the purpose of which is social revolution by peaceful means. On the other hand, we have allowed our fear of Communism to drive us into supporting a number of governments whose policies, to put it charitably, are inconsistent with the aims of the Alliance, and on three occasions – Guatemala in 1954, Cuba in 1961, and the Dominican Republic in 1965 – we resorted to force, illegally, unwisely, and in as much as each of these interventions almost certainly strengthened the appeal of Communism to the younger generation of educated Latin Americans, unsuccessfully as well … The Alliance for Progress encouraged the hope in Latin America that the USA would not only tolerate but actively support domestic social revolution. The Dominican intervention at least temporarily destroyed that hope. The facts remain that the USA engaged in a unilateral military intervention in violation of inter-American law, the 'good neighbor' policy of 30 years' standing and the spirit of the Charter of Punta del Este; that the [OAS] was gravely weakened as the results of its use – with its own consent – as an instrument of the policy of the USA.

SOURCE G

A cartoon published in the *Chicago Sun Times*, May 1965. Copyright by Bill Maudlin (1965). Courtesy of Bill Maudlin Estate LLC.

What is Source G trying to say about Johnson's foreign policy?

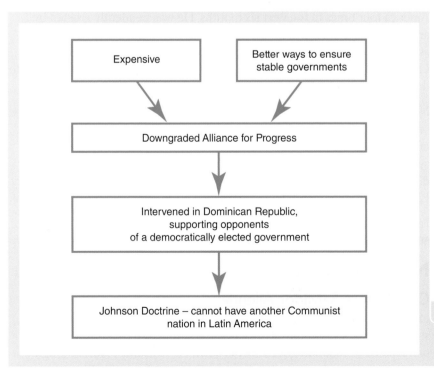

SUMMARY DIAGRAM

President Johnson and Latin America

173

President Nixon and control of the Western hemisphere

> ▶ **Key question:** *Was the USA losing control of the Western hemisphere in the mid-1970s?*

The foreign policy of the Republican Richard Nixon was both different from and similar to that of the Democrat Johnson. Nixon's preoccupations differed from Johnson's in that he wanted to end the Vietnam War and initiate *détente* with the USSR and China (see pages 116–21), which was different from Johnson. However, on Latin America there was more similarity, including opposition to a democratically elected government. Although Nixon's national security adviser Henry Kissinger said Latin America was, 'a dagger pointed at the heart of – Antarctica … What happens in the South is of no importance', during the **Ford presidency** (1974–7), Kissinger began to fear that the USA was losing control in the Western hemisphere.

KEY TERM

Ford presidency Nixon resigned in 1974 in order to avoid impeachment and Vice President Gerald Ford became president.

The Rockefeller Report

> Why was the Rockefeller Report important?

Richard Nixon had long considered Latin America important and problematic (see pages 81–7) and on his first day as president he asked New York Governor Nelson Rockefeller to go to consult with Latin American leaders and make recommendations for US policy. Rockefeller visited Latin America four times in the next six months. He was frequently greeted by angry demonstrators, and the governments of Peru, Chile and Venezuela asked him to stay away. Rockefeller reported to Nixon that the USA and Latin America were drifting apart and suggested that the USA would have to demonstrate more tolerance for authoritarian rule in Latin America.

Not everyone agreed with Rockefeller. In the June 1969 Senate Subcommittee on Western Hemisphere Affairs hearings, there was a great deal of criticism of US aid to Latin American military forces since the Kennedy years. A sympathetic *New York Times* editorial said that Americans 'need to be disabused of the notion that the Alliance for Progress has failed because lazy Latins simply squandered billions provided by an over-generous Uncle Sam'.

Faced with the options of giving more economic aid or assisting authoritarian governments, the Nixon administration opted for the latter.

Nixon and Chile

Chile before Salvador Allende

> Why did the USA oppose Allende's democratically elected government, and how far was the USA responsible for its overthrow?

In the early twentieth century, Chilean socialism and Communism grew in strength. Chile's Communist Party was the strongest in Latin America, and participated in coalition governments between 1938 and 1946. Although outlawed in 1948, the party remained confident and popular. From the

1950s, Chile's most prominent leftist politician was Salvador Allende Gossens (1908–73), a doctor and Socialist Party leader who repeatedly stood for the presidency and came close to victory in the elections of 1952 and 1958. His Socialist Party was Marxist but opposed Chile's more moderate and pro-Soviet Communist Party.

The Cold War made Chilean political rivalries more polarized. Leftists increasingly believed that Castro's way of violent revolution was best and viewed the Christian Democrat opposition as the tools of the Roman Catholic Church and US imperialism, while more conservative political parties such as the Christian Democrats felt that the Communist Party would make Chile a Communist state within the Soviet empire.

In 1964, the Christian Democrat leader, Eduardo Frei Montalva (1911–82) was elected president. Frei did not always please the Americans, as when he nationalized the copper mines, but the USA felt he was better than Allende. Allende stood for the presidency in 1952, 1958, 1964 and 1970 and the CIA funded Allende's opponents on each occasion (such contributions had been made throughout Latin America since the Truman years).

In 1970, US companies with interests in Chile feared that Allende might get elected and contributed money to his political opponents. Allende aimed to improve the living standards of less affluent Chileans and to decrease the massive economic inequality in Chile, which would entail decreasing the power, wealth and influence of large landowners and of US multinational corporations. The erosion of the power and influence of multinational corporations had begun before Allende came to power, but the US-owned copper mining companies and the US communications giant International Telephone and Telegraph thought they would lose more under him.

The Nixon administration also feared an Allende victory. Nixon quoted an Italian businessman as saying, 'If Allende should win the election, and then you have Castro in Cuba, what you will in effect have in Latin America is a red sandwich, and eventually it will all be red.' So, anxious about the psychological and political impact of the first democratically elected Marxist leader in the Western world, Nixon decided an Allende regime was 'not acceptable' and granted the CIA $10 million to prevent his coming to power or to unseat him if he did.

The Allende government

To the dismay of the USA, Allende was elected president of Chile on his fourth attempt. Once elected, Allende formed a leftist Popular Unity coalition that had many successes, including improvements in health care and education, but it also had many problems.

Allende's coalition suffered from great internal divisions. Some members favoured armed struggle as the route to socialism and felt that Allende proceeded too slowly. However, when he began to accelerate land redistribution, his more moderate support in both the coalition and in the nation haemorrhaged. Increased government control over the media and education further alienated the Chilean middle class, as did a long and greatly publicized visit by Fidel Castro in November 1971.

Chile had great economic problems that further increased Allende's unpopularity. Copper exports were crucial to the Chilean economy, but copper prices were falling. Partly in response to Allende's nationalization of industries without compensation, and partly in response to his Marxism, the Americans blocked credits and loans to Chile. Allende made the situation worse. He printed money and inflation rose to 300 per cent, but as an elected Marxist, he felt he could not cut back public spending or lower wages. The Chilean economy appeared to be on the verge of meltdown. Stores ran out of items such as coffee and toilet paper. In response, thousands of women took to the streets in 1971 in 'the march of the empty pots', protesting against prices and scarcities by banging their pots and pans. Although Allende supporters physically attacked them, the women held more marches, many of them at night.

SOURCE H

Castro (centre) on a visit to Allende's Chile in 1971.

Nixon administration's opposition to Allende

The Nixon administration had worked to prevent Allende's election, and after his victory it worked to destabilize his government. The US companies that had contributed funds to his opponents in the election urged intervention but Nixon was motivated more by fears that Allende's Chile could develop into a Soviet satellite, a second Cuba, and that he and the USA would look weak if nothing was done. Kissinger said the situation in Chile was 'a challenge to our national interest', and described Nixon as 'beside himself' with fury in fear lest he get the blame for having 'lost Chile'.

In order to get rid of Allende, the Nixon administration waged economic warfare on Chile. Since the 1960s, the USA had given Chile $70 million aid per year, but Nixon said he wanted 'to make the economy scream', so he stopped all aid and World Bank and Inter-American Bank loans to Allende. On the other hand, US economic warfare was not the only reason the Chilean economy was in trouble, as has been seen (see page 176) and Chile obtained loans from other sources such as Canada, the USSR and China.

Along with the economic warfare, the CIA funded media criticism and strikes by truckers and taxi drivers, and encouraged the demonstrations by middle-class housewives in an attempt to destabilize the Allende government. Subsequently, the CIA chief Richard Helms testified before Congress that the CIA had not intervened in Chile, but he was fined for lying and given a two-year suspended sentence.

As Chile appeared to be descending into chaos, General Augusto Pinochet Ugarte (1915–2006) led a bloody coup in September 1973. It is thought that Allende killed himself in his palace after the air force bombed it and troops invaded it.

To what extent was the USA responsible for the overthrow of Allende?

The overthrow of Allende's democratically elected government generated debates about the extent to which the USA had undermined Allende's government and bore responsibility for Pinochet's coup. It is difficult to say whether the coup would have succeeded without American aid. Leftists throughout the world were convinced that the CIA was directly responsible for the coup, despite a great deal of evidence to the contrary. Those who believe in the US involvement in the coup cite it as the worst case of imperialism in Nixon's presidency and there is no doubt that the Nixon administration had no qualms about the morality of overthrowing democratically elected governments. When asked about this, Kissinger replied: 'I don't see why we need to stand by and watch a country go Communist due to the irresponsibility of its own people. The issues are much too important for the Chilean voters to be left to decide for themselves.'

A significant assessment of the US role in Chile came from the US Senate investigation into the matter in 1975. The committee concluded that US economic policy under Nixon was 'a significant factor' in Chile's economic problems, that the US had made 'massive' efforts to destabilize Allende's government with financial aid to the media and opposition political parties, and that while there was 'no hard evidence' of direct US involvement in the

1973 coup, the US attitude to Allende had probably stimulated the opposition (see Source I). It should be borne in mind that the committee, led by the Democratic Senator Frank Church, consisted of six Democrats and five Republicans, reflecting the balance of power in the Senate in 1975. The committee was investigating the policies of a Republican president, but a president who was unpopular with Republicans as well as Democrats because of his involvement in the Watergate scandal (see page 120), at a time when Congress felt that the 'imperial presidency' had got out of hand and needed to be reined in.

(see Source I)

(see page 120)

SOURCE I

Extracts from the Church Report of 1975.

Covert US involvement in Chile in the decade between 1963 and 1973 was extensive and continuous ... The CIA attempted, directly, to foment a military coup in Chile [in 1970] ... The pattern of US covert action in Chile is striking but not unique. It arose in the context not only of American foreign policy, but also of covert United States involvement in other countries within and outside Latin America. The scale of CIA involvement in Chile was unusual but by no means unprecedented ... We had moved finally to advocating and encouraging the overthrow of a democratically elected government ... Did the threat posed by an Allende presidency justify covert American involvement in Chile? Did it justify the specific and unusual attempt to foment a military coup to deny Allende the presidency [in 1970]? ... On these questions the Committee members may differ ... Given the costs of covert action, it should be resorted to only to counter severe threats to the national security of the United States. It is far from clear that that was the case in Chile.

> **?** Using Source I and your own knowledge, how far would you consider the extracts from the report of the Church committee to be a fair assessment of US policy in Chile?

Pinochet's regime in Chile

Pinochet's regime aimed at political stability and economic improvement. He let the '**Chicago boys**' run the Chilean economy. Great believers in deregulation, they sold off state companies and cut government expenditure and trade barriers in what could be called a right-wing economic revolution, one result of which was an increased gap between rich and poor.

Pinochet's regime was exceptionally brutal. Tens of thousands were put in prison camps, several thousand executed, and around 30,000 Popular Front supporters fled the country. Pinochet ordered the hunting down and killing of opponents – even on the streets of Washington, DC. Chile was diplomatically ostracized by many in the international community because of such violations of human rights. Significantly, although Secretary of State Henry Kissinger's speech at the 1976 OAS meeting in Santiago, Chile, called for all member states to respect human rights and was interpreted as implicit criticism of Pinochet, Kissinger privately assured Pinochet of his support.

By the early 1980s there was widespread domestic opposition to Pinochet, but the economy had done reasonably well on his watch, which was

> **🔑 KEY TERM**
>
> **Chicago boys** Economists trained at the University of Chicago by economist Milton Friedman, who believed in a pure form of capitalism with minimal government intervention.

probably why he decided to hold elections in 1988. To his surprise he lost, and to the surprise of everyone else, he accepted the will of the electorate.

Operation Condor

Operation Condor was a Chilean initiative, officially launched in 1975 by the right-wing dictatorships in the **Southern Cone** of Latin America. It was an integrated intelligence system, designed to counter 'transnational subversive elements', to get rid of socialist and Communist influence, and to control opposition to the participating governments. As with so many other Cold War counterinsurgency operations, Operation Condor gave states an unprecedented repressive capability. Pinochet used Condor to kill or terrorize political opponents who might challenge his rule. The countries involved in Operation Condor co-operated closely in political assassinations and the kidnapping and 'transfer' of political refugees to their countries of origin. The military governments exchanged information about leftists residing in each other's countries so that, for example, a foreign leftist might 'disappear' in Chile. Operation Condor officially ended in 1983, with the fall of the Argentine dictatorship. It was responsible for the death, torture and disappearance of thousands. It has been estimated that around 50,000 died.

KEY TERM

Southern Cone Argentina, Brazil, Chile, Paraguay and Uruguay.

US involvement in Operation Condor

'Today, no one can seriously deny the atrocities the USA either committed or condoned in order to wage the Cold War in Latin America,' wrote historian Greg Grandin (2006). These 'atrocities' include US involvement in Operation Condor.

The USA has been slow to declassify information on the Cold War. For example, much remains to be learned about CIA activity in Argentina leading up to the 1962 military coup against Arturo Frondizi. However, information released in the last decade reveals the importance of the US provision of important organizational, financial and technical aid to Operation Condor. Historian Peter Kornbluh (2003) studied declassified documents that revealed that Kissinger not only knew about Condor but also covertly encouraged and perhaps abetted Pinochet's behaviour. In the twenty-first century, several Latin American courts and a French judge have tried but failed to obtain information from Kissinger on Operation Condor.

Nixon, Kissinger and US influence in the Western hemisphere

Was the USA losing influence in the Western hemisphere by the mid-1970s?

Chile was not the only problem in the Western hemisphere as far as Nixon was concerned. Countries such as Cuba and Mexico demonstrated an infuriating independence from US influence.

Cuba and revolutionaries

Nixon's best (some say only) friend Charles 'Bebe' Rebozo was a Cuban exile who hated Castro, but Nixon needed no encouragement to worry about

Castro and revolutionaries. He authorized the continuation of covert CIA operations against Cuba. These included pinprick raids, sabotage, recruitment and the organization of resistance cells.

Despite his hostility to Castro's Cuba, Nixon privately confirmed to the Soviets that he would never invade Cuba so long as they never based offensive missiles there. The Soviets were improving and expanding their base at Cienfuegos, but as there were no missiles there, Nixon did not object. The Cuba problem remained, but the situation was stable.

Although Cuba had greatly decreased its efforts to stimulate revolution in Latin America in the Nixon years (see page 210), the Nixon (1969–74) and Ford (1974–7) administrations were faced with increased terrorism and guerrilla activity there. Their response was to support military regimes such as that of Brazil.

Mexican declarations of independence

Mexico never waged the Cold War in the way that the USA would have liked. In 1954, Mexico was unwilling to back the USA over Guatemala and an American poll of Mexicans in 1956 found that 71 per cent of respondents did not favour either side in the Cold War. When Castro came to power in Cuba in 1959, President Adolfo López Mateos (1958–64) declared his desire to uphold the principles of self-determination and non-intervention, and US anti-Castro actions were openly criticized in the Mexican National Congress. After the Bay of Pigs, there were anti-American demonstrations in Mexico. Although Mexico was supportive of the US blockade during the Cuban Missiles Crisis, Mexico never joined the US crusade against Cuba. President Gustavo Díaz Ordaz (1964–70) sought an amicable relationship with the USA while nevertheless maintaining Mexican independence. Along with other Latin American leaders, he refused to approve the US intervention in the Dominican Republic in 1965.

In 1969, Nixon had problems with Díaz Ordaz, who criticized his policy of intercepting drugs along the US–Mexican border, as this policy adversely affected trade. Historian Burton Kirkwood (2000) claimed that Mexico then demonstrated 'a growing willingness to act independently of the USA', but Mexico's Cuban policy suggests that that had always been the case.

In answer to the question as to how Mexico was able to maintain relative independence in foreign policy, Lorenzo Meyer (2004) has argued that as long as Mexico's long-entrenched ruling party maintained stability (through a combination of repression and social reform), the USA refrained from criticism.

Venezuela and Canada

By 1975, Kissinger was expressing anxiety that the Latin Americans and others in the developing world were 'tending to form a rigid bloc of their own', which was 'particularly inappropriate for the Western hemisphere'. The nation leading this developing bloc in Latin America was wealthy Venezuela, one of the world's major oil producers at a time when oil prices were rocketing. Canada was also flexing its muscles. Half of Canadian companies were US owned, and Prime Minister Pierre Trudeau (whom Nixon hated) greatly increased controls on foreign investment in 1973. This was the first time that Canada had ever behaved thus, and the policy was clearly aimed at the USA. Trudeau also initiated trade with China and signed several trade treaties with the USSR.

'Hemispheric unity fragmented'?

According to historian Walter LaFaber, 'Hemispheric unity, which Americans tended to take for granted, had fragmented.' However, that is perhaps an exaggeration. Continuing unity was demonstrated by Operation Condor and the large number of Latin American countries with a US military group administering military assistance and advising the local military forces. For example, Guatemala's counterinsurgency unit was US trained, while Argentina, Chile and Brazil's national intelligence agencies were all funded and trained by the USA. On the other hand, as has been seen, there had long been frequent divergences of purpose and unease in US–Latin American relations, of which Mexico is an excellent example. Hemispheric unity had never been total, but it was certainly not fragmented.

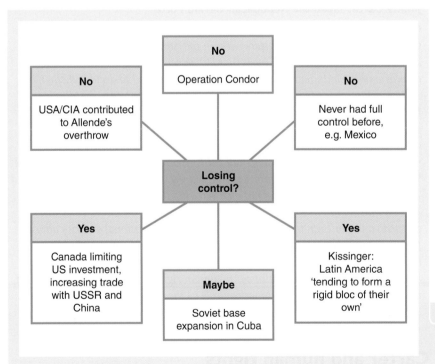

SUMMARY DIAGRAM

President Nixon and control of the Western hemisphere

President Carter, human rights, the Panama Canal and Nicaragua

▶ **Key question:** *What implications did President Carter's policies have for Latin America?*

When campaigning for the presidency in 1976, the former Democrat Governor of Georgia, Jimmy Carter, promised a very new and different kind of foreign policy from his Republican predecessors, Nixon and Ford. He said the USA should 'replace balance of power politics with world order politics'. During his first two years as president (1977–9), and in keeping with his campaign promise to introduce a new kind of foreign policy, he emphasized human rights, 'North–South dialogue' on economic issues, and an end to the 'cynical' and 'dangerous' sale of arms to foreign countries.

SOURCE J

An extract from Robert Schulzinger, *U.S. Diplomacy Since 1900*, published in 2002, describing the 1976 presidential election, in which the Democrat Jimmy Carter faced the Republican Gerald Ford.

Carter's apparent sincerity, his promise 'I'll never lie to you,' and his ostentatious Christianity won many supporters early in the campaign; late August polls showed him ahead of Ford by more than 30 percentage points. Then disillusionment with both candidates set in as voters had to decide whether, in Arthur Schlesinger's words, to choose a candidate afflicted with the 'dumbness factor' (Ford) or the 'weirdness factor' (Carter). They chose a change … Shortly after the election, Carter's aide Hamilton Jordan explained that the new administration's diplomacy would mark a clean break with the discredited policies and tired individuals who had led American diplomacy since the Second World War. 'If after the inauguration you find Cy Vance as Secretary of State and Zbigniew Brzezinski as head of national security, then I would say we failed. And I'd quit … You're going to see new faces, new ideas.' In December, Carter selected Vance for Secretary of State and Brzezinski as national security adviser. Jordan did not quit. A new administration came to town vowing to put Vietnam behind the United States, open a dialogue between the rich and poor nations, recapture the American commitment to human rights, place the Soviet Union on the defensive, and reduce the American role as the major arms supplier to the world.

How far did Carter promote human rights?

→ Carter and human rights

During the 1970s, the human rights records of Latin American governments that received military and economic aid from the USA were increasingly debated. Congress was critical of Nixon's support for repressive foreign governments and in 1973 and in 1975 put legal limitations on US aid to such governments. Carter was very much in sympathy with this mood. When campaigning for the presidency, he suggested that the Republicans had not shown an appropriate interest in human rights violations and promised that his commitment to the promotion of human rights was 'absolute' and that human rights would be 'the soul of our foreign policy'.

Human rights: successes

Encouraged by Congress, Carter created a Bureau of Human Rights within the State Department. The bureau published an annual account of the state of human rights in foreign countries and, in contrast to the Nixon administration, criticized nations such as the Philippines, South Korea, Chile, Brazil and Argentina for human rights abuses. Carter called for these countries to release political prisoners and used US economic power against them, cutting economic aid, and pressuring the World Bank, the IMF and the Inter-American Development Bank to halt assistance. Carter's emphasis on human rights encouraged military regimes such as those in Argentina, Brazil and Chile, to moderate their behaviour, and helped persuade President Joaquín Balaguer of the Dominican Republic to step down after an electoral defeat.

Human rights: failures

Carter's human rights campaign did not always go well. He encouraged Soviet dissidents such as Andrei Sakharov who were demanding more political freedom but this damaged the possibility of progress in the arms reductions talks that he was simultaneously conducting with the USSR. Furthermore, the Soviets pointed out that because Carter was trying to improve relations with China, he said little about the thousands of political prisoners there. Carter's pro-China policy even led him to support the Chinese-backed Pol Pot regime in Cambodia, which had millions of Cambodians murdered in the 'killing fields'.

Carter's ambassador to the UN, Andrew Young, subsequently admitted that Carter's human rights policy was never 'thought out and planned' and therefore ineffective. The greatest problem was that Carter felt he had to continue to support extremely unpleasant regimes when he considered that US interests were at stake. He favoured the repressive Shah of Iran because of Iranian oil. At a formal dinner in which the Shah was the guest of honour, Carter congratulated him on making Iran 'an island of stability' in the Middle East and for deserving 'the respect and the admiration and love which your people give you'. Within a year, the Shah was overthrown by a popular revolution. Carter also supported the brutal dictatorship of Jean-Claude 'Baby Doc' Duvalier in Haiti, which was considered a bulwark against Castro and Communism.

Refugees

Carter had to deal with tens of thousands of immigrants fleeing from countries where their human rights had been abused. Again, his record was mixed. Anxious to score points in the Cold War, Carter allowed 100,000 Cubans to enter the USA because he disapproved of Castro's regime. This went down badly with voters in states such as Florida which were ill-equipped to handle such an influx (see page 207). Carter also let in tens of thousands of 'boat people' who took to the seas to flee the Communist governments of Vietnam, Laos and Cambodia. However, when thousands of Haitian refugees from tyranny landed on Florida's shores, they were unwelcome because of US support for Duvalier. Carter was also ambivalent about the Nicaraguan dictator Somoza (see page 185).

While Carter's record on human rights was mixed, he played a vital part in the restoration of Panamanian sovereignty.

How new was Carter's Panama Canal policy?

Carter and the Panama Canal

There had been a long history of Panamanian resentment against the Canal Zone, the five-mile wide strip of territory alongside the canal (see the map on page 147). In the Canal Zone, Panamanians were treated as second-class citizens. They could be jailed under American law in US courts where proceedings were conducted in English, a language many Panamanians did not understand. The Panamanians had the low-paid, unskilled jobs in the zone, while Americans operated the locks and piloted the ships. The Panamanian government said US actions in the Canal Zone constituted an outstanding example of 'Yankee colonialism', and other Latin American nations joined Panama in putting pressure on the USA to give up its control of the zone and the canal.

President Ford and the Panama Canal

In 1975, the Ford administration expressed willingness to sign a treaty yielding the US perpetual lease on the Canal Zone. Panama wanted the Americans out in 20 or 30 years. However, the prospects for any treaty getting through the US Congress were bleak: 38 senators signed a letter opposing any forfeit of US sovereignty, and only 33 votes were needed to block Senate ratification of the treaty. When Ronald Reagan ran against Ford for the Republican nomination for the presidency in 1976, he accused Ford of 'giving away our canal', so Ford halted the negotiations. When the talks stopped, the Panamanian leader Omar Torrijos made life difficult for the US United Fruit Company, and there were more anti-American riots.

President Carter and the Panama Canal treaties

Determined to demonstrate his new and more moral foreign policy, Carter signed two treaties with Panama. One treaty gave legal jurisdiction over the Canal Zone to Panama, said the USA would continue to operate and to defend the canal until 31 December 1999 when Panama would take over, and guaranteed the jobs of Americans operating the canal. The second treaty gave the USA the right to defend the 'neutrality of the waterway' in perpetuity.

Carter's treaties met great opposition in Congress and among the public, 78 per cent of whom opposed them. However, his administration conducted an effective campaign to change minds. Carter himself took questions on a radio phone-in. Eventually, Congress was won over. In 1978 the Senate ratified both treaties, although Carter and Panama had to accept a violation of Panamanian sovereignty in a clause that said US forces would keep the canal open after 1999.

Here, Carter had lived up to all his promises of a new and more decent foreign policy. It was a considerable triumph to obtain congressional assent to this American retreat from empire. According to historian Walter LaFaber (2008), 'Carter and the Senate had scored the most important advance in USA–Latin American relations since the 1930s.'

President Carter and Nicaragua

← **What was new about Carter's policy toward Nicaragua?**

Nicaragua was one of the most impoverished nations of Latin America. Its three million people had suffered under the rule of the Somoza family dictatorship since 1936. While the Somoza regime was strengthened by the USA, ordinary Nicaraguans suffered some of the worst problems in Latin America. Life expectancy was less than 50 years, and half the population was illiterate. The Alliance for Progress improved the Nicaraguan economy, but only the middle and upper classes benefited, in particular the Somoza dynasty and their friends.

Anastasio Somoza Debayle

The Somoza dynasty was loyal to the USA. In 1961, the CIA trained the Cuban invasion force in Nicaragua, and in 1965, Nicaragua sent troops to aid the US invasion of the Dominican Republic. Anastasio Somoza Debayle came to power in 1972 and he had particularly close relations with the USA. He had been educated there and had influential friends in the US Congress. He prided himself on being a great American ally, asking, 'Who else votes with the USA in the United Nations one thousand percent of the time?' The USA trained his officers at the jungle warfare schools at Fort Bragg and in the Panama Canal Zone.

Despite his popularity with the US government, Somoza was hated by most Nicaraguans. He was probably the most corrupt and greedy member of the dynasty. When a large earthquake in Managua killed 10,000 people and left 50,000 homeless in 1972, Somoza illegally appropriated $500 million sent from all over the world to help relieve the suffering. Under continuous US pressure to be democratic, Somoza held and won a fixed election in 1974 (he famously talked of 'ballots for my friends, bullets for my enemies'). In January 1978 Pedro Joaquín Chamorro was assassinated. Chamorro was a member of an old élite family, editor of the leading Nicaraguan newspaper *La Prensa*, and a leading opponent of Somoza. Nicaraguans received small fees for giving blood, and in a series of articles emotively entitled the 'Vampire Chronicles', Chamorro had denounced Somoza for selling it to the USA. Everyone assumed Somoza was behind the assassination, which was the last straw for many upper-class Nicaraguans. While willing to overlook Somoza's mistreatment of Indians and peasants, they decided that if Chamorro could be assassinated, none of them were safe.

Frente Sandinista de Liberación Nacional

From the mid-1970s, Somoza faced considerable opposition from an urban middle-class Marxist guerrilla movement called the Frente Sandinista de Liberación Nacional (Sandinista National Liberation Front or FSLN).

The Sandinista movement had been established in 1961, inspired by and named after Augusto César Sandino (1895–1934), an impoverished Marxist guerrilla leader who had described the USA as 'the enemy of our race' and conducted an effective guerrilla campaign against the central government and against the US troops that occupied Nicaragua. The Sandinistas had few supporters until the mid-1970s, when they gained publicity and funds (a $5 million ransom) through taking diplomats and other important individuals hostage at a party in 1974. From this point onwards, the FSLN became important opponents to Somoza.

In 1975, there were around 150 Sandinista guerrillas, many trained and encouraged in Cuba. Cuba, Panama and Costa Rica supplied the revolutionaries with arms and they also received Soviet aid. In 1977, their numbers increased in response to Somoza's brutal counter-insurgency operations. They gained a great deal of support from the poor and the Catholic Church. From 1968, Archbishop Miguel Obando y Bravo was an outspoken critic of the Somoza regime and advocate of social change. He was one of a group among the Catholic clergy who were determined that religion should help to improve the lot of the poor in this life, not just the next life, and their **liberation theology** (see box) helped to politicize and mobilize many poor Nicaraguans.

Fall from power

Basically, Anastasio Somoza Debayle fell from power in 1979 because he had alienated most of the population, but it was the Sandinistas who played the largest part in his overthrow and they came to dominate the new revolutionary government. Carter's response to this new revolutionary government would prove a good test of his new and moral foreign policy.

 **KEY TERM**

Liberation theology Latin American Catholic clergy movement, inspiring parishioners to work for change in this life, rather than waiting for their reward in heaven.

Liberation theology

Liberation theology was a minority Catholic movement that emerged in Latin America in the 1950s. It grew rapidly in the 1960s inspired by the Second Vatican Council (1962–5) and the conference of Latin American bishops at Medellín, Colombia (1968), both of which looked afresh at the Church's role in the modern world and urged the Catholic clergy to work with the poor. Latin America had the biggest concentration of Catholics in the world, so where the Church (or some members of it) led, it was likely that many people would follow. Priestly followers of liberation theology emphasized Jesus Christ the revolutionary: 'The spirit of the Lord is upon me, because he hath anointed me to preach the gospel to the poor; he has sent me to heal the broken hearted, to preach deliverance to the captives, and recovering of sight to the blind, to set at liberty them that are bruised' (Luke 5:18).

When priests stopped telling their impoverished flocks to be patient and to wait for their reward in heaven, and urged them to work for change in this world, the potential for mass participation in revolutionary movements greatly increased. The socially revolutionary words of Christ, 'The meek shall inherit the earth', were potentially explosive in the Latin American context. The 'theology of liberation' said that Christian charity had to be interpreted as a commitment to work for the liberation of the poor and downtrodden, by violence if necessary. This theology was influenced by Marxist ideas of class struggle, exploitation and imperialism. Radical Catholics allied with revolutionary socialists in the 1960s and 1970s, often working alongside the poor in factories in shanty towns. Some clergy supported armed insurrection, and some even joined Marxist guerrillas: Camilo Torres died fighting alongside a guerrilla force in Colombia in 1966. Radicalism was not confined to the lesser clergy. Several distinguished bishops, such as Dom Hélder Câmara of Brazil, gained world-wide publicity by their support for strikers.

Naturally, the Catholic Church was divided over liberation theology. The vast majority of the clergy and laity disliked it. In 1980, Pope John Paul II visited Brazil, forbade the clergy from holding political office, and condemned violence as a means of social change.

A moral foreign policy and the Sandinistas

Carter's attitude to the Sandinistas was always ambivalent, both when they led the opposition to Somoza, and when they were in government themselves.

Carter and Somoza's overthrow

From 1977 onwards, Carter became increasingly critical of Somoza and his human rights abuses. He withdrew financial and military aid. Historian Edwin Williamson (2009) claimed this was crucial to the Sandinistas' success in overthrowing Somoza but that is arguable. As has been seen, Somoza generated large-scale opposition. Furthermore, although Carter cut off US financial and military aid, he was unwilling to see the end of this staunch Cold War ally and tried, unsuccessfully, to mobilize the OAS for an intervention that would save Somoza.

The US ambassador to the UN, Andrew Young, worked to make the USA more sympathetic to the poor in Latin American states and he persuaded the Carter administration to accept the demise of the Somoza dictatorship. When in 1978 the OAS called for the 'immediate and definitive replacement of the Somoza regime' by 'a democratic government', Carter reluctantly endorsed the call but then worked, again unsuccessfully, to arrange a new government that would exclude the Sandinistas. The Somoza dictatorship was finally overthrown in July 1979 and a coalition government containing moderates and Sandinistas was established.

Carter and the Sandinista regime

Carter supported the new revolutionary government with an aid package worth over $80 million. In September 1980, he promised to continue giving aid to Nicaragua, but was developing doubts about the new regime. The Sandinistas had come to dominate the government and moderates and even some revolutionaries had left it in protest against their domination. Carter increasingly perceived their rhetoric and policies as damaging to the USA. The Nicaraguan representative at the UN said some Americans sought a Somozan restoration, and although Nicaragua had initially sought to follow a non-aligned foreign policy, the Sandinistas were moving closer to Cuba. Cuba had helped the Sandinista revolution and sent thousands of teachers, health experts and military advisers to help their new regime. Also, the Sandinistas began to supply revolutionaries in El Salvador in 1980. Carter himself had demonstrated disapproval of the vicious Salvadoran regime, cutting off aid to the government after four American Catholic churchwomen were sexually assaulted and murdered by the Salvadoran military, while the Salvadoran authorities did nothing. However, Carter feared that the Sandinistas might promote further revolutions in Latin America. Finally, Carter's aid to the Sandinistas was causing him problems during the 1980 presidential election campaign. The Republican candidate Ronald Reagan accused him of assisting the development of another Cuba and promised that if he were elected he would replace the Sandinistas with a 'free and independent' government.

Historian Walter LaFaber (2008) concluded that at the end of Carter's presidency, his Latin American policy 'lay in fragments'. The problem was, as Che Guevara had said, that if the USA unleashed the forces of reform in Latin America, those forces were likely to work against what the USA perceived to be its economic and security interests. For one brief shining moment, in the Panama Canal treaties, Carter had clearly and selflessly put a new and moral foreign policy into place, but traditional perceptions of the responsibilities of presidential power and the wishes of the American electorate ensured that this would be a rare occurrence. Carter's uncertain response to the Sandinistas saw him dithering between the old and the new.

SOURCE K

Extract about Jimmy Carter from *The Contemporary History of Latin America* by Argentine historian Tulio Halperín Donghi, published in 1996.

A considerable number of Latin Americans probably owe their lives to his efforts – something that cannot be said of any other US president – and he is no doubt the only former chief executive of that country ever to be greeted cordially by ordinary citizens on a private visit to the streets of a Latin American city, as occurred in Buenos Aires in 1984.

> Looking at what this famous Argentine historian writes in Source K and elsewhere (see page 88), what would you infer about his viewpoint on US foreign policy and how much would you value his opinions? **?**

New		Old
Emphasized human rights	*but*	Supported some dictators
Returned canal to Panamanian sovereignty	*but*	Congress inserted clause violating Panamanian sovereignty
Gave some support to Sandinistas	*but*	Often half-hearted

SUMMARY DIAGRAM

President Carter, human rights, the Panama Canal and Nicaragua

Chapter summary

From Kennedy to Carter: US foreign policy in Latin America 1961–81

Kennedy attempted to introduce a more constructive US approach to Latin America. His Alliance for Progress had limited success there, but his less ambitious Peace Corps was more successful. Kennedy inherited from Eisenhower the plan for a US-sponsored invasion of Cuba by Cuban exiles. The invasion was a humiliating disaster that strengthened Castro. Cuba continued to be a focal point in the Cold War when despite Kennedy's warnings the Soviets put missiles in Cuba in 1962, motivated by balance of power considerations and by Cuba's vulnerability to US invasion. Kennedy chose to 'quarantine' Cuba and Khrushchev backed down because of US military superiority and Kennedy's promise not to invade Cuba. The Cuban Missiles Crisis humiliated Castro, played a part in Khrushchev's fall, frightened the USA and the USSR into a Cold War thaw, and helped lead to a multipolar world.

Johnson downgraded Kennedy's Alliance for Progress because it was expensive and because military governments seemed better for stability. He intervened in the Dominican Republic to support a junta against the democratically elected government, motivated by fear of Communism and, some say, a desire to demonstrate strength.

Nixon contributed to the overthrow of a democratically elected Marxist government in Chile, then supported Pinochet's brutal military regime and Operation Condor. Nevertheless, some people thought the USA was losing its power and influence in the Western hemisphere by the mid-1970s.

Carter came to the presidency having promised a new kind of foreign policy. He talked of promoting human rights, but compromised with dictators when it suited US interests. He reluctantly gave up on the brutal Somoza dictatorship in Nicaragua and then equally reluctantly supported the revolutionary Sandinista government. However, he got Congress to agree to give Panama the Panama Canal.

 Examination advice

How to answer 'why' questions

Questions that ask <u>why</u> are prompting you to consider a variety of explanations. Each of these will need to be explained in full. It is also possible to question the question. This means that you can disagree with the basic premise of the question. In this case, you must present full counter-arguments and be prepared to expound on these.

Example

> <u>Why</u> was the Bay of Pigs invasion a foreign policy disaster for President Kennedy?

1. To answer this question successfully, you should first explain what took place at the Bay of Pigs in April 1961. Next discuss the various reasons the invasion was a foreign policy disaster. These might include:
   - humiliation in the eyes of the world

- an increase in Castro's popularity
- closer relations between Castro and the USSR
- a seeming violation of international law by the USA.

Stronger answers will provide the historical context in which Kennedy acted, as well as how President Kennedy attempted to recover from the fiasco. Do not spend a great deal of time, however, on discussing the Cuban Missiles Crisis. Your primary focus should be on the Bay of Pigs.

2. Before writing the answer take at least five minutes to write a short outline. In your outline for this question, you could include key points about the invasion and supporting evidence for it being a disaster for Kennedy, such as:

- *Kennedy inherited the CIA plan from Eisenhower. Trapped by his own anti-Communist rhetoric.*
- *April 1961: 1600 Cuban exiles trained and equipped by the CIA landed at the Bay of Pigs (Playa Girón). Plan was to stimulate an uprising against Castro. Military disaster. Completely overwhelmed by Cuban army within two days.*
- *Kennedy humiliated by failure and US complicity in an illegal action.*
- *Castro's popularity in Cuba and elsewhere soared. He was able to defeat 'Yankee imperialism'.*
- *Castro's position in Cuba secured.*
- *Cuba moved closer to the Soviet Union. Signed economic and defence links with USSR.*
- *Britain, a key US ally, unsupportive of the invasion.*
- *USSR became more involved in Latin America because it felt the USA was weaker than originally supposed.*
- *Aftermath: CIA unleashed Operation Mongoose. Covert operations against Cuba. Soviet missiles placed in Cuba. Dangerous crisis resulted.*
- *Increased Latin American distrust of the USA.*

3. In your introduction, you should:
   - Briefly define the Bay of Pigs invasion.
   - State your thesis. This might be: 'The failure of the US-backed Bay of Pigs invasion represented an enormous foreign policy fiasco for President Kennedy.'
   - Provide the general themes you will use to support this idea.

   An example of a good introductory paragraph for this question is given on page 192.

In April 1961, a force of US-trained and armed Cuban exiles invaded Cuba. The goal was to foster an uprising against Fidel Castro. The attempt was disastrous from the beginning of the operation. Consequently, the recently elected President Kennedy suffered what was to become a terrible foreign policy disaster. Castro became ever more popular, the USA was humiliated by backing such a poorly planned adventure, and the USSR stepped up its involvement in Latin America. The failure at the Bay of Pigs also led to further CIA covert activities in Cuba and may have been partially to blame for Khrushchev's decision to place missiles on the island.

4. In the body of your essay, write at least one paragraph on each of the major themes you raised in your introduction.
5. In the conclusion, you should tie together the themes you have explored and how they relate directly to the idea that the Bay of Pigs invasion was a foreign policy disaster for President Kennedy.
6. Now try writing a complete answer to the question following the advice above.

Examination practice

Below are two exam-style questions for you to practise on this topic.

1 Assess the successes and failures of Kennedy's Alliance for Progress plan.
   (For guidance on how to answer 'assess' questions, see page 39.)

2 Compare and contrast Nixon's and Carter's foreign policy in Latin America.
   (For guidance on how to answer 'compare and contrast' questions, see page 129.)

CHAPTER 8

Cuba in the Cold War

This chapter continues the study of the Cold War in Cuba. It looks at Castro's domestic policies, and his relations with Latin America, the USA, the USSR and the 'Third World'. You need to consider the following questions throughout this chapter:

✪ How were Castro's domestic policies affected by the Cold War?

✪ How and why was Cuba important in the Cold War?

✪ How successful was the Cuban Revolution?

 ## Castro's domestic policies

▶ *Key question: How were Castro's domestic policies affected by the Cold War?*

The consolidation of the regime

Castro's 1959 revolution had not been a Communist revolution. He had made his ideological position clear before 1959:

- Castro was a Cuban nationalist, desirous of independence from foreign domination.
- He sought a fairer society. His 'History will absolve me' speech (see page 138) had called for land reform, rent reductions, and better and more widely available health care and education.
- He wanted to modernize and diversify the economy.
- Castro favoured the restoration of the 1940 Cuban constitution, which had included provision of democratic elections.

Although his brother Raúl and Che Guevara were at the very least Communist sympathizers, this was not a Communist manifesto and Fidel Castro's relationship with the Communist party was strained. Indeed, after Batista's overthrow, Castro seemed willing to work with political moderates. He put middle-class figures into prominent positions, including the anti-Communist liberal Manuel Urrutia, whom Castro declared to be President of Cuba. For a few months reform seemed to be proceeding smoothly. The new regime introduced lower prices for medicines, phone calls and electricity, a minimum wage for cane cutters and moderate land redistribution (June 1959).

However, by November 1959 most of the moderates such as Urrutia had either resigned or been forced out of office and Cuba was being governed by

> **What were the causes and consequences of Castro's domestic policies?**

a cabinet containing Castro and his close friends and associates. Despite having called for the restoration of the Cuban constitution of 1940 and for elections, Castro now rejected elections and the idea of a multi-party state, partly because that would empower pro-American Cubans and the USA had quickly demonstrated its dislike of Castro's policies. The basic issue between the USA and Fidel Castro was the nature of the Cuban economy.

? Look at Source A. What point was Fidel Castro trying to make?

SOURCE A

Cuba's leader, Fidel Castro, cutting sugarcane in 1965.

Economic problems and solutions

The Cuban economy was highly problematic, dependent on sugar and dominated by the USA. Castro and many of his followers deeply resented the American stranglehold on the Cuban economy:

- The USA had more investments in Cuba than in any other Latin American country. Between 1953 and 1958 US investment in Cuba increased from $686 million to $1 billion.
- Ninety per cent of Cuba's telephone and electricity services, all of its oil, railways and nickel mines, and most of its banks, were US-owned.
- The US Mafia ran Cuba's gambling and brothels and dominated the tourist industry.
- Forty per cent of Cuban sugar was produced in US-owned refineries.
- The USA bought 58 per cent of Cuba's annual sugar production.
- Sugar constituted 80 per cent of all Cuba's exports, and two-thirds of Cuban sugar went to the USA.
- Three-quarters of Cuban imports were from the USA.

- While the sugarcane **monoculture** was highly profitable for the plantation owners, many of whom were American, it left Cuba having to spend a great deal on American grain, flour and rice, in order to feed the Cuban population. Cuba took one-third of all US-produced rice.
- 150,000 relatively prosperous Cubans worked for American firms.

Another problem for Castro was that his new regime was short of trained economists and of **entrepreneurs**, most of whom had quickly fled to the USA. He therefore turned to the UN Economic Committee for Latin America (see page 29), which urged Cuba to industrialize. As it was difficult to industrialize with a population that was 40 per cent illiterate, Castro used teenage teachers fired with revolutionary enthusiasm to teach people to read. This was done speedily and effectively and gained favourable world-wide publicity in 1961.

Cuban economic problems were exacerbated in November 1960 when the USA put an embargo on trade with Cuba in response to Castro's confiscations of American properties and businesses (see page 148) and his increasing economic contact with the USSR. Castro tried several solutions to Cuba's economic problems, including diversification, nationalization and moral motivation for the workforce, but by the late 1960s he decided that the answer lay in the **Sovietization** of Cuba. American hostility to Castro's rejection of US economic domination helped ensure that, given the Cold War context, Cuba would become Communist.

When did Castro's Cuba become Communist?

Fidel Castro's ideological evolution has been much debated. Had he always planned a Marxist revolution rather than liberal democratic reform? Some argue that he was a secret Communist who, once in power, 'stole' the revolution from other opponents of Batista. Others argue that it was the influence of his brother Raúl and of Che Guevara that made him a Marxist while in the mountains. Some claim he became Marxist in his early days in power because liberals were opposed to fundamental change. Others argue that Castro was a patriot first, and Communist second. Finally, and probably most persuasively, some suggest he was essentially a pragmatist, who became a Marxist because he needed Soviet aid in the face of American hostility.

In the first year of Castro's rule, his relations with the Cuban Communist Party were frequently hostile, and there were some signs that US–Cuban relations might be relatively amicable. It is quite difficult to pinpoint the turning points in these initially fluid relationships, but the stiff American protest against Castro's initial and moderate land reform in the summer of 1959 was significant. During 1960 it became increasingly clear that the Cuban Communist Party was developing into Fidel Castro's friend and that the USA had developed into his enemy. By early 1960, he had marginalized, imprisoned or exiled all except those who were publicly socialist and anti-

KEY TERM

Monoculture
Concentration and dependency on a single crop.

Entrepreneurs Innovative and ambitious business people.

Sovietization Modelling the economy, in particular, on the USSR's.

American. In April 1961, following American air raids on Cuba, Castro spoke for the first time of 'our socialist revolution'. From December 1961, he began to describe himself as a Marxist–Leninist.

Why did Castro's Cuba become Communist?

Castro's Cuba went Communist for several reasons. He was sympathetic to a Communist-style **command economy** that redistributed wealth. The Cuban Communist Party was a well-organized political party, and as Castro's regime lacked such organization and structure, he found the expertise of the Communists useful. Finally, and perhaps most important of all, going Communist was a way of declaring independence from US domination.

The Eisenhower administration quickly indicated its disapproval of Castro's regime, as when Eisenhower avoided meeting the Cuban leader (see page 146). The American obsession with whether or not Fidel Castro was a Communist was offensive to Cuban nationalism, suggesting as it did that only a non-Communist regime in Cuba would be acceptable to the USA. Given the American attitude, it is hardly surprising in the Cold War context that Castro turned to, and was welcomed by, the USSR.

Castro was very much in the nationalist tradition of José Martí and while there was a fund of anti-Americanism for Castro to draw on and to use to unite the Cuban people, there was no anti-Soviet feeling or tradition. Economic or defensive arrangements with the Soviets were less likely to arouse Cuban nationalism and to disrupt national unity. From July 1959, the USSR bought more and more Cuban sugar and in early 1960, Khrushchev made it clear to Castro that he did not see the Cuban Communist Party as 'an intermediary' between Castro and the Soviet government. So, Castro had nothing to fear from the Cuban Communist Party if he were to go Communist, and a great deal to lose if he did not.

Significantly, after having declared himself a Marxist–Leninist, Castro had frequent doctrinal disagreements with both the USSR and the Cuban Communist Party, which he reorganized in 1965 in order to ensure his control. His was personal rather than party rule and, without the Cold War, Castro's Cuba might not have taken the direction it did. The tradition of US domination and intervention probably made great tension between the USA and Castro's nationalist regime inevitable, but the Sovietization of Cuba was surely a product primarily of Cold War tensions – ostracized by the USA, Cuba naturally turned to the other side in the Cold War. The Soviets, for their part, were happy to have a Communist state under 100 miles from the USA.

The Soviet economic solution

The Soviets advised Castro to forget about the emphasis on diversification and industrialization, encouraged the tradition of monoculture, and provided a guaranteed market for the Cuban sugar crop. In 1972, Castro made an economic agreement with the USSR, receiving a massive Soviet subsidy that the Cuban leader characterized as 'a model of truly fraternal, internationalized and revolutionary relations'.

From 1975 to 1985, Cuba experienced great economic growth, funded by Soviet subsidies. When he reorganized the Cuban Communist Party along more orthodox Soviet lines in 1975, a grateful Castro publicly confessed that he had previously lacked the humility to take advantage of 'the rich experience of socialism elsewhere'. Soviet subsidies helped fund an education system and medical care that were second to none in Latin America although, as always in Cuba's past, there were those who voted with their feet and fled to the USA (see page 206) in search of greater prosperity and to get away from what had become essentially a one-party state in the Soviet mould.

Castro and the retention of power

There were many in the USA who found it difficult to understand how Castro could retain power. He survived the Bay of Pigs invasion, CIA assassination attempts, and periods when the Cuban people did not have enough food and might have been expected to attempt another change of regime. The following subsections explain why.

> ← What methods did Castro use to retain power?

Charisma

Many observers agreed on Castro's charisma. The *New York Times* correspondent Ruby Hart Phillips observed him making a victory speech in Havana in January 1960, and wrote, 'As I watched Castro I realized the magic of his personality … He seemed to weave a hypnotic net over his listeners.'

Many people found his speeches impressive. Castro could speak for four or five hours, in pouring rain or blazing sun, outlasting members of his audience who sometimes had to be carried away by paramedics.

Control of the media

Castro handled the media well. Another *New York Times* reporter, Tad Szulc, wrote in 1986 that '[Castro] always insisted that propaganda was vital in mobilizing the masses for a revolution … He was a natural television personality and, literally, he sold the revolution on TV.'

All criticisms in the media were silenced by May 1960.

Ruthlessness

Although there were no bloodbaths under Castro, he was ruthless when necessary. The American media estimated that around 500 Batista's supporters were killed on Castro's accession to power. He quickly developed several state organs of repression, notably the political police or G-2 and a secret service, the *Dirección General de Inteligencia* or DGI, which was organized with help from the **KGB**. Saboteurs and opposition groups were tracked down by 800,000-strong Committees for the Defence of the Revolution (CDRs). Again, the Cold War had an impact on domestic politics,

KEY TERM

KGB The Soviet secret service.

both in the intensity of the opposition to Castro, which was encouraged by the USA, and in the intensity of the repression, which was inspired both by the US hostility and by Soviet practices. Former friends and allies were marginalized if they were considered too bourgeois or too radical. Che Guevara's expedition to Bolivia in 1966 probably owed a great deal to his desire to get away from disagreements with Castro.

The Cuban army

By 1962, Commander-in-Chief Fidel Castro had the largest army in Latin America. With more than a quarter of a million men, the army was exceptionally loyal to Castro. The officers were well aware that Cuban exiles in the USA repeatedly said that they would purge the military hierarchy if Castro was overthrown. There was also the Cuban **militia**, which served as an important counterbalance to the power of the army. Castro's lightly armed militia of 100,000 citizens was decisive in repelling the Bay of Pigs invasion, after which their numbers rose to 300,000.

Mass organizations

Castro mobilized and wooed mass organizations in support of his regime. Well aware of the potential of trade union and student power, he carefully monitored the leadership of the Federation of University Students and in 1970 was willing to admit to trade unionists that his economic policies would benefit from more consultation with them.

Exiles

Castro allowed those who disliked his regime to leave the country, which decreased the number of potential opponents. By 1962 around a quarter of a million had departed, and more were to follow. Most went to the USA, and their identification with the national enemy helped strengthen Castro's regime. The American threat was used to rally and unite Cubans and to increase, justify and sustain Castro's control. Castro successfully exploited nationalist resentment against the USA, particularly at the time of the Bay of Pigs (1961) (see page 162).

Popular policies

Many Cubans greatly admired and revered Castro. He had rid Cuba of Batista and many of his policies were popular. Cuba's social services developed into the best in Latin America. Castro's land redistribution policy won him a great deal of support and gave many Cubans a vested interest in the continuation of Castro's regime because if the anti-Castro exiles were to return and take charge of Cuba, they would reclaim their land. While many Latin American dictators enriched themselves shamelessly, Castro was not interested in financial gain. He even ordered the expropriation of his family farm, leaving his mother with only the living quarters. As well as improving the standard of living of Cubans, his foreign policy gave them a pride and a sense of identity that none of his predecessors had managed. After many

KEY TERM

Militia Reserve citizens' army.

years under US domination, Castro's Cuba had successfully declared and maintained its independence from its giant neighbour.

Soviet support

Soviet support helped Castro retain power. Given the history of US interventions in Cuba, the USA would probably have got rid of Castro had it not been for fear of a clash with the USSR. Soviet subsidies were vital to the Cuban economy and funded the social services that many Cubans so greatly valued.

Conclusions

Fidel Castro would have instituted a leftist regime even without the Cold War, but the Cold War did have an impact on his domestic policies. American antagonism contributed to Castro's rejection of the multi-party state model, although the unimpressive performance of the different parties in early twentieth-century Cuba and his own authoritarian tendencies also affected his decision.

When the USA stopped buying Cuban sugar, the Cold War encouraged and enabled Castro to turn to the USSR for support and aid. Indeed, the American antagonism and trade embargo left him with little choice, and contributed greatly to his decisions to follow the Soviet command economy model and to concentrate upon sugar production. For their part, the Soviets funded Castro's social services.

The Soviets frequently found him extremely irritating (see page 205) but continued to support him because he was a useful Cold War trophy – a Communist regime under 100 miles from the USA. Soviet support inevitably made Castro declare Cuba to be a Communist country and part of the Soviet bloc. Given Castro's nationalism, his following of the Soviet line, for example over the Soviet invasion of Czechoslovakia in 1968, would surely have been an unthinkable development without the Cold War context. The Cold War thus had a great impact on his domestic policies, in conception, execution and success.

> **To what extent did the Cold War have an impact on Castro's domestic policies?**

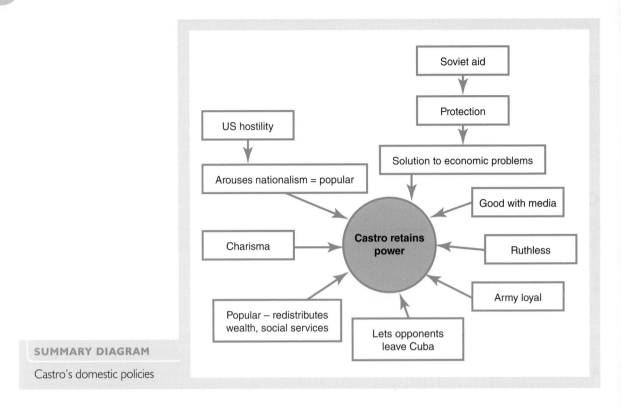

Castro's domestic policies

② Cuban foreign policy

▶ Key question: How and why was Cuba important in the Cold War?

Without the Cold War, a leftist revolution on a Caribbean island would surely not have made a global impact, but the Cold War context gave Cuba the opportunity to play a vital role in international relations.

Was Cuba a Soviet satellite?

Cuba and the superpowers

Relations with the USA and USSR 1959–60

At first, Castro attracted considerable support from American liberals, including the revisionist historian William Appleman Williams (see page 21). However, given US–Cuban history, conflict with Castro's radical nationalist government was surely inevitable, even without the Cold War.

In the early months of Castro's regime, it seemed possible that US–Cuban relations could be relatively cordial. The USA recognized Castro's government immediately and crowds greeted him warmly during his spring 1959 visit to the USA. On the other hand, despite Castro's poor relations with the Cuban Communist Party, there was much talk of Castro's supposed Communism in the American media and in the Eisenhower administration.

It could be argued that the first great turning point in relations between Castro and the USA came with the land reform of June 1959, which prompted the Eisenhower administration to agree to 'accelerate the development of an opposition in Cuba which would bring about … a new government favorable to US interests'. Sometimes the USA advocated land reform, as in the Alliance for Progress (see page 154) and Vietnam (see page 96), which raises the question as to whether the prime American motivation in opposing Castro was the desire to protect US economic interests rather than to combat Communism.

The Soviets had disliked Batista because of his anti-Communist stance and had broken off diplomatic relations with Cuba, but they recognized Castro's government immediately. The initial Soviet reaction to Castro's triumph seemed to be one of surprise. Although the USSR considered Latin America part of the American sphere of interest, and was relatively ignorant of the area, it responded to Castro's overtures about the purchase of Cuban sugar, agreeing to buy some in July 1959, then more in February 1960. Between those months, Castro's attitude to the Cuban Communist Party became far more positive.

Economic relations

Cuba's economic contacts with the USSR prompted US retaliation. In April 1960 the USA ordered US oil companies not to process Soviet crude oil in the US-owned refineries on Cuba. The Cubans then confiscated the companies' assets, and the USA stopped buying Cuban sugar. 'They will take away our [sugar] quota pound by pound,' said Castro, 'and we will take away their sugar refineries one by one.' The Soviets and the Chinese quickly stepped in and bought up the sugar and in August 1960 Castro began to nationalize all major US properties on the island: sugar mills, oil refineries, electricity and telephone companies, banks, railways, port facilities, hotels and casinos. One month later in a speech that became known as the First Declaration of Havana, Castro placed the Cuban Revolution in the Latin American tradition of struggles for freedom against American imperialism (see Source B, page 202). By the end of 1960, there was no Cuban–American trade, no American businesses operated in Cuba, and there were no Christmas trees or Santa Claus (they had become popular in Cuba in the 1930s when Cubans had visited the USA and brought the customs back with them, but were abolished in December 1959 as 'imperialist').

As Cuba moved slowly but surely into the Soviet camp, Khrushchev triumphantly declared, 'We consider that the Monroe Doctrine has outlasted its time [and] has died.' However, the Monroe Doctrine was alive and kicking, as attested by Eisenhower's plan for, and Kennedy's implementation of, a US-sponsored Cuban exile invasion of Castro's island.

SOURCE B

Extracts from Castro's First Declaration of Havana, September 1960.

*The People of Cuba strongly condemn the imperialism of North America for its
gross and criminal domination, lasting for more than a century, of all the peoples
of Latin America, who <u>more than once have seen the soil of Mexico, Nicaragua,
Haiti, the Dominican Republic and Cuba invaded; who have lost to a greedy
imperialism such wide and rich lands as Texas, such vital strategic areas as the
Panama Canal, and even, as in the case of Puerto Rico</u>, entire countries converted
into territories of occupation.*

*That domination, built upon <u>superior military power</u>, upon <u>unfair treaties</u>, and
upon the <u>shameful collaboration of traitorous government</u>, has for more than
100 years made of Our America – the America that [Latin Americans such as]
<u>Martí</u> wished to see free – a <u>zone of exploitation, a backyard in the financial and
political empire of the United States, a reserve supply of votes in international
organizations</u> …*

*In this fight for liberated Latin America, there now rises with invincible power
against the obedient voice of those who hold office as usurpers, the genuine voice
of the people, a voice that breaks forth from the depths of coal and tin mines,
from factories in sugar mills, from feudal lands where … <u>the heirs of Zapata and
Sandino</u>, take up the arms of liberty … To this voice of our brothers, the
Assembly of the People of Cuba responds: We are ready! Cuba will not fail.*

The Bay of Pigs and the missiles crisis: the Cuban viewpoint

The Bay of Pigs

The unsuccessful US-supported invasion at the Bay of Pigs (see page 162)
had a massive impact on Castro, Cuba and Latin America. The invasion
demonstrated the extent of American hostility to Castro, and helped push
him further into the Soviet camp. In his funeral oration for the victims of the
US bombing that had preceded the invasion, Castro spoke for the first time
of the socialist character of his revolution: 'This is what they cannot forgive,
that we should here, under their very noses, have made a socialist
revolution.'

The invasion increased the Cuban nationalism and anti-Americanism with
which Castro was very much associated, and confirmed his image as the
defender of the national honour, all of which served to reinforce his control
and to help ensure the permanence of his revolution. The relative ease with
which the invasion was repulsed made Castro and his revolution appear
successful to Cuba, Latin America and to the world. Castro had humiliated
the USA, confirming the Soviet belief that he was worth cultivating. The Bay
of Pigs was a major trigger of the Cuban Missiles Crisis, prompting the
USSR to put the missiles on Cuba (avowedly in order to protect Castro),
inspiring Castro to agree to have them (in order to forestall another US
invasion), and helping ensure Kennedy would stand firm on the removal
of the missiles.

The missiles crisis

Although in December 1961 Castro declared that he was and always had been a Marxist–Leninist, the Russians still had doubts about his reliability as an ally. Some felt he sounded too much like Mao, as in his Second Declaration of Havana speech in early 1962, in which he responded to the US-generated OAS expulsion of Cuba by urging revolution in Latin America and the 'Third World'. There was further Soviet unease over Castro's March 1962 attacks on some of the old pro-Soviet Communist Party. However, despite all the doubts, Khrushchev liked Castro and feared Soviet prestige would suffer (particularly in the 'Third World') if the USSR allowed his overthrow. So, in spring 1962, Khrushchev decided on full support of the Cuban Revolution. Castro expected that support to take the form of a military pact, but Khrushchev preferred nuclear missiles, probably to counter American supremacy in ICBMs as much as to protect Cuba. Castro was not keen. He felt the missiles would make Cuba a Soviet military base and damage Cuba's standing in the 'Third World'. He feared the American response if they saw the build-up and construction. However, the Soviets assured him that the Americans would not notice. If they did, Khrushchev said, 'I'll grab Kennedy by the balls and make him negotiate. There will be no problems from the United States.'

While the Bay of Pigs was a triumph from Castro's viewpoint and a disaster from that of the USA, the Cuban Missiles Crisis (see page 164) saw the positions reversed. Castro emerged humiliated; Kennedy emerged triumphant.

Throughout the missiles crisis, Castro feared a US invasion and waged a verbal propaganda war with Kennedy. In his 22 October televised address, Kennedy tried to frighten Latin America into supporting the USA, listing the cities (such as Mexico City and Lima) that could be reached by the missiles from Cuba. Kennedy said Cuba had 'a special and historical relationship to the USA' and the installation of missiles constituted 'a deliberately provocative and unjustified change in the *status quo* which cannot be accepted by this country'. He appealed to Cuban nationalism, describing Castro's regime as 'puppets and agents of an international [Communist] conspiracy'. In his televised response, Castro agreed that there was a 'special and historical relationship', but one in which the USA had always tried to undermine Cuban independence and sovereignty. He listed American efforts against his regime – diplomatic pressure, economic aggression, 'a Guatemalan-type invasion' and now 'trying to prevent us from arming ourselves' with Soviet aid. He derided the US suggestion of UN inspectors overseeing the withdrawal of any offensive missiles.

Kennedy appeared to have won the battle for the hearts and minds of the OAS when the members approved Kennedy's 'quarantine' of Cuba (see page 166) by 19 to nil, with Uruguay abstaining because the Uruguayan ambassador had not received his instructions. Whatever their political leanings, the Latin American leaders probably considered the installation of the missiles provocative, and/or that the safest bet was to side with the most powerful country in the world.

The Soviets had put the missiles in Cuba despite Castro's doubts and removed them without consulting him. In a 28 October speech Castro implicitly criticized the Kennedy–Khrushchev agreement that ended the crisis, saying the USA should end its subversive activities and its violation of Cuban airspace and waters, and get out of Guantánamo Bay (see page 133).

In a 20 November press conference, Kennedy said the USA would not invade Cuba, but would never cease its 'political, economic and other efforts' to 'halt subversion from Cuba'. Kennedy authorized CIA sabotage of Cuban power plants, oil refineries and sugar mills. Such attacks continued for the rest of the century, a perpetual irritant to Castro and the Cuban population – and an excellent excuse for Castro to maintain an ever more powerful and intrusive secret police. However, subsequent administrations kept Kennedy's promise not to invade Cuba, even when the USSR collapsed in 1990–1.

Using Source C and your own knowledge, how seriously would you take Castro's accusations about US biological warfare?

SOURCE C

In 1999 the People of Cuba brought a case in a Havana court seeking compensation against the US government for the financial and human costs of years of 'covert operations'. In this case, the Cubans accused the USA of biological warfare against Cuba, alleging that in May 1981, US agents released a type of dengue fever virus that led to an epidemic affecting around 350,000 Cubans, out of whom 158 died, including 101 children. The following is a private message from Castro complaining to the East German leader, Erich Honecker, in May 1980.

We have had some very strange plagues appearing here recently. It is our view that the three major plagues have been acts of sabotage. One of these was a fungus on the tobacco plantations, which destroyed 90 per cent of this year's tobacco production and forced us to import tobacco ... It involved blue mould. We also had a very serious plague on the sugar plantations ... It caused a loss of roughly 1,000,000 tonnes of sugar... Then we had the African swine fever.

Soviet–Cuban relations, 1962–8

In his biography of Castro, the journalist Volker Skierka (2004) described the Soviet–Cuban relationship as a 'forced marriage' rather than a 'love match'. This was well illustrated during the Cuban Missiles Crisis, when Castro was furious with Khrushchev, the streets of Cuba rang with the anti-Khrushchev chant, '*Nikita, mariquita, lo que se da no se quita*' ('Nikita, you sissy, don't give and then take away'), and Soviet personnel in Cuba were referred to as *bolos* (idiots). The Soviets for their part were convinced that they had saved Cuba from US aggression and resented Castro's ingratitude. Khrushchev tried to repair the damage by inviting Castro to visit the USSR in May 1963. Khrushchev also hoped to distract attention from his own domestic troubles, gain popularity by his association with the charismatic revolutionary leader, and ensure Castro did not align himself with the Chinese.

Castro's visit to the USSR was significant. Khrushchev successfully persuaded him to give up on economic diversification and to concentrate on sugar production again. Furthermore, the visit increased US antagonism. As Kennedy noted, 'No satellite leader has ever spent 40 days in Russia, basking in such glory and getting so much of Khrushchev's personal attention.' During a second visit, in 1964, the emphasis on sugar was confirmed, and Castro and Khrushchev agreed there could be peaceful as well as revolutionary routes to socialism.

Despite Castro's visits, Cuban–Soviet relations remained uneasy. While the USA publicly declared Castro to be a Soviet puppet, in private the State Department noted that Soviet officials 'muttered about pouring funds down the Cuban rat hole', and that Castro frequently acted independently of the USSR, especially over the promotion of revolution in Latin America (see page 207).

Soviet support for revolution in Latin America

Khrushchev had mixed feelings about Castro's support of revolution throughout Latin America. The Soviet leader did not consider the use of force as the best way to achieve socialism, but feared that if he did not support armed combat in Latin America, Castro might ally with the Chinese. Also, there was a chance that armed struggle might succeed, thereby weakening the USA. So, Khrushchev tried to give just enough aid to the armed struggles so as to ensure that the USSR would not be accused of refusing to support national liberation movements, yet not enough to provoke a US backlash.

After Khrushchev's fall in 1964, the USSR decreased support for the armed struggles in Latin America. Soviet pressure on Castro to do likewise culminated in a slowing down of Soviet oil supplies to Cuba in 1967, all of which infuriated Castro. Volker Skierka suggested that Cuban–Soviet relations might have been near breaking point at this time, as Castro arrested pro-Soviet members of the Cuban Communist Party and his brother publicly accused some Soviets of conspiring to overthrow the Cuban regime. However, when in 1968 radicals throughout the world protested against their governments and looked to Castro for approval, he disappointed them when he supported the Soviet invasion to crush the liberalization movement in Czechoslovakia and increased repression in Cuba ('counter-revolutionary' small businesses were closed down and political debate was silenced). Castro had made his choice. The bottom line was that he needed Soviet aid, and he got a great deal of it. By the mid-1970s, nearly half of Soviet development aid was given to Cuba and Cuba was clearly an orthodox Soviet satellite. In 1972, Cuba joined **Comecon**, and gained a massive Soviet subsidy.

US–Cuban relations after the Cuban Missiles Crisis

Relations between Castro and the USA were greatly embittered after the Bay of Pigs and the Cuban Missiles Crisis. Another major and continuing cause of antagonism was the number of Cubans who fled to the USA.

 **KEY TERM**

Comecon Soviet bloc economic organization.

Exiles

The first wave of Cuban migration to the USA occurred in the immediate aftermath of Castro's triumph in 1959. These were pro-Batista middle-class white businessmen and professionals. The second wave consisted of middle-class liberals for whom the revolution had become too radical. Under Operation Pedro Pan (Peter Pan) in 1961–2, 14,000 children were sent to the USA by Cuban parents anxious that they should not grow up being indoctrinated with Communist ideas. Some of those children never saw their parents again. In 1965, Castro allowed several thousand Cubans to leave under Johnson's US–Cuban Adjustment Act. Castro and Johnson agreed on regular airlifts, and there were six years of these 'freedom flights' until Nixon stopped them.

The exodus had advantages and disadvantages for Castro's Cuba. Some historians suggest the stability of revolutionary Cuba was due to the departure of the opposition, but the refugees constituted a great loss to the Cuban economy and their departure was a humiliating rejection of Castro's regime. Furthermore, they continually damaged US–Cuban relations. In October 1976 the Cuban fencing team flew back from Venezuela to Cuba. Their plane exploded in mid-air, the first instance of a civilian airliner being blown up by a terrorist bomb, and the worst act of terrorism in the Americas prior to **9/11** acts. All 77 passengers died, and it was thought two Cuban exiles who had worked with the CIA were responsible. The two were arrested and charged in Venezuela, but one was acquitted and the other was sprung from jail. The incident increased Castro's anxiety about American support for terrorists and he began to try to improve relations with the USA.

Relations under Nixon and Ford 1969–77

There had been no chance of improved relations under Nixon (1969–74) who reportedly said, 'There will be no change toward that bastard while I am president' (a Cuban newspaper replaced the 'x' in Nixon with a swastika). The Senate Foreign Relations Committee voted for the restoration of diplomatic relations and an end to the trade embargo in 1974 but any hopes of improvement under Nixon's successor, President Ford (1974–7), were dashed by American hostility toward the Cuban intervention in Angola (see page 211). However, the presidency of Jimmy Carter (1977–81) seemed to give cause for optimism.

Relations under Carter 1977–81

During his presidential election campaign, Carter had advocated talks with Cuba. In his presidency, US **reconnaissance flights** over Cuba were halted, travel restrictions were eased, and 'interest sections' (embassies by another name) were opened in Havana and Washington.

However, there was no further progress, due to:

- Castro's support of Mengistu (see page 212).
- The USA's failure to do anything about exile terrorism.

KEY TERM

9/11 On 11 September 2001, a terrorist attack on the USA led to thousands of deaths.

Reconnaissance flights Aerial spying missions.

- US national security adviser Zbigniew Brzezinski's unremitting hostility to the USSR and what he perceived to be its Cuban pawn.
- US legislation that demanded compensation to nationalized companies before trade with Cuba could be restored, and decreed that the embargo should continue until the USA 'determined that Cuba is no longer dominated or controlled by the foreign government or foreign organization controlling the world Communist movement'.

When Castro decided that he was not going to make much progress over the terrorism through dealing directly with the USA itself, he turned to Bernardo Benes, a wealthy Cuban banker who had fled to Miami in 1960 and was a great supporter of Carter. After negotiations with Benes, Castro released some political prisoners and eased restrictions on exile visits to Cuba (100,000 Cuban-Americans visited in 1979). The results of the increased visits were mixed. Cuba earned a great many dollars from the exiles, exile terrorism decreased somewhat, and Cuban families benefited. However, although the tension with the USA decreased a little, the US–Cuban hostility did not end, and the extra visitors had a deeply disturbing effect on Cuban society, increasing the number who wanted to leave the country, as shown in the **Mariel boatlift** in 1980.

By the 1980s, around a million Cubans (10 per cent of the population) had left for the USA. Many families were divided, and Cuba lost many skilled and enterprising individuals. The exile opposition was a serious threat to Castro, especially as exiles increased US antagonism toward his regime. On the other hand, their opposition helped maintain Castro's regime as those Cubans who remained behind resented the exiles' American connections.

> **KEY TERM**
>
> **Mariel boatlift** In 1980, Castro allowed thousands of discontented Cubans to depart for the USA from the port of Mariel.

Cuba, Latin America and Africa

← Did Castro successfully export revolution?

Since 1917 and the foundation of the USSR, Communists had disagreed as to whether or not a Communist country should promote revolution abroad. Some believed that Communist countries should promote revolutions abroad as that would gain them allies. Others felt that Communist countries should concentrate on consolidation at home. Before Castro came to power, Latin American Communists worked on the principle that socialism could be promoted through the ballot box. However, Castro advocated the revolutionary road to socialism and this had a dramatic impact on Latin America and Africa.

Cuba, revolutions and Latin America

Like his hero Martí, Fidel Castro had always felt kinship with other Latin Americans and from the first he talked of toppling Caribbean and South American dictatorships. Within days of taking power he said, 'How much do the peoples of our continent need a revolution like this one which has been made in Cuba!' Che Guevara also wanted to replicate the Cuban revolutionary experience to the south and his handbook for guerrillas, *Guerrilla Warfare* (1961), was read throughout Latin America. According to historian Richard Gott (2004), Che Guevara made a great error in failing to recognize the massive gulf between the 'frail mini-states' of the Caribbean and Central America, and the substantial economies and armies of South American nations that had centuries of experience in crushing native rebellions. Nevertheless he and Castro promoted guerrilla warfare in Latin America.

SOURCE D

An extract from Che Guevara's *Guerrilla Warfare*, published in 1961.

The example of our revolution for Latin America and the lesson it implies, have destroyed all the café theories. We have shown that a small group of resolute men, supported by the people and not afraid to die if necessary, can take on a disciplined regular army and completely defeat it.

? Using Source D and your own knowledge, explain whether 'we' had really 'shown that a small group of resolute men' could defeat a 'disciplined regular army'?

The urge to remake Latin America was intensified by the behaviour of the USA. After Castro declared himself a Marxist–Leninist, US pressure encouraged 13 Latin American governments to break off diplomatic relations with Havana. At the OAS summit in January 1962 at Punta del Este in Uruguay, Cuba was expelled in a vote of 14 to 7 (the USA had to promise to finance an airport in order to gain Haiti's vote). The OAS announced that 'ties to Marxism–Leninism' were 'incompatible with the inter-American system'. Increasing isolation in the Western hemisphere gave Castro a further reason to promote revolution: it could gain him allies.

Impact of the Cuban Revolution

Inevitably, the Cuban Revolution had a great impact on Latin American revolutionaries. The CIA station chief in Caracas observed Castro's 1960 visit to Venezuela, noting, 'that something like a chain reaction was occurring all over Latin America after Castro came to power. I saw … that a new and powerful force was at work in the hemisphere.'

Thousands of young Latin Americans were inspired by Castro and Guevara and there was an upsurge of revolutionary activism in the 1960s. Marxist guerrillas were active in many Latin American countries, including Brazil, Chile, El Salvador and Uruguay. Of course, the violent overthrow of dictatorships had a long tradition in Latin America, and the guerrillas also gained inspiration from the native tradition of revolt against oppressors. The Tupamaros of Uruguay took their name from Túpac Amaru II, who had led an eighteenth-century Indian uprising against white Spanish domination. Still, there was usually some Cuban involvement, however minimal, in all Latin American guerrilla activity.

In the early months of the Cuban Revolution, small-scale expeditions were launched from Cuba against the dictators Trujillo (in the Dominican Republic), and Somoza (in Nicaragua). Although Guevara encouraged them, these expeditions did not have any other kind of support from the Cuban regime. Revolutionaries were also encouraged in Guatemala, Peru,

Venezuela, Bolivia and Argentina. Argentine guerrillas began training in Cuba in 1962 and arrived in Argentina in 1963, but a moderate government had just taken power there, making it far less fertile soil for the revolutionaries who were surrounded by government troops, betrayed then destroyed.

Castro provided guerrillas with some financial aid, weapons, advice and military training (over 1500 were trained by Cuba between 1961 and 1964). A few Cuban guerrillas (never more than 100) fought alongside the guerrillas in Argentina, Bolivia and Venezuela. From 1963 to 1967, the Cubans concentrated on training and supplying Venezuelan guerrillas, although to Castro's fury, the Venezuelan Communist Party was totally opposed to guerrilla warfare, and the Kremlin sympathized with them.

Latin American Communist parties

The Cuban guerrilla experience did not necessarily fit other Latin American countries. For example, in Peru in 1968 a progressive military government came to power through a coup and in Chile in 1970, the Marxist Salvador Allende came to power through the ballot box. Latin American Communist parties were not always on good terms with the Cubans. The Communist parties of Chile, Argentina and Venezuela were particularly antagonistic (see Source E).

SOURCE E

A Venezuelan Communist Party statement from 13 March 1967.

Cuba has creditably followed a hard revolutionary path … but we want to make it clear that we were never and will never be Cuba's agents in Venezuela … We … never accept being told what to do. Fidel Castro enjoys … again playing the role of judge over revolutionary activities in Latin America, the role of the super-revolutionary who has already carried out the revolution in the place of the Latin American Communists … We categorically reject his claim to be the only one who decides what is and is not revolutionary in Latin America.

Quoting from Source E, how would you describe the attitude of the Venezuelan Communists toward Castro and Cuba?

Guevara, Bolivia and improved relations with Latin America

Despite all the guerrilla activity it was clear by the mid-1960s that the conservative forces (the 'counter-revolutionaries') were in the ascendant. In 1965, revolutionary groups were crushed in Peru. The Guatemalan revolutionaries struggled, and the Colombian Revolution, which had begun in the early 1950s and had been given a new lease of life by the Cuban Revolution, stuttered as the revolutionaries were driven into the mountains.

In 1966, Guevara led some Cubans to Bolivia where he fell out with the Bolivian Communist Party leadership, and in October 1967 found himself marooned in the mountains with a handful of followers, and was captured and killed by Bolivian army rangers trained in counterinsurgency by the USA. His body was photographed (see Source F) and then buried near where he had been killed.

Why do you suppose that the Bolivian authorities did all they could to ensure that the world saw Source F?

SOURCE F

The Bolivian authorities show off Che Guevara's corpse in 1967.

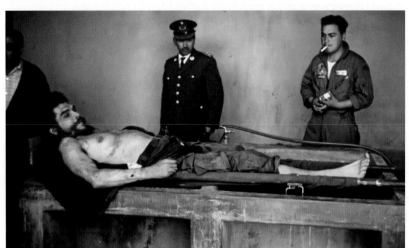

In his final published message in 1967, Che Guevara had given 'a battle cry against imperialism, and a battle hymn for the people's unity against the great enemy of mankind, the United States of America'. However, his death and Soviet pressure combined to help turn Castro against assisting Latin American guerrillas who fought against repressive, pro-American governments. Khrushchev wanted peaceful coexistence with the West, so he tied aid to Cuba to the condition that Cuba stop instigating revolutions.

After Castro dropped the emphasis on the promotion of revolution in Latin America, relations between Cuba and Latin America improved. By the mid-1970s, Cuba had reopened embassies in Venezuela, Colombia, Ecuador, Panama and Honduras, and embassies were opened for the first time in former British Caribbean possessions such as Jamaica.

Cuba's failure to trigger successful revolutions in Latin America

Although Castro was keen to promote revolutions elsewhere, and although he inspired many leftist guerrilla movements in Latin America, it was not until 20 years after the Cuban Revolution that Latin America saw another effective revolutionary movement. There were several reasons for this. The Marxist guerrillas of the 1960s and 1970s were often bitterly divided among themselves, largely cut off from the masses and lacking popular support. They often clashed with the established working-class organizations, as in Argentina where, in September 1973, the guerrillas assassinated the secretary-general of the Peronist labour confederation. Supported by the army and the trade unions, Perón crushed the guerrillas. In Argentina, as in Brazil, Chile and Uruguay in the 1970s, the guerrillas added to the disorder in already disorderly states and gave the armed forces the excuse to smash them. The established Latin American regimes were strong, particularly those that were military dictatorships such as that of Pinochet in Chile. These right-wing regimes usually got US military aid, which ironically helped ensure that leftist revolutions would be violent, because those dictatorships made liberal reform impossible.

Cuba and Africa

The CIA contended that Castro expended more effort in Africa than in Latin America because he was 'canny enough to keep his risks low' in Latin America. There, he was operating against legal governments and flouting international law, in the backyard of the USA. Africa was less risky. There, Castro would be confronting colonial powers or defending established states, and the USA would pay little attention to his activities.

In 1961, Castro promised aid to radicals in Africa. In the 1960s rebels from Guinea-Bissau, Mozambique and Angola were given aid in their struggles against Portuguese colonialism, as were Algerian revolutionaries who were fighting the French. After Algeria gained independence in 1962, Cuba sent a 55-person medical mission. 'It was like a beggar offering his help, but we knew that the Algerian people needed it even more than we did, and that they deserved it,' said the Cuban Minister of Public Health. When Morocco threatened Algeria in 1963, Cuba sent 686 men to their aid, even though Morocco had just signed a contract to buy a million tonnes of Cuban sugar. However, it was in the 1970s that Castro's Cuba really had an impact on Africa.

Guinea-Bissau and Angola

Cuban military instructors were in Guinea-Bissau from 1966 to 1974, and the first president of that country credited 'the heroic people of Cuba' as the most important factor in his country's successful war of independence. By 1975, Angola too had won its independence from Portugal, but the country was riven by faction. While Cuba and the USSR supported the Popular Movement for the Liberation of Angola (or MPLA), the Chinese, Americans and South Africans favoured a rival faction, the National Union for the Total Independence of Angola (UNITA).

The impact of Cuban aid was significant. Between 1975 and 1991 around a quarter of a million Cubans served in Angola. They helped the MPLA to defeat a South African invasion. The liberal South African newspaper, the *Rand Daily Mail*, noted the implications of that South African defeat in Angola: 'White elitism has suffered an irreversible blow.'

The Angolan intervention greatly added to Castro's standing in the developing world, and confirmed his belief that Africa was more fertile ground for revolution than Latin America. In 1978, Cuban exile Bernardo Benes (see page 207) recorded Castro as saying to him that Latin America's 'rigid social structures' and 'organized interest groups' (the military, the Church, business corporations, trade unions and political parties) made revolution far less likely there than in Africa, which was 'poor and lacked such forces'.

Ethiopia

Inspired by his success in Angola, Castro toured Africa in 1977 and was impressed by the Ethiopian leader Mengistu Haile Mariam, whose successful coup had led to the establishment of a Marxist–Leninist regime, and who had requested Soviet aid. Initially Castro was in a dilemma. Ethiopia had a clash of territorial interests with Somalia, which had been in the Soviet sphere and friendly with Castro since 1969. He opted for Ethiopia and Mengistu, and sent troops and weapons that were decisive in Ethiopia's defeat of Somalia. Such troops inspired a popular joke amongst Cuban exiles in Florida in 1980:

Question: Why is Cuba the largest country in the world?

Answer: Because its army is in Africa, its population is in Florida, and its government is in Moscow.

Castro's motivation

Although Castro's African wars had a considerable impact on that continent, it could be argued that other than in terms of national prestige, they were not particularly helpful to Cuba. They were an expensive diversion of resources and definitely damaged the chance of a *rapprochement* with the USA. What then had motivated Castro? Castro rejected US accusations that he was doing the bidding of the Soviet Union in Africa, and the Soviet archives confirm that Cuban intervention in Angola was done 'on their own initiative and without consulting us'. Indeed, the Soviet leader Leonid Brezhnev opposed the despatch of Cuban soldiers to Angola. The CIA sometimes attributed Castro's motivation to 'his thirst for self-aggrandizement', but more usually the CIA emphasized the motives of self-defence and revolutionary fervour. Piero Gleijeses (2008) concluded that Castro sent troops to Angola 'because he was committed to racial justice … I do not know of any other country, in modern times, for which idealism has been such a key component of its foreign policy'. From that viewpoint, the foreign policy was an extension of the desire to create a better and fairer society at home, although Gleijeses' explanation does not illuminate Castro's Ethiopian policy. Perhaps the latter was an aberration that can be explained by overconfidence after the Angolan triumph (see Source G).

SOURCE G

Castro speaking after his visit to Africa in 1977.

I could say that I discovered Africa, just as Christopher Columbus discovered America.

What does Castro mean in Source G, and what does it tell us about him?

212

Castro's international standing, 1975–80

The late 1970s: optimism

The 1970s saw a great improvement in Cuba's international position. Relations with Latin America improved (see page 209) and in 1977 the OAS relaxed restrictions on contacts with Cuba. Castro's reputation in the 'Third World' grew because of his intervention in Africa and the doctors and teachers that he sent to help developing countries. Thirty-five countries were receiving civil and military support from Cuba and a conference of **non-aligned nations** was held in Havana in 1979. A stream of national leaders visited Cuba, not only Communists such as Brezhnev of the USSR and Honecker of East Germany, but also Canada's Pierre Trudeau and Mexico's Echeverria.

Nicaragua

In 1979, Castro gained a foreign ally when Sandinista guerrillas overthrew the dynastic dictatorship of the Somozas in Nicaragua (see page 185). Although this was a Cuban-style revolution (an initially small band of guerrillas defeated a regular army, in tandem with a popular rising), the responsibility of Cuba for the Nicaraguan Revolution was minimal. Nicaragua had a long history of revolutionary struggles. The guerrillas had some aid from Cuba, but it was insignificant. Nevertheless, the victorious Sandinistas looked eagerly to Castro for help and inspiration and an uninvited delegation arrived in Cuba. This made Castro uneasy, as he had long since given up promoting Latin American revolutions, but he was aware that Nicaragua might be a useful ally and he was glad to see the end of the Somoza dictatorship. He advised the Nicaraguans to avoid antagonizing the USA, lest that prompt US intervention.

1980: pessimism

In many ways, 1980 was a disastrous year for Fidel Castro. There was unrest in the Soviet bloc, and Castro's loyal support of the Soviet invasion of Afghanistan (begun in May 1979) provoked world-wide criticism. The sugar crop was poor, there was rationing and austerity and 125,000 Cubans left to live in the USA.

The new exodus was triggered when 10,000 unhappy Cubans sought asylum in the grounds of the Peruvian Embassy in Havana. Castro invited anyone who wanted to leave to do so and President Carter said all of them could come to the USA (more than he had expected took him at his word and his poll ratings plummeted). Miami Cubans organized the exodus, picking up passengers from the Cuban port of Mariel. To the dissatisfaction of the older exile community, many of these migrants were black and poor, and fulsome in their praise of the free health care, education and sports facilities available in Cuba but not in the USA. However, the fact that so many still sought to flee Castro's Cuba was a humiliation and by the time Carter stopped the

Was Cuba's international position cause for optimism in 1975–80?

KEY TERM

Non-aligned nations
Nations independent of the USA and the USSR in the Cold War.

influx, there was little prospect of the US–Cuban *rapprochement* that had seemed possible when Carter first became president (see page 206).

What was the relationship between Cuba and the Cold War?

Cuba and the Cold War: conclusions

Cuba was very important in the Cold War. Although the Cuban Revolution was not initially a product of the Cold War, the continued existence of revolutionary Cuba owed much to the Cold War context and helped shape the course of the Cold War.

Cuba helped to shape the Cold War in that it helped focus superpower attention on the importance of the 'Third World' when it encouraged guerrilla movements in Latin America. Those movements in turn contributed to repressive counter-revolutionary regimes on that continent (see page 229). More importantly, the Soviet–American tug of war over Cuba intensified the Cold War, and the most dangerous crisis of the conflict took place in and because of Cuba.

Just as Cuba helped shape the Cold War, so the Cold War helped shape Cuba. The USA played an important part in triggering the Cuban revolution, and the opposition of the USA and the support of the USSR were important in sustaining it. The opposition of the USA served to increase Castro's popularity with many Cubans and stimulated Soviet support for Cuba. Without the Cold War and Soviet help, Castro's Cuba would probably have faced another and better organized American invasion. But while the Cuban Revolution was shaped and made Communist by US opposition and Soviet support, it was also very much in the Cuban tradition, which probably explains why it was able to survive the withdrawal of Soviet military and economic aid in the 1980s, and the collapse of the Soviet bloc between 1990 and 1991. The Cold War had not triggered Fidel Castro's revolution, nor did it bring about its end. Significantly, with the collapse of the Soviet empire, Castro's 1992 constitution dropped references to Marxism–Leninism and he stopped promoting revolution abroad ('Military assistance outside our borders is a thing of the past'), which suggests that Castro's revolution might have taken a very different course had it not been for American enmity and the Cold War.

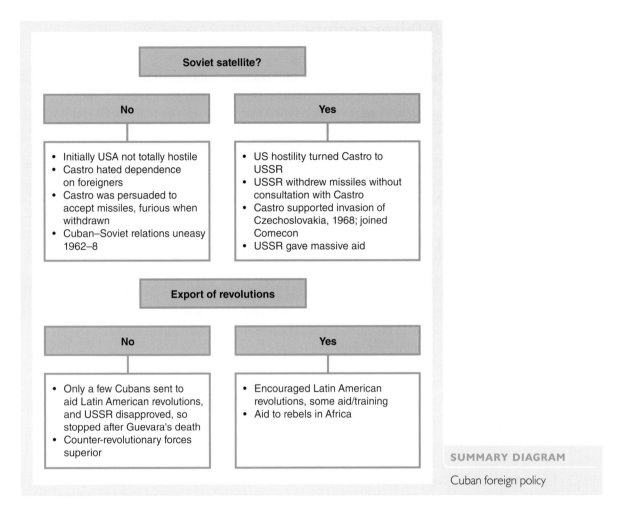

SUMMARY DIAGRAM

Cuban foreign policy

③ Castro's Cuba: conclusions

▶ *Key question: How successful was the Cuban Revolution?*

Assessments of the success of the Cuban Revolution depend very much on one's viewpoint. Castro sought a fairer, more economically advanced Cuba, free from foreign domination and able to inspire those in other countries who were pursuing their own revolutions. Even if it could be asserted that he had successfully achieved all those aims, Cuban exiles and their American supporters would still consider the Cuban Revolution to be a failure, as their goals were different. Around 10 per cent of the island's population voted with their feet and left revolutionary Cuba.

How successful were
Castro's domestic
policies?

→ # A fairer society

Democratic elections

In the Cold War, the USA and its allies would have included democratic elections as one of the characteristics of a fairer society, and by those standards Castro's Cuban Revolution failed. However, the Cold War-era USSR and its allies defined fairness in terms of a more equal distribution of wealth than was characteristic of Western societies. By those standards, the Cuban Revolution succeeded. Castro's view of democratic elections was that there was no point in having them if elected governments did nothing to help the people, and he argued with considerable justification that this had been the case in Cuba in the first half of the twentieth century.

Living standards

With or without elections, many reforms in the early years of the Castro regime made Cuba a fairer society. Land was more fairly distributed. Many plantation workers and peasants quickly gained 67-acre plots when the larger estates were broken up. Sugarcane cutters were given a minimum wage. In the cities, Castro ensured the fair distribution of food through rationing, and rents and the prices of utilities were reduced in 1959. Living standards certainly rose under Castro. Unemployment was ended. Free health care was widely available, and by 1980 the infant mortality rate had fallen and diseases such as tuberculosis were far less prevalent. Castro tried to improve housing, but gave priority to hospitals and schools which, combined with problems in the construction industry, severely damaged the prospects of success.

Social advancement

Educational standards greatly improved in revolutionary Cuba. In 1961, idealistic students taught over a million Cubans to read and write. During this time, 3000 schools were built in a year and over 300,000 children attended school for the first time. Adult education was given great prominence. Overall, Cuba's education system, like its health care system, was the best in Latin America. This was an educational revolution.

Under Castro, life improved for women. They had easier access to divorce, abortions and family planning. More were in employment, where they often got equal pay, and more were educated. Sexism was combated by the Federation of Cuban Women (FMC), established in 1960 under Vilma Espín, wife of Raúl Castro. The FMC helped get the Family Code established in 1975. That code required men to do half of household chores, although traditional sexism ensured limited success. Similarly, women remained underrepresented in politics. In 1980, only a fifth of Communist Party members and officials were women.

Castro worked from the first to decrease racial discrimination. Cuban blacks were among the poorest members of society, but their standard of living improved so much under Castro that his government became more popular with them than with whites, even though whites dominated the top positions in Cuban society. In 1979, only 16 of the 146 members of the Central Committee were black.

Despite the enlightened attitudes toward women and blacks, the revolutionary regime discriminated against homosexuals until attitudes began to change in the late 1970s.

Economic advancement

Throughout the 1960s there were problems in agriculture, but production improved greatly in the 1970s. This rise owed much to the USSR, which helped modernize the sugar industry and provided a stable, secure market for the sugar. However, Castro's dreams of economic diversification and industrial development were not fully realized, and again this owed much to the USSR, which urged Cuba to concentrate on the production of sugar.

A revolutionary foreign policy

Freedom from foreign domination

Castro aimed to end US domination of Cuba, and in this he succeeded, although in some ways it could be argued that he replaced it with Soviet domination. There were times when he suffered great humiliation at the hands of the Soviets, as in the Cuban Missiles Crisis in 1962, and in 1967 when his oil supplies from the USSR were threatened. On the other hand, he frequently said and did things that infuriated Moscow. With the collapse of Communism and the Soviet bloc, the media in what had been the Soviet bloc were highly critical of Castro. One Hungarian newspaper said that the golden boy of 'tropical socialism' could afford to be ideologically radical because Cuba was 'eating the bread of others and building socialism at the expense of another country'.

> How successful was Castro's foreign policy?

Revolutionary inspiration and aid

Fidel Castro's Cuba inspired and gave (limited) assistance to revolutionaries in Latin America, although guerrillas usually prompted a counter-revolutionary reaction. Castro had a considerable impact on Africa, helping the MPLA in Angola and Mengistu in Ethiopia. South African leader Nelson Mandela said Castro's rescue of Angola from South Africa's attack helped stimulate the collapse of the racist regime in his country. With his interventions in Africa and his defiance of the USA, Castro was a great inspiration to other developing nations.

National pride

Castro could be said to have humiliated the USA when his regime stubbornly refused to collapse, despite great and incessant pressure from successive administrations. The Cold War and Castro's alignment with the USSR gave Cuba an importance that its size did not merit. This world prominence did not necessarily make life materially better for the Cubans, but it increased national pride in a country that had long suffered from foreign domination.

Citing phrases from Source H, how would you describe this historian's attitude to Cuba's foreign policy?

SOURCE H

An extract from a chapter by Piero Gleijeses in *In from the Cold: Latin America's New Encounter With the Cold War*, edited by Gilbert Joseph and Daniela Spenser, published in 2008.

Cuba's role in the world since 1959 is without precedent. No other Third World country has projected its military power beyond its immediate neighborhood. Brazil's mighty generals sent a small troop to the Dominican Republic in 1965 as the United States' junior partner; Argentina's generals briefly helped Somoza's defeated cohorts in 1980–81 … even the Soviet Union sent far fewer soldiers beyond its immediate neighborhood than did Cuba. In this regard, Cuba is second only to the United States.

Did Castro's success depend on the USSR?

Postscript: Cuba after 1981

During the 1980s, Soviet aid to and support for Cuba slowly decreased and ultimately ended as the USSR collapsed. Castro steered Cuba through incredible economic problems and slowly restored the economy in the 1990s.

To the surprise and dismay of the European Union, which hoped to re-establish an amicable relationship and more trade with Cuba, the end of the Cold War failed to improve US–Cuban relations. Indeed, they worsened, suggesting that the Cold War was not the key factor in the American hostility to Castro.

The Cuban exiles were very important in keeping the antagonism alive. They had become politically important in electorally pivotal states, such as Florida and New Jersey, and the American political parties were well aware of the importance of their votes. This helped ensure that there would be no real improvement of relations with Castro. Also, American pride was at stake: a previously quite insignificant Caribbean island had made the superpower look rather foolish when it survived frequent attempts at destabilization. The USA found it hard to change its mind-set with regard to Cuba, a country in which it had so long interfered and dominated. The 1996 Helms–Burton Act contained the declaration that the USA had the right to define the nature of Cuban democracy, which aroused Cuban nationalism and helped maintain Castro's regime. Not all Americans, and not even all Cuban-Americans, were hostile to Castro's Cuba. Seventy per cent of voters favoured lifting the economic embargo in the 1990s. However, the militantly anti-Castro minority were more influential.

The Castro brothers are but mortal, and it may be that with the death of Fidel and/or Raúl, Cuba will revert to the status of an American protectorate.

Success?	Failure?
• Equalization of wealth • Free health care • Better education • Better for women • Better for blacks • Sugar industry modernized	• No elections • Frequent rationing • Loss of entrepreneurs • Still macho • Still monoculture
• Free from US domination • Inspired Latin American revolutionaries • World prominence, great national pride	• Greatly dependent on USSR • Counter-revolutionaries triumphed • Many fled to USA

SUMMARY DIAGRAM

Castro's Cuba: conclusions

Chapter summary

Cuba in the Cold War

Castro aimed to end corrupt politics and the economic dominance of the USA, and to improve the lives of Cubans through a fairer distribution of wealth and better education and health care. Castro tried but failed to diversify the Cuban economy, which remained highly dependent on sugar production and Soviet aid. Castro Sovietized Cuba because of economic weakness, Western hostility, and because there was much about Soviet socialism with which he sympathized. His regime was repressive, but Cubans got the best education and social services in Latin America. Nevertheless, around 10 per cent of the population left Castro's Cuba to live in the USA, where they became politically important and ensured continuing American hostility to Castro. On the other hand, the exodus helped ensure the stability of Revolutionary Cuba. While the Cuban Revolution was shaped by the Cold War, it was also very much in the Cuban tradition, which is probably why it survived the collapse of the USSR.

Another of Castro's early aims was to export revolution to other Latin American countries, but a combination of the death of Che Guevara in the Bolivian Revolution, the increasing strength of counter-revolutionary regimes in Latin America, and Soviet doubts about the wisdom of promoting guerrilla activity in Latin America, led Castro to concentrate instead on assisting revolutionary regimes in Africa, where Cuban intervention had a massive impact.

Castro's Cuba became a focal point of the Cold War world after the US-backed invasion by Cuban exiles at the Bay of Pigs, and the Cuban Missiles Crisis. American hostility was vital in the process whereby Castro's Cuba became a Soviet satellite. Castro joined Comecon and supported the Soviet invasions of Czechoslovakia and Afghanistan. Ever since the Ford years there have been some Americans who have wanted to improve relations with Castro's Cuba, but the political importance of anti-Castro Cuban exiles in the USA has ensured continuing US antagonism. Castro and the Cold War put Cuba on the map, and although this did little to help the Cuban people in practical terms, it gave them a sense of national pride and achievement unheard of in the pre-Castro era.

Examination advice

How to answer 'in what ways and with what effects' questions

In questions such as these, stay focused on what is being asked. <u>In what ways and with what effects</u> is really asking two questions. Be sure to discuss both. You should explain several ways and several outcomes or results.

Example

> <u>In what ways and with what effects</u> did Castro attempt to export his revolution?

1. A question of this sort is asking you to do several tasks. You are to discuss **both** the ways Castro tried to export the Cuban Revolution and the effects of these efforts. Be sure to provide supporting evidence that discusses the two. You might be tempted to divide your essay in two: the first section that deals with the ways and the second section with the effects, but this will not score as highly as an essay that synthesizes the two. In other words, discuss in one paragraph one way Castro tried to export his ideas and in the same paragraph analyse the effects of the action. It would also help to explain why Castro chose certain policies even if this is not specifically stated in the question. Finally, this question is a good one in which to offer historians' interpretations of Castro's actions.

2. First take at least five minutes to write a short outline. In a question that asks for 'in what ways and with what effects', one strategy might be to make a chart that illustrates the ways and the effects. An example of a chart is given on the next page.

Ways	Effects	Reasons
Some aid to Latin American guerrillas in Uruguay, Brazil, Bolivia, for example. 1960s	Local Communist parties resented Cuban interference They were often more beholden to the USSR	Add to his revolutionary credentials Gain allies
Che Guevara's mission to Bolivia. 1967	Guevara executed. USSR put pressure on Castro to cease aiding guerrillas. Wanted improved relations with West. Created Guevara as a martyr	Supported small mission to Bolivia because Guevara thought it was ripe for revolution
Aid to revolutionaries in Africa. This included doctors and teachers. 1961	Initially, only small impact	Castro felt Africa was where revolution might succeed, more so than in Latin America
Military intervention in Angola. 250,000 Cubans served there from 1975 to 1991. Supported the Marxist MPLA	Defeated apartheid-era South African army and rival UNITA guerrilla faction. Won world-wide praise from Socialist camp for his aid to revolutionary forces. Helped to end racist regime in South Africa. Brought medical care and education to thousands of Angolans	To prove that Cuba was at the forefront of nations promoting revolutions, even if the country was poor Committed to racial justice (Gleijeses)
Support for Ethiopian dictatorship in 1977. Troops fought against Somalia	Propped up Mengistu dictatorship. Ethiopia defeated Somalia	Not thoroughly clear why he aided a foe of Somalia, a Soviet ally. Wanted to support a fellow leftist who overthrew a corrupt regime
Support for Sandinista government in Nicaragua after it came to power in 1979. Doctors, teachers, military advisers	Provided a counter-balance to US government aid to anti-Sandinista forces	Important to support a fellow leftist government in the Americas

3. In your introduction, briefly state the major points you plan to raise in your essay.
4. In the body of the essay, you need to discuss each of the points you raised in the introduction. Devote at least a paragraph to each one. Be sure to make the connection between the points you raise and the major thrust of your argument. An example of how one of the points could be addressed is given on page 222.

Fidel Castro made a major effort in the 1970s to export revolution to Africa. He sent 250,000 soldiers, doctors and teachers to Angola beginning in 1975. Their primary goals were to ensure that the MPLA, a Marxist guerrilla group, maintained control of the government after winning independence from Portugal, and to bring tangible social benefits to the Angolan people. South Africa and the USA supported UNITA, a rival group. Cuban soldiers were key in defeating South African troops and helping to ensure that the MPLA was victorious. Castro felt strongly that his standing and that of the Cuban nation would be helped by taking such a major stand against what he viewed as Western imperialism. At the time of the Cuban intervention, US policy-makers viewed this as Castro working on behalf of his Soviet patrons. However, this appears not to be the case according to Soviet documents released after the collapse of the USSR. Castro often acted independently of his major benefactor. He was able to demonstrate that a small nation could support revolutionary movements abroad in significant ways.

5. Your conclusion should tie together the major points you raised in the essay and how these relate to the question.
6. Now try writing a complete answer to the question following the advice above.

 Examination practice

Below are two exam-style questions for you to practise on this topic.

1 Castro's relationship with the Soviet Union was a troubled one. To what extent do you agree with this assessment?
(For guidance on how to answer 'to what extent' questions, see page 67.)

2 Analyse the successes and failures of Castro's domestic policies.
(For guidance on how to answer 'analyse' questions, see page 90.)

CHAPTER 9

The impact of the Cold War on Latin America

This chapter comes to tentative conclusions about the impact of the Cold War on Latin America, focusing on the debate over the extent to which the development of Latin America has been affected by external factors (such as foreign intervention) rather than internal factors (domestic politics). You need to consider the following questions throughout this chapter:

✖ Was foreign intervention the most important factor in the development of Latin America?

✖ To what extent did the USA dominate Latin America in the Cold War?

 1 The debate over the external connection

▶ *Key question: Was foreign intervention the most important factor in the development of Latin America?*

 **KEY TERM**

External connection
Foreign involvement in Central and South America since 1492.

Some scholars have seen the '**external connection**' as the most important factor in the history and development of Latin America. Generally, these scholars are on the left or the far right of the political spectrum. At their most extreme, they blame foreign powers for most Latin American problems, especially for the great disparities in wealth and status between rich and poor. They look at the impact of the external connection in three phases of Latin American history.

The three phases of the external connection

First and second phases

The first 'external connection' was the colonial period, the legacy of which still has a great impact on twenty-first-century Latin America, as in the massive landed estates owned by descendants of the white colonists. The second phase of external connection was the nineteenth century, when Britain and the USA exerted great political and economic influence on Latin America.

> When and with what results did the external connection have an impact on Latin America?

Third phase

The third period of external connection was the twentieth century, when the USA developed from the pre-eminent regional power into the world's greatest power and frequently intervened in Latin American affairs. While the Monroe Doctrine (see page 9) meant little in practice in the nineteenth century, the early twentieth-century USA had the will and the power to intervene in Latin America whenever it felt its interests were threatened. Along with increased political power, US economic domination of Latin America also increased in the early twentieth century. For example, the Chilean copper mining industry and the Cuban sugar industry were dominated by US companies, and by the Second World War the USA was Latin America's greatest export market. In both the Second World War and the Cold War, the USA was anxious to retain access to Latin American natural resources, to defend its investments in the region, and to ensure that no other foreign power became dominant there.

Historian Marshall Eakin (2007) described the Cold War as 'an era of unprecedented US power and influence in Latin America' but the extent to which the USA and the Cold War (the 'external connection') dominated Latin American development is controversial, and Section 2 investigates this, looking back at examples already covered in the book and at some new case studies.

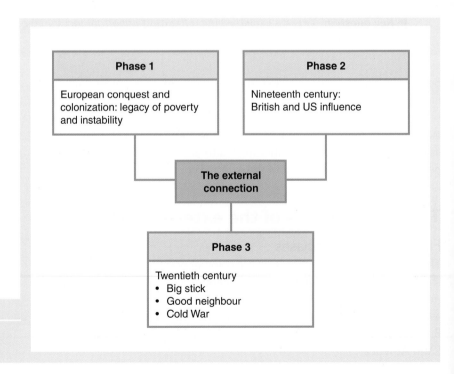

The three phases of the external connection

Conclusions about the impact of the Cold War on Latin America

▶ *Key question: To what extent did the USA dominate Latin America in the Cold War?*

The Cold War sometimes seemed to produce a polarized world in which the Latin American countries faced two choices:

- The first option was to have a capitalist economy, friendship with the USA, and continued economic and social inequality.
- The second option was to have a socialist economy, alignment with the USSR, and the elimination of inequality via state intervention and authoritarianism.

In the polarized world of the Cold War, the danger for Latin American nations or parties that attempted or advocated any kind of socialism, was that the USA would intervene to stop the reforms. In countries such as Cuba (see page 204) and Chile (see page 177), experiments with socialism suffered because of the Cold War polarization that made the pursuit of equality seem 'Communist'. Conservative Latin American political élites found it easy to get aid out of the USA by convincing it that the reformers who opposed them were Communist leftists trying to seize power. So, due to the Cold War context, most Latin American revolutionary leftist movements were defeated, usually with US assistance. Only Cuba (1959) (see Chapter 8) and to a lesser extent Nicaragua (1979) (see page 185) managed leftist revolutions.

However, it is dangerous to generalize about the impact of the Cold War on Latin America, as demonstrated by the complex interrelationship between distinctively Cuban traditions and the Cold War struggle (see Chapter 8). The dominant factor in the relationship between local conditions and the Cold War varied widely from nation to nation and decade to decade.

Conditions in Latin America

> Did the external connection dominate Cold War Latin America?

Although it sometimes seemed that the Cold War dominated Latin American politics, much depended on existing conditions in Latin America. The greatest and longest struggle in Latin American history was that between the poor masses and the élite (mostly landowners). In the Cold War, the struggle between capitalism (led by the USA) and Communism (led by the USSR) was superimposed on that Latin American struggle.

Internal divisions

It is too easy to overestimate the primacy of the 'external connection'. As Castro's 1959 triumph demonstrates (see Chapter 6), there were times when the traditional Latin American struggle between the poor and the élite was more important than the Cold War in determining the course of events, but also times when both were of equal importance (see page 202). During the Cold War era, many scholars made the argument that foreign powers, especially the USA, were to blame for the inequality, poverty and political instability that bedevilled many Latin American nations, but it is unrealistic to deny that Latin Americans themselves played a large part in their countries' histories.

Latin American anti-Communism

Latin Americans frequently chose to collaborate with foreign powers, for example Batista and Castro in Cuba, Trujillo in the Dominican Republic, and the military regimes in countries such as Argentina, who exchanged information with the USA in the 1970s in Operation Condor (see page 179). Historian John Lewis Gaddis (1997) made the valid point that left-wing historians have failed to recognize the 'strong base of popular support, confirmed repeatedly' for the American presence in Western Europe and Asia. His point can be applied to Latin America, where there was a great deal of support for anti-Communism, as seen in Brazil (see page 169). There were also important tensions between two or more Latin American countries (such as Brazil and Argentina) that continued and developed quite independently of the Cold War.

Trade and aid

While there was often resentment of US power and influence, Latin American nations frequently sought trade with and aid from the USA. The USA was often willing to give arms, military training and economic aid in exchange for raw materials and an anti-Communist stance and this often affected the behaviour of Latin American regimes. The desire for US aid prompted some Latin American governments to ban Communist parties or to exclude them from power, as in Chile in 1948. In 1946, the Chilean economy was dependent on copper. Copper mining was controlled by US companies and when the miners went on strike, the USA put pressure on the Chilean government to eliminate Communist influence in both the unions and the government. When the Chilean government responded by outlawing the Communist Party in 1948, the American companies announced expansion plans, and the US government and the World Bank offered Chile new loans. The desire for aid inspired some Latin American countries to try to please the USA by holding elections, as with Vargas in Brazil, Batista in Cuba, and Perón in Argentina.

Twentieth-century Latin American revolutionary and reformist movements

There were multiple revolutionary and reformist movements in Latin America in the twentieth century. Many were opposed and some halted by the USA. The success of such movements was affected by several variables. It was easier for large countries such as Mexico to withstand external pressures than it was for smaller countries such as Nicaragua and Cuba. The USA inevitably had more impact on the Caribbean and Central American countries because of their closer geographical proximity and weaker governments. The following case studies illuminate the variety of movements and their varied success.

← **What impact did the US have on Latin American revolutionary and reformist movements during the Cold War?**

Successful revolutions and reforms

The Mexican and Bolivian revolutions

The Mexican Revolution, the first and arguably the most successful of the twentieth-century Latin American revolutions, was essentially socialist, and characterized by anti-American rhetoric. Given the subsequent US history of halting Latin American revolutions, this raises the question as to why the Mexican Revolution succeeded. One reason was that the outbreak of the Mexican Revolution predated the Bolshevik Revolution of 1917 and the American fears of Communism. It has been seen that, in contrast to Guatemala, a Bolivian Revolution survived. Both emerged during the Cold War but while Guatemala became a casualty of it, the Bolivian Revolution (see page 79) survived because Bolivia was further away and the USA had far fewer economic interests at stake there.

The Cuban Revolution and Marxists

Cuba was strategically and economically important to the USA, but despite US opposition, the Cuban Revolution survived (see page 214), a survival that owed much to the Cold War.

The success of the Cuban Revolution renewed interest in Marxist theory which up until 1961 had played a minimal role in Latin American politics. Before Castro, the USSR had shown relatively little interest in Latin America because it was predominantly agrarian (traditional Marxist theory declared that the revolution would be led by the industrial proletariat) and within the American sphere of influence. Without much contact with Moscow, Latin American Communist parties had been cautiously reformist. Then the success of the Cuban Revolution identified socialism with the long-established Latin American tradition of armed rebellion and inspired in some the belief that socialism and nationalism could solve the political, economic and social problems in Latin America. For a time it seemed as if Castro had triggered leftist revolutions throughout Latin America.

Cuba and the New Left

Events in Cuba contributed to the rise of the intellectual 'New Left' in Latin America. The New Left adopted the popular Latin American belief of the 1950s that the USA and Europe exploited the natural resources of Latin America, selling more profitable manufactured goods to Latin America in return. The New Left then adapted that theory, superimposing two new ideas on the 'external connection' thesis: first, that the local élites collaborated in this exploitation of Latin America, and second, that the answer to these problems should be to mobilize the working classes and the peasants. The New Left argued that only a socialist revolution could bring about true national sovereignty and balanced national development.

In short, the Cuban Revolution stimulated fresh thinking about the 'under-development' of Latin America, and provided an answer to the problem: Cuban-style socialism. This answer was particularly appealing at a time of severe rural misery, increasingly large shanty towns, massive income

? What do you think the cartoonist in Source A is trying to say about Castro, Cuba and Brazil?

SOURCE A

'What You Need, Man, Is a Revolution Like Mine', an Ed Valtman cartoon published in the *Hartford Times* in 1961.

disparities, mass unemployment, rampant inflation, and an enlarged university-educated middle class that sought an answer to Latin America's problems. However, despite Castro's success and the consequent encouragement of revolutionary socialism, there were no successful revolutions for the next two decades. Indeed, events in Cuba probably helped trigger right-wing military coups throughout Latin America, as in Brazil (1964) then Uruguay and Chile (1973). The USA responded to those military coups with considerable approval and assistance.

Left-wing revolutionaries: best for reform?

Latin American military regimes retained power through repression but historian Gilbert Joseph (2008) attributed the stability of the right-wing regimes of the 1970s 'at least in part' to their implementation of programmes of moderate social reform, as with the military regimes in Brazil, Chile and Uruguay. In Uruguay, the military adapted and built on a long-standing welfare state tradition. Just as Joseph gives a cautionary reminder of the dangers of painting the military regimes in totally black colours, so the political scientist Jorge Castañeda (1993) suggested that the Cuban-inspired revolutionary road radicalized Latin American politics and led 'absolutist revolutionaries' to provoke a right-wing repression, which moderate reformers would not have done.

Leftists kept from power by the USA

The USA played an important role in the demise of reformist regimes in Guatemala (see page 76), in the Dominican Republic (see page 171), in Chile (see page 174) and in Honduras.

Honduras

In the early twentieth century, US-based multinational companies took control of Honduran banana plantations. Honduras was a typical 'banana republic', with foreign companies dominating the economy and sometimes overthrowing governments they disliked. In the 1970s and 1980s, the USA used Honduras as a base for its military operations in Nicaragua, El Salvador and Guatemala. This served to reinforce the military governments and to ensure the absence of leftist guerrillas.

The USA, right-wing regimes and the persecution of the left

Uruguay

Uruguay had a long tradition of democratic, stable politics. However, economic problems (inflation neared 200 per cent in 1968) contributed to the rise of armed middle-class urban guerrillas, the Tupamaros. Inspired by Marx, Lenin, Guevara and the Cuban revolution, the Tupamaros robbed banks, kidnapped diplomats, and executed a US official who was training the Uruguayan police force.

The USA supported the counter-insurgency campaign and the 1973 military coup that developed into a brutal dictatorship. The new military government

KEY TERM

Banana republic Small nations, especially in Latin America, usually dependent on one crop and politically unstable.

saw the world in terms similar to the Truman Doctrine (see page 23). They saw a polarized world, one Christian, democratic and led by the USA, and the other authoritarian, Communist and led by the USSR. They believed that the USSR was behind leftist revolutionaries such as the Tupamaros who needed to be destroyed. Completed by the mid-1970s, the destruction of the revolutionaries was brought about by a plan known as the National Security Doctrine (NSD), which was greatly influenced by training in the USA and US instructors working in Latin America. Revolutionaries were either killed or imprisoned. At one time, one out of every 600 Uruguayan inhabitants was a political prisoner. In 1984, with the leftists wiped out and severe economic problems, the Uruguayan military allowed elections.

Argentina

Argentina in the 1970s is an excellent example of a Latin American regime that sought to wage the Cold War fiercely yet not at the behest of the USA, which the Argentine regime actually considered remiss in dealing with the Communist threat.

After the fall of Juan Perón in 1955 (see page 82), Argentina became increasingly unstable, both economically and politically. Terrorist groups active from the 1950s were radicalized in the mid-1960s by events in Cuba and especially by the Argentine Che Guevara. The revolutionary Montoneros robbed banks and undertook political kidnappings of the 'enemies of the people'. The Revolutionary Army of the People (ERP) focused on the rural north-west, trying to emulate Castro's winning over of the peasantry in the Sierra Maestra (see page 140). The right counter-attacked with 'death squads' that avenged the death of family and friends. In 1974, the government began a campaign of counterterrorism, led by the Argentine Anti-Communist Alliance (AAA). The AAA identified suspects then kidnapped or assassinated them. Even moderate left-wingers were targeted.

By 1975, the Argentine military had had enough. They eliminated the 'subversives' and their sympathizers in the 'Dirty War'. Union activists, leaders of community aid groups and even student activists who had petitioned the authorities for paper and pencils for use in schools, were targeted and thousands 'disappeared'. The government worked closely with other dictatorships in Chile, Brazil and Uruguay, as part of Operation Condor (see page 179). Believing that the Carter administration had neglected the anti-Communist struggle in the Western hemisphere, the military regime undertook a crusade against Communism:

- When Carter halted military aid to the Nicaraguan dictator Somoza at the beginning of 1979, Argentina, along with South Africa, Brazil, El Salvador, Guatemala and Israel, provided Somoza with military equipment and advice in his struggle with the leftist Sandinistas.
- The Argentines provided training in counterinsurgency and military aid to El Salvador, at the request of the government of General Carlos Humberto

Romero (1976–9). A Salvadoran counterinsurgent said, 'The Argentines are the only ones in the world who fought an urban guerrilla war and won it. So they are just naturally recognized as the best.'

- In 1980, an Argentine military mission was sent to Guatemala where Romeo Lucas García's regime sought assistance in counterinsurgency warfare. This Argentine taskforce did sterling work in the assassination and disappearance of Guatemalan political dissidents.
- After the Sandinista victory in Nicaragua, the Argentines assisted their opponents in Honduras where it was agreed in 1981 that the Argentines would contribute the organization, administration and military instruction and the CIA would supply covert financial aid.
- Argentina participated in a military coup in Bolivia in 1980. 'We had to do the dirty work in Bolivia,' said an Argentine naval officer.

Historian Ariel Armony (2008) concluded that Argentina played a very important part in 'a formidable transnational political nexus' that included the governments of Chile, Uruguay, Paraguay, Bolivia, Brazil, Ecuador and Peru, along with Cuban terrorist organizations based in Florida, right-wing political parties in Guatemala and El Salvador, paramilitary organizations, religious organizations such as the Moral Majority in the USA, and business groups from Argentina and many other countries in the Western hemisphere. These governments and groups pursued Communists with a fanaticism worthy of Senator McCarthy.

SOURCE B

An extract from a chapter on the right-wing Argentine government in the late 1970s by historian Ariel Armony, in *In From the Cold: Latin America's New Encounter With the Cold War*, edited by Gilbert Joseph and Daniela Spenser, published in 2008.

The Argentine case represents the anti-Communist counterpart of Cuban activism in the Third World. The cases of Argentina and Cuba reveal that certain Latin American states designed and carried out forms of intervention in the Third World independently of the great powers … These cases show that the United States and the Soviet Union should not be considered as the only principal, external actors in Central America during the Cold War.

> What position does Source B take on the external connection in the Cold War?

What had motivated Argentina's military regime? The Argentines were militantly anti-Communist and believed that their international efforts were a continuation of the war that they had fought within Argentina against leftist revolutionaries, some of whom were in exile in Nicaragua. They feared that 'other Cubas' might emerge in the Western hemisphere. They sought international influence and prestige, and were particularly proud when they seemed to be equal partners to Reagan's USA in the struggle against Communism.

In conclusion, Argentina was too large and too powerful to suffer US domination, and in the late 1970s and early 1980s waged its own Cold War quite independently of the USA, although the USA certainly influenced the course of events.

Anti-Communist but independent

Like Argentina, Venezuela and Brazil are good examples of how larger, more powerful Latin American countries could be anti-Communist yet develop and act quite independently of the USA.

Venezuela and the OAS

Along with Argentina, Brazil, Colombia, Ecuador, Paraguay and Peru, Venezuela was one of the South American nations that enjoyed freedom from US domination. The size of the country and massive oil reserves enabled Venezuela to steer a relatively independent, yet anti-Communist, course in the Cold War and in the OAS.

While historian Gaddis Smith (1994) saw the OAS as dominated by the USA, historian Carolyn Shaw (2004) argued that there were varying degrees of co-operation between the USA and Latin Americans within the organization. While the Eisenhower administration sought to use the OAS against Cuba in 1960, the Latin Americans were more interested in opposing the Dominican Republic dictator Trujillo. The Venezuelan leader Rómulo Betancourt let Eisenhower know that he considered Trujillo, who dropped anti-Betancourt leaflets over Caracas and tried to get Betancourt assassinated, more of a threat than Castro.

In January 1961, the USA broke off diplomatic relations with Cuba and sought to persuade other countries to follow its lead, but it took several years and the intervention of other Latin American nations before Cuba was ostracized. Initially, Venezuela and Colombia were the only nations that had joined the USA in breaking off diplomatic relations with Cuba. Peru and Colombia put the problem of Castro's aggression and association with the USSR on the agenda at the Punta del Este conference in Uruguay in 1962, but Mexico and the Southern Cone opposed economic sanctions on Cuba. US offers of aid resulted in the suspension of Cuba from the OAS, but by a very narrow vote. It took Venezuelan co-operation with the USA to bring about the diplomatic isolation of Cuba. Betancourt was infuriated by Castro-trained revolutionaries who disrupted the Venezuelan presidential election in 1962. The Venezuelan campaign in the OAS led to all the Latin American nations, with the exception of Mexico, breaking off diplomatic relations with Cuba by 1964. Here, Castro's export of revolution and Betancourt's resentment of it, were the driving force behind OAS action – not the USA.

Brazil

Like many other Latin American states, Brazil saw the slow growth of a small Marxist movement in the 1920s. During the Depression, the Communist Party joined with the Socialists and radical liberals in a popular front, but this was crushed in 1935 by Getúlio Vargas, who used the mirage of Communist plots to increase his powers.

Cold War Brazilians were deeply divided about the USA. There were advocates of outright opposition, of neutrality, and of co-operation. Some, such as Juscelino Kubitschek, desperately wanted US aid (see page 85). One of the great problems for Latin American leaders was that while American aid and trade were incredibly important, trade unions and nationalists resented the American connection. In 1961, President João Goulart's plan for the economic stabilization of Brazil required a $1.5 billion loan from the USA and the IMF. Kennedy agreed to support this funding under the Alliance for Progress (see page 157), but Goulart could not obtain the domestic support necessary for the loan's acceptance. He then tried to increase his popularity by adopting a radical, nationalist leftist stance. The Brazilian right declared that this was an example of Communist subversion, and when Goulart nationalized the oil industry and legalized the Communist Party, there was a military coup. Historians disagree as to whether the USA bore any responsibility for that coup (see Source C).

SOURCE C

An extract on the downfall of the Goulart government from *A Concise History of Brazil* by Boris Fausto, published in 1999.

To understand the government's demise, it is necessary to consider several factors, and to give weight to the situation within Brazil. It is true that the United States government supported that coup and knew about it beforehand. It even dispatched a naval task force to support the revolutionary movement in the event of a prolonged struggle. But that measure was not necessary, given the ease with which the military came to power. João Goulart and his advisers had a mistaken vision of Brazil's politics.

> How far does the historian in Source C see the external connection as important in the downfall of the Goulart government?

From 1964 to 1984, Brazil was under military rule. The military did not need US prompting to be militantly anti-Communist and anti-revolutionaries. Urban guerrilla warfare broke out in 1968 and the guerrillas even managed to kidnap the US ambassador, but by 1973 the army had brutally crushed them.

Overall then, Brazil had an ambivalent reaction to the USA. Brazil had developed relatively independently from the USA, although less so than Venezuela, because it was less affluent.

The impact of the end of the Cold War

> Had the Cold War both impoverished and damaged democracy in Latin America?

During the late 1980s, the Cold War came to an end. By this time, the Marxist challenge in Latin America had receded because:

- Communism had collapsed in Eastern Europe.
- Cuba lost political prestige in the 1970s, due to revelations about the repression of dissent and to economic stagnation.
- Latin American nations were exhausted by guerrilla struggles.
- The repressive Latin American military regimes had fuelled the desire for democracy.

- The military regimes had not always provided economic progress.
- The efficacy of state planning was questioned, especially after the collapse of the planned economies of Communist Eastern Europe.

The end of the Cold War triggered a new phase of representative, electoral politics in Latin America, which has led some to conclude that the struggle between the USA and the USSR had retarded the development of democracy there. On the other hand, the Latin American republics had struggled for stability ever since the end of colonial rule in the early nineteenth century, and representative democracies had usually been the exception rather than the rule.

It has also been argued that the Cold War bore responsibility for Latin American poverty, but it is perhaps significant that the end of the Cold War did not see any great amelioration of the poverty of the masses. It was perhaps all too easy to blame that which was visible – the landowners and US business interests – for Latin American poverty. This is not to argue that the Cold War did not have a great impact on Latin America, but to agree with those who argue that it was not the 'external connection' alone that shaped the history of Latin America. It was the interrelationship with internal Latin American issues, individuals and groups that ensured that the external connection – the USA and the Cold War – had such a dramatic but also variable impact.

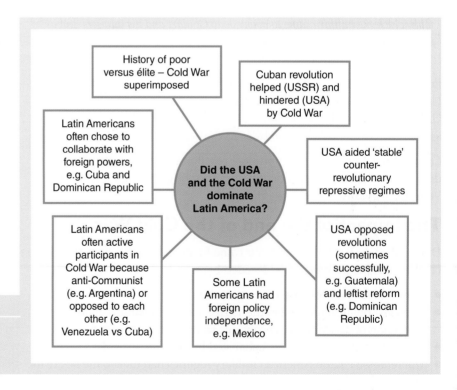

SUMMARY DIAGRAM

Conclusions about the impact of the Cold War on Latin America

Chapter summary

The impact of the Cold War on Latin America
Some historians emphasize the external connection as the most important factor in Latin American history and development. The first external connection came in the colonial period, the second in the nineteenth century with American and British influence, and the third in the twentieth century, when the USA became the most powerful country in the world.

In the twentieth century, the USA exercised a great deal of economic power over Latin America and frequently intervened in Latin American politics, motivated by the desire to retain access to Latin American natural resources, to defend its investments in the region, and to ensure that no other foreign powers such as Germany or the USSR became dominant there. The Latin Americans frequently co-operated with the USA, but there was considerable resentment of US power.

The Cold War sometimes seemed to dominate Latin American politics, partly because of US involvement and partly because the issues raised by the Cold War had long been controversial in Latin America. These issues included the unequal distribution of wealth and power and the extent of US power and influence in Latin America. The USA aided anti-Communist governments and usually opposed leftist governments, but historians differ as to whether this 'external connection' governed the course of events in Cold War Latin America. Sometimes the USA appeared to be the vital factor in the overthrow of a leftist government, as in Guatemala in 1954 and Chile in 1973. At other times the USA seemed tolerant of leftist governments, as in Bolivia in the 1950s. When US opposition to leftist revolutions failed to bring about the end of the revolution, the USA nevertheless caused the revolutionary regime a great deal of trouble, as in Cuba. The USA all too frequently supported brutal dictatorships, as with Chile and Uruguay in the 1970s. Some larger Latin American nations were sufficiently powerful to avoid undue US influence, as can be seen in Venezuela, Brazil and Argentina.

During the 1980s, the Marxist challenge in Latin America receded. This was due to the collapse of the Soviet bloc, disillusionment with the Cuban Revolution, exhaustion from guerrilla struggles, and disappointment and disgust with the repressive military regimes. Capitalism and democracy became much more widespread. Historians argue over whether the Cold War retarded the development of democracies in Latin America and over whether the USA and the Cold War bore responsibility for Latin American poverty, but Latin American politics had frequently been unstable before the Cold War, and Latin American poverty continued after the Cold War. Perhaps the most persuasive argument is that it was not simply the external connection alone that shaped the history of Latin America. Internal factors played an important part, as demonstrated so well by Cuba.

Timeline

Cold War timeline

1917	Communists seized power after the Russian Revolution
1941–5	USA and USSR allied in Second World War
1945 August	USA dropped atomic bombs on Japan
1947 March	Truman Doctrine said the USA would oppose Communism
June	Marshall Plan
July	Mr X article said Communism must be contained
September	Rio Treaty
1948	OAS set up in Bogotá
1949 April	NATO established
August	USSR tested atomic bomb
October	China became Communist
1950 February	Start of McCarthyism
June	Outbreak of Korean War
1952	Eisenhower criticized containment and advocated rollback of Communism in presidential election campaign
1953 July	Armistice signed in Korea
October	Eisenhower's 'New Look' defence policy accepted by National Security Council
1954 January–March	Eisenhower administration's speeches about massive retaliation to halt aggression
March	OAS condemned Communism in Caracas conference
April	Eisenhower's Domino Theory
June	US involvement in replacement of left-wing President Árbenz of Guatemala by right wing pro-US Castillo Armas
July	Geneva Accords temporarily divided Vietnam
August	Quemoy and Matsu crisis
September	SEATO formed
1958 May	NORAD established
	Vice President Nixon attacked by anti-American mob in Caracas, Venezuela
September	OAS Foreign Ministers discussed OPA in Washington
1959 January	Fidel Castro came to power in Cuba
1960 September	Act of Bogotá (OAS recommendations for economic and social development)
1961 January	USA broke off relations with Castro's Cuba
March	President Kennedy announced Alliance for Progress and Peace Corps
April	Bay of Pigs fiasco
1962 January	OAS excluded Cuba from its activities
October	Cuban Missiles Crisis
1964 January	Panama Canal riots
1965 March	First US ground troops sent to Vietnam
April	US invasion of Dominican Republic

May	Johnson Doctrine against Communism in Latin America
1968 January–February	US escalation in Vietnam ended after Tet Offensive
August	Castro supported Soviet invasion of Czechoslovakia
1969 June	Senate Subcommittee on Western Hemisphere Affairs hearings criticized US aid to Latin American military
1970 September	Salvador Allende became Latin America's first democratically elected Marxist leader
1973 January	Paris Peace Accords ended the USA's involvement in Vietnam
September	Allende overthrown by Pinochet in military coup in Chile
1975 November	Operation Condor established by right-wing dictatorships of Southern Cone

December	Church Report said the USA bore great responsibility for overthrow of Allende in Chile
1976 March	Establishment of militantly anti-Communist Argentine military government
1977 January	President Carter's inauguration speech emphasized human rights and a 'new start' for the USA
September	Carter signed treaties transferring Panama Canal to Panamanian control by 2000
1979 July	Somoza dictatorship in Nicaragua overthrown by revolutionaries led by leftist Sandinista guerrillas
1980 April–October	Tens of thousands of Cubans fled Castro's regime

Organization of American States (OAS) timeline

1826	Pan-American movement became active
1889	USA first active in Pan-American movement at First International Conference of American States
1947	Rio Treaty, hemispheric defence agreement
1948	The Union of American Republics re-established as Organization of American States (OAS) at Bogotá
1948–55	OAS handled border disputes between Costa Rica and Nicaragua
1954	OAS did not give go-ahead for US intervention in Guatemala; gave Guatemalan representative's anti-US speech a standing ovation
1958	OAS established committee to discuss OPA
1959	Full OAS agreement on Panama: small invasion force, mostly Cuban, persuaded to surrender by OAS intermediaries. Inter-American Commission on Human Rights, autonomous organ of OAS, established
1960	USA sought condemnation of Castro's activities in Cuba, others disagreed; compromised with condemnation of Sino-Soviet attempts to subvert legitimate governments of Western hemisphere, without specific mention of Cuba
	Dominican Republic condemned, sanctions imposed, because of attempted assassination of Venezuela's President Romulo Betancourt
	Act of Bogota contained recommendations for social and economic improvements
1961	Adopted the Charter of Punta del Este, which established the Alliance for Progress
1962	Unanimous OAS opposition to Soviet missiles in Cuba; support for Kennedy's blockade of Cuba; banned participation of Cuba in OAS, despite great Mexican opposition
1964	More sanctions imposed on Cuba for intervention in other Latin American states
1965	US intervention in Dominican Republic greatly supported by Colombia, Haiti and Paraguay, denounced by Mexico, Chile and Uruguay; 10,000-man Inter-American Peace Force helped restore order in Dominican Republic
1967	Even more sanctions on Cuba for intervention in Venezuela
1969	Threat of economic sanctions helped end war between El Salvador and Honduras
1974	Proposed lifting of sanctions on Cuba failed to obtain necessary two-thirds vote
1975	Despite the USA's opposition, economic sanctions on Cuba removed
1978	USA tried to persuade OAS that US-led peacekeeping force necessary for stability in Nicaragua, but other foreign ministers rejected that and urged Nicaraguan people to rid themselves of Somoza dictatorship. Inter-American Commission on Human Rights condemned Somoza
1979	Inter-American Commission on Human Rights condemned abuses in Argentina

Glossary

Alliance for Progress   Kennedy's plan to advance economic development, democratic institutions and social justice in Latin America.

American way of life   Americans greatly valued their political democracy, economic opportunities and general prosperity.

Amphibious assault   Attack in which land and sea forces combine.

Andes   Mountain range in Latin America. Andean states include Peru and Bolivia.

Appeasement   Policy of conciliating a potential aggressor by making concessions, as Britain and France did to Nazi Germany in the 1930s, before the outbreak of the Second World War.

ARVN   Army of the Republic of Vietnam.

Balance of payments deficit   When the value of a country's imports exceeds that of its exports.

Banana republic   Small nations, especially in Latin America, usually dependent on one crop and politically unstable.

Berkeley   University of California at Berkeley, an important state university.

Berlin Wall   Wall built by the Communists in August 1961 to halt the haemorrhage of people from Communist East Berlin to capitalist West Berlin.

Big stick   President Theodore Roosevelt had said that the USA should 'speak softly' but 'carry a big stick' when dealing with Latin Americans.

Bogotazo   A massive popular uprising in 1948 in Bogotá, Colombia, over the assassination of a populist politician, Jorge Eliécer Gaitán.

Brinkmanship   Creating the impression that one is willing to push events to the point of war rather than concede.

Canal Zone   Territory within the Republic of Panama, consisting of the Panama Canal and land extending roughly five miles on each side of the waterway.

Chapultepec   Castle in Mexico City where the 1945 Act of Chapultepec was signed.

Chicago boys   Economists trained at the University of Chicago by economist Milton Friedman, who believed in a pure form of capitalism with minimal government intervention.

Chinese Nationalists   Chiang Kai-shek's party, the Guomindang.

CIA   The Central Intelligence Agency was established in 1947 to conduct counter-intelligence operations outside the USA.

Cold War   A state of extreme tension between the USA and the USSR from about 1946 to 1989.

Collective security   System whereby nations promised to intervene to help if one of them was a victim of aggression.

Colossus of the North   Phrase used to signify the greater power of the USA relative to its southern neighbours.

Comecon   Soviet bloc economic organization.

Command economy   National economy totally controlled by the central government; the opposite of capitalism.

Commander-in-chief   Under the US Constitution, the president commands the US armed forces.

Commitment trap   Historians' theory that successive US presidents were committed to Vietnam by the actions of their predecessors.

Communists   Supporters of the ideology that emphasized large-scale redistribution of wealth in order to attain economic equality.

Congress   Elected US legislative body consisting of the Senate and the House of Representatives.

Containment   The Truman administration's policy of preventing the spread of Communism.

Conventional forces   Soldiers, tanks, ships, etc.

Council on Foreign Relations   American non-profit, non-partisan think-tank specializing in US foreign policy information and publications.

Counterfactual   History that asks 'what if' a particular event had or had not happened.

Coup   The illegal overthrow of a government, usually by violent and/or revolutionary means.

Court-martialled   Tried by an army court for breaking army regulations.

Covert operations   Secret warfare, for example sabotage.

Democrat   US political party that tends to favour big government in matters relating to the health and welfare of the population.

Détente   A relaxation in Cold War tensions.

Domino theory Eisenhower believed that if one country fell to Communism, surrounding countries might follow, like falling dominoes.

Draft Compulsory call-up to military service.

Economic imperialism Dominating other countries through trade rather than by territorial conquest.

Entrepreneurs Innovative and ambitious business people.

Expropriated Took possession without compensation.

External connection Foreign involvement in Central and South America since 1492.

FBI The Federal Bureau of Investigation was established in 1935 in order to investigate federal crime and to collect intelligence.

Ford presidency Nixon resigned in 1974 in order to avoid impeachment and Vice President Gerald Ford became president.

Fragging When enlisted men tried to kill officers by throwing fragmentation grenades at them.

Free World The West (countries such as the USA and its allies).

General Assembly UN body where every single UN member has representation.

Geneva Accords Agreements reached at Geneva in 1954 by France, China, Ho Chi Minh and the USSR, that Vietnam should be temporarily divided, with national elections held in 1956.

Gestapo Nazi Germany's feared secret police force.

'Good neighbor' President Franklin Roosevelt's repudiation of past US use of force in Latin America.

Grand Alliance The USA, USSR and Britain were allied to oppose Nazi Germany in the Second World War.

Great Depression World-wide economic depression starting in 1929.

Great Society President Johnson's policy to bring about greater social and economic quality in the USA.

Ground commander MacArthur was in overall charge of the UNC, but Walker then Ridgway were in charge on the ground in Korea itself.

Ground troops Regular soldiers (rather than just 'advisers') in Vietnam.

Grunts Ordinary ground troopers or foot soldiers.

Gubernatorial Pertaining to governors.

Guerrilla movement Irregular fighting force that concentrates on activities such as sabotage and raids.

Gulf of Tonkin Resolution Congressional resolution giving the president power to do as he saw fit in Vietnam.

Gunboat diplomacy Foreign policy aims pursued through military force rather than negotiation.

Hamburger Hill A 1969 battle where the quantity of blood and guts spilled reminded soldiers of raw hamburgers.

Ho Chi Minh Trail Route through Cambodia and Laos, by which Hanoi sent troops to South Vietnam.

Hotline Direct telephone line between the White House and the Kremlin.

ICBM Intercontinental ballistic missile.

IMF International Monetary Fund. An organization of 187 countries which works to secure financial stability and reduce poverty around the world.

Imperial presidency Continuous Cold War emergencies increased presidential authority, and some contemporaries felt the president was becoming dangerously powerful.

IRBM Intermediate range ballistic missile.

Iron Curtain Former British Prime Minister Winston Churchill used this term in 1946 when he said that Soviets had separated Eastern Europe from the rest of Europe.

Joint Chiefs of Staff Heads of the US army, navy and air force.

Justice Department The part of the federal government with special responsibility for monitoring the enforcement of laws and the administration of justice.

KGB The Soviet secret service.

Kremlin Location of the Soviet government in Moscow.

Labour unions Trade unions that negotiated for better pay and working conditions for their members.

Land reform A more equal distribution of land.

League of Nations A global organization, set up in 1920, to resolve international disputes.

Left-wing radicalism Enthusiastic leftists who believe in a more equal distribution of wealth and political power.

Left-wingers Those sympathetic to the ideals of socialism and Communism, favouring government activism.

Liberation theology Latin American Catholic clergy movement, inspiring parishioners to work for change in this life, rather than waiting for their reward in heaven.

Linkage Linking American concessions to the USSR and China to their assistance in ending the Vietnam War.

'Loss of China' Belief that Truman could have prevented Communist victory in China in 1949 with more aid to Chiang Kai-shek.

Mandate Legitimate authority given for action.

Mariel boatlift In 1980, Castro allowed thousands of discontented Cubans to depart for the USA from the port of Mariel.

Marshall Plan US economic aid programme for post-war Western Europe, also known as Marshall Aid.

Marxist–Leninist Someone who follows the Communist ideology of Karl Marx and Vladimir Lenin.

Mestizo Person of mixed race.

Middle class Businessmen, professionals, landowners.

Military junta Government by a group of army officers.

Military–industrial complex Belief that the vested interests of the military and industry encouraged them to escalate tensions and the production of weaponry.

Militia Reserve citizens' army.

Monoculture Concentration and dependency on a single crop.

Moratorium In this context, suspension of normal activities, in order to protest.

More bang for a buck Eisenhower's belief that greater dependence on nuclear weaponry would save the USA money and protect it as effectively as conventional forces.

MRBM Medium-range ballistic missile.

Napalm Flammable liquid used in warfare.

NATO The North Atlantic Treaty Organization, established in 1949, as a defensive alliance against the USSR.

Neo-colonialism A new form of colonialism in which a country was dominated economically rather than territorially.

New Left Political movement of the 1960s that favoured confrontational tactics in order to achieve radical change in government, politics and society, particularly popular among Latin American, European and American students.

New Look Eisenhower's defence policy emphasized the use of nuclear weaponry rather than conventional forces.

9/11 On 11 September 2001, a terrorist attack on the USA led to thousands of deaths.

NLF Communist National Liberation Front in Vietnam.

Non-aligned nations Nations independent of the USA and the USSR in the Cold War.

NORAD North American Aerospace Defense Command.

NSC-68 Sixty-eighth National Security Council planning paper.

OAS Organization of American States, established in 1948 to combat Communism.

Oligarchies Unrepresentative élites.

OPA Brazilian President Juscelino Kubitschek's proposed Operation Pan America was a Marshall Plan for Latin America that never really came to anything.

Orthodox In the Cold War context, a Western historian who sees the West as always right and blames the USSR for the conflict.

Pan-American Covering North and South America.

'Peace with honor' Nixon wanted Thieu's government to stay in power in a viable South Vietnamese state, so that the USA could withdraw from Vietnam with its dignity intact.

Pearl Harbor The US naval base in Hawaii.

Pink Cold War Americans referred to Communists as 'Reds' or as 'pink'.

Platt Amendment US amendment to the Cuban constitution, named after US Senator Orville Platt who proposed it. It gave the USA the right to intervene in Cuba.

Post-revisionist In the Cold War context, a historian who argues that both the USA and the USSR bore responsibility for the Cold War.

POWs Prisoners of war.

Protectionist Economic policies designed to protect the domestic economy, for example, through the imposition of tariffs on imports from other countries.

Protectorate Country whose foreign affairs and domestic stability are 'looked after' by another more powerful nation.

'Pseudo-Republic' Castro's term for 'independent' Cuba, 1901–59.

Pusan Perimeter An area 100 by 50 miles in the south-eastern corner of the Korean peninsula, where retreating US/UN/ROK troops were pinned around the port of Pusan in summer 1950.

Putsch Attempted revolution.

Quagmire theory Belief that the USA got slowly and increasingly trapped in Vietnam, due to ignorance, overconfidence and credibility concerns.

Reconnaissance flights Aerial spying missions.

Red Scare An outburst of anti-Communist hysteria, in which Communists (real and imagined) were seen everywhere ('Reds under the bed').

Republican US political party that tends to favour minimal government and big business.

Revisionist In the Cold War context, a Western historian who blames the USA for the conflict.

Rollback Pushing back Communism in places where it was already established.

Rolling Thunder Sustained US bombing of North Vietnam from March 1965 to November 1968.

Sabotage and subversion Destruction of property, designed to damage and undermine Batista's regime.

Search and destroy General Westmoreland's tactics included finding and killing groups of Vietcong guerrillas.

SEATO South East Asia Treaty Organization; defensive alliance of USA, UK, France, Australia, New Zealand and Pakistan, who agreed to protect South Vietnam, Cambodia and Laos.

Secretary of State US government official with responsibility for foreign affairs.

Security Council UN body that has responsibility for the maintenance of international peace and security. It has five permanent members and 10 non-permanent members. Each member can veto an action.

Shanty towns Collections of poorly built dwellings containing poverty-stricken populations.

Sino-American Chinese–American.

Sino-Soviet split Chinese–Soviet mutual hostility became increasingly obvious to the rest of the world in the 1960s.

Socialism Political philosophy that advocated redistribution of wealth. Some contemporaries used the words Communism and socialism interchangeably.

Southern Cone Argentina, Brazil, Chile, Paraguay and Uruguay.

Soviet Pertaining to the USSR.

Soviet bloc The countries in the USSR's Eastern European empire (East Germany, Czechoslovakia, Poland, Romania, Bulgaria and Hungary).

Sovietization Modelling the economy, in particular, on the USSR's.

Stalemate theory Belief that the USA continued to fight an unwinnable war in Vietnam, simply to avoid being seen to be defeated.

State Department The US federal government department that deals with foreign affairs.

Strongmen Dictators – often Latin American.

Surgical air strike Bombing aimed at highly specific targets.

Tet The most important Vietnamese festival. Americans use the word 'Tet' as shorthand for the 'Tet Offensive'.

Third World During the Cold War, the USA and its allies considered themselves the 'first' world, the Communist bloc the 'second', and the less developed nations the 'third'.

38th parallel Line of latitude dividing northern Korea from southern Korea.

Tickertape parade When national heroes returned to the USA, New Yorkers would shower them with bits of paper (tickertape) as they drove through the streets of the city in an open-top car.

Truman Doctrine Truman's March 1947 speech that said the USA would help any country under attack from Communists.

United Nations International organization established after the Second World War to work for international peace, co-operation and progress.

Urban revolutionaries Revolutionaries based in Cuba's cities, rather than in the mountains with Castro.

US Information Agency Established by President Eisenhower in 1953 to educate foreigners about the USA.

USSR Communist Russia called itself the Union of Soviet Socialist Republics (USSR).

Vietcong Vietnamese Communists in South Vietnam.

Vietminh Vietnamese nationalists led by Ho Chi Minh.

Vietnamization Nixon's policy under which South Vietnam's government and forces took the main responsibility for the war.

Wake Island A US base in the middle of the Pacific Ocean.

Watergate scandal In 1973, the Nixon administration tried to cover up the burglary and wiretapping of the Democratic national headquarters at the Watergate building in Washington, DC.

West Point US military academy for officer training.

Western Cold War term for the anti-Communist alliance led by the USA.

Further reading

Chapter 1: US foreign policy pre-1945

Robert D. Schulzinger, *U.S. Diplomacy Since 1900*, Oxford, 2007

Walter LaFaber, *America, Russia and the Cold War*, McGraw-Hill, 2008

These are two excellent overviews of twentieth-century US foreign policy, both written with engaging style, both critical of their country, both good on Latin America.

Chapter 2: President Truman and the Cold War

Martin McCauley, *The Origins of the Cold War*, Longman, 2003

Solid, detailed post-revisionist account of the 'two competing systems', the USA and the USSR.

James Patterson, *Grand Expectations: The United States, 1945–74*, Oxford, 1996

Part of the excellent Oxford History of the United States; particularly good on the homefront and McCarthy during the Korean War.

William Appleman Williams, *The Tragedy of American Diplomacy*, W.W. Norton, 1962

Interesting to read the first great American critic of US foreign policy, founder of the revisionist school.

Chapter 3: The Korean War 1950–3

Bruce Cumings, *The Origins of the Korean War*, Princeton, 1981–90. Two volumes

Early revisionist account with emphasis on Korean civil war context.

Michael Dockrill and Michael Hopkins, *The Cold War*, Palgrave, 2006

Clear, conventional overview.

John Lewis Gaddis, *The Cold War*, Penguin, 2005

An accessible writer, and interesting to compare this with his earlier revisionist works.

Melvyn Leffler, in Odd Arne Westad (editor), *Reviewing the Cold War*, Frank Cass, 2001

Brief, stimulating overview of different approaches to the history of the Cold War.

Peter Lowe, *The Korean War*, Macmillan, 2000

Detailed, balanced account, good international perspective.

James Matray in Robert Schulzinger (editor), *A Companion to American Foreign Relations*, Blackwell, 2003

Sees the Korean War as a great Cold War turning point.

Vivienne Sanders, *Access to History: The USA in Asia 1945–75*, Hodder Education, 2010

Includes an account of the Korean War; aimed at 16–19-year-old students.

William Stueck, *The Korean War: An International History*, Princeton, 1997

Useful corrective to the more usual US-centred accounts.

Robert Wood in Melvyn Leffler and David Painter (editors), *The Origins of the Cold War: An International History*, Routledge, 2005

Revisionist viewpoint, critical of US aggression.

Chapter 4: President Eisenhower and the 'New Look'

Stephen Ambrose, *Nixon: Volume 1: The Education of a Politician, 1913–61*, Simon & Schuster, 1987

Detailed and fascinating account of Vice President Nixon's Latin American visits.

Leslie Bethell and Ian Roxborough, *Latin America Between the Second World War and the Cold War*, Cambridge, 1997

Bethell is the solid author of multiple volumes in the Cambridge histories of Latin America.

Nick Cullather, *Secret History: The CIA's Classified Account of its Operations in Guatemala, 1952–54*, Stanford, 1999
Detailed study of the awesome power and influence of the CIA and the USA.

Piero Gleijeses, *Shattered Hope: The Guatemalan Revolution and the United States, 1944–54*, Princeton, 1991
Stresses the ideological motivation behind US policy in 1954.

Greg Grandin in Jean-Christophe Agnew and Roy Rosensweig (editors), *A Companion to Post-1945 America*, Blackwell, 2006
Blames the USA for post-Second World War demise of democracy and other Cold War 'atrocities' in Latin America.

Tulio Halperín Donghi, *The Contemporary History of Latin America*, Duke, 1993
Interesting left-wing Argentine perspective, highly critical of the impact of the USA on Latin America.

Henry Raymont, *Troubled Neighbors: The Story of US–Latin American Relations from Roosevelt to the Present*, Westview, 2005
Written by a journalist, passionately critical of US failure to aid Latin America; not good history, but some interesting insights.

Stephen Schlesinger and Stephen Kinzer, *Bitter Fruit: The Untold Story of the American Coup in Guatemala*, Harvard, 1990
Detailed study of the importance of the United Fruit Company.

Edwin Williamson, *The Penguin History of Latin America*, Penguin, 2009
A masterly overview, but as with all such ambitious overviews, it is often difficult to trace the chronology of the different countries.

Chapter 5: US involvement in the Vietnam War

Stephen Ambrose, *Eisenhower: The President*, HarperCollins, 1984
Well-written and favourable biography.

David Anderson, *Trapped by Success: The Eisenhower Administration in Vietnam*, Columbia, 1993
Highly critical of Eisenhower's Vietnam policy.

David Anderson, *The Vietnam War*, Palgrave Macmillan, 2005
Balanced, comprehensive account.

Mark Byrnes, *The Truman Years*, Longman, 2000
Solid entry in the student-friendly Longman Seminar Studies series.

Lawrence Freedman, *Kennedy's Wars*, Oxford, 2000
Detailed study of Berlin, Cuba and Laos leads to conclusion that Kennedy would have got out of Vietnam.

Lloyd Gardner, *Approaching Vietnam: From World War II Through Dienbienphu*, W.W. Norton, 1989
Useful on the significance of the French withdrawal.

Leslie Gelb and Richard Betts, *The Irony of Vietnam: The System Worked*, Brookings Institution, 1979
Proponents of stalemate theory.

David Halberstam, *The Making of a Quagmire: America and Vietnam During the Kennedy Era*, Knopf, 1964
US journalist who covered the Vietnam War in lively and increasingly hostile fashion.

George Herring, *America's Longest War*, Temple, 2001
Clear, classic account.

David Kaiser, *American Tragedy: Kennedy, Johnson, and the Origins of the Vietnam War*, Harvard, 2000
Blames everyone but Kennedy for the escalation during Kennedy's presidency. Yet another example of a historian who finds it hard to find fault with Kennedy.

Stanley Karnow, *Vietnam: A History*, Penguin, 1997
A fascinating, highly readable account of the war by an American journalist who covered it.

Gabriel Kolko, *Anatomy of a War: Vietnam, the United States, and the Modern Historical Experience*, Pantheon, 1983
Highly influential revisionist account.

Fredrik Logevall, *The Origins of the Vietnam War*, Longman, 2001
While sympathetic about the context in which successive presidents made their decisions, realistic about their errors.

John Newman, *JFK and Vietnam: Deception, Intrigue, and the Struggle for Power*, Warner, 1992
Believes Kennedy would have got out.

Vivienne Sanders, *Access to History: The USA and Vietnam 1945–75*, Hodder Education, 2007
Detailed account of the Vietnam War; aimed at 16–19-year-old students.

David Schmitz, *The Tet Offensive*, Rowman & Littlefield, 2005
Unusually sympathetic to Johnson, caught in the commitment trap.

Robert Schulzinger, *A Time for War: The United States and Vietnam, 1941–75*, Oxford, 1997
Clear, lively.

Anthony Short, *The Origins of the Vietnam War*, Longman, 1989
Critical of Eisenhower's rejection of the Geneva Accords.

Chapter 6: The Cuban Revolution

Richard Gott, *Cuba: A New History*, Yale, 2004
Sympathetic and detailed, particularly good on Castro's ambivalent relations with Communists.

Volker Skierka, *Fidel Castro: A Biography*, Polity, 2005
Concentrates on Castro's motivation.

Hugh Thomas, *Cuba: A History*, Penguin, 2001
Has classic status; although good coverage of Cuban history up to the mid-1960s, nothing much on the highly Sovietized years.

Chapter 7: From Kennedy to Carter

Hugh Brogan, *Kennedy*, Longman, 1996
Favourable account.

Robert Dallek, *John Kennedy: An Unfinished Life*, Penguin, 2004
Exhaustive, balanced account.

James Giglio, *The Presidency of John F. Kennedy*, Kansas, 1991
Part of the excellent Kansas University Press series on American presidents.

Michael Grow, *U.S. Presidents and Latin American Intervention*, Kansas, 2008
Emphasizes the importance of image and credibility in US foreign policy.

Burton Kirkwood, *The History of Mexico*, Palgrave, 2000
A volume in the excellent Palgrave Macmillan histories of Latin American nations.

Peter Kornbluh, *The Pinochet File*, New Press, 2003
Author who doggedly and repeatedly exposes the dark side of US foreign policy.

William LeoGrande, *Our Own Backyard: The United States and Central America*, North Carolina, 2000
Critical account of US foreign policy; author frequently consulted by the US government.

Lorenzo Meyer in Daniela Spenser (editor), *Espejos de la Guerra Fria: Mexico, America Central y el Caribe*, Porrula Miguel Angel, 2004
Explains Mexico's independent foreign policy (in Spanish).

Stephen Rabe, *The Most Dangerous Area in the World: Kennedy Confronts Communist Revolution in Latin America*, North Carolina, 2000
Interesting in that it records the unhappy impact of US policies, while nevertheless excusing Kennedy because he meant well.

Chapter 8: Cuba in the Cold War

See also Chapter 6.

Piero Gleijeses in Gilbert Joseph and Daniela Spenser (editors), *In From the Cold: Latin America's New Encounter With the Cold War*, Duke, 2008
Highly sympathetic to Castro.

Chapter 9: The Impact of the Cold War on Latin America

Ariel Armony in Gilbert Joseph and Daniela Spenser (editors), *In From the Cold: Latin America's New Encounter With the Cold War*, Duke, 2008
Argentine historian, useful corrective to accounts that neglect Latin American anti-Communism.

Jorge Castañada, *Utopia Unarmed: The Latin American Left After the Cold War*, Random House, 1993
Controversially claims that the Cuban Revolution retarded the progress of democracy in Latin America.

Marshall Eakin, *The History of Latin America*, Palgrave, 2007
An interesting overview of the clash of cultures in Latin America.

Boris Fausto, *A Concise History of Brazil*, Cambridge, 1999
Classic history that reminds us that Latin American life and politics often went on unaffected by and without much interest in the Cold War.

Gilbert Joseph and Daniela Spenser (editors), *In From the Cold: Latin America's New Encounter with the Cold War*, Duke, 2008
A strange mixture of excellent articles, coupled with some that seem to be in there to fill up the space.

Carolyn Shaw, *Cooperation, Conflict and Consensus in the OAS*, Palgrave, 2004
Useful corrective to those who see the USA dominating OAS.

Gaddis Smith, *The Last Years of the Monroe Doctrine*, Farrar, Straus & Giroux, 1994
Emphasizes US domination of OAS.

Internet sources

www.casahistoria.net
An invaluable portal for IB students. Many excellent links to topics for students studying the Cold War.

www.wilsoncenter.org/program/cold-war-international-history-project
This site has an excellent digital archive with many hard to find sources.

http://avalon.law.yale.edu/subject_menus/coldwar.asp
More great sources on the Cold War. There are particularly helpful sources on the Cuban Missiles Crisis.

www.gwu.edu/~nsarchiv/
The National Security Archive at George Washington University provides access to many hitherto secret government documents. Many important sources on the USA's role in Latin America, including the CIA in Guatemala and Chile.

http://lanic.utexas.edu/la/region/history/
The Latin American Network Information Center serves as a portal for hundreds of Latin American-related websites. Students will find many useful sites here although not all are in English.

www.fordham.edu/halsall/
Wonderful collection of documents and links that range from the ancient to the modern world.

Internal assessment

Internal assessment

The internal assessment is a historical investigation on a historical topic. Below is a list of possible topics on the Cold War that could warrant further investigation. They have been organized by chapter theme.

Chapter 2: President Truman and the Cold War
1. Charlie Chaplin and the FBI. What were the circumstances that led to Chaplin's exile from the USA?
2. Why was the Organization of American States founded?

Chapter 3: The Korean War 1950–3
1. Analyse Truman's decision to dismiss General MacArthur.
2. What role did Canada play in the Korean War?

Chapter 4: President Eisenhower and the 'New Look'
1. What was the significance of Vice President Nixon's trips to Latin America?
2. Why did Guatemalan President Jacobo Árbenz seize United Fruit Company property?

Chapter 5: US involvement in the Vietnam War
1. How successful was the North Vietnamese and Vietcong offensive during Tet 1968?
2. Why did President Nixon bomb North Vietnam during Christmas 1972?

Chapter 6: The Cuban Revolution
1. Why was the 1953 uprising in Cuba a failure?
2. To what extent were Herbert Matthews' newspaper articles a factor in the success of the Cuban Revolution from 1957 to 1959?

Chapter 7: From Kennedy to Carter: US foreign policy in Latin America 1961–81
1. To what extent was the USA involved in Operation Condor?
2. How successful was President Kennedy's Alliance for Progress?

Chapter 8: Cuba in the Cold War
1. To what extent was Castro involved in decision-making during the Cuban Missiles Crisis?
2. Analyse Che Guevara's revolutionary activities in Africa.
3. Why and how did Castro intervene in Ethiopia?

Chapter 9: The impact of the Cold War on Latin America
1. What role did the USA play in the 1964 Brazilian military coup?
2. How did the Uruguayan military crush the Tupamaro guerrilla movement?

Index